THE POLITICS OF RIGHTS

D1824594

Since the late 1990s, development institutions have increasingly used the language of rights in their policy and practice. This book explores the strategies, tensions and challenges associated with 'rights work' from a feminist perspective. Articles on the Middle East, Africa, Latin America, East and South Asia examine the dilemmas that arise for feminist praxis in these diverse locations, and address the question of what rights can contribute to struggles for gender justice. They explore the intersection of formal rights – whether international human rights conventions, constitutional rights or national legislation – with the everyday realities of women in settings characterised by entrenched gender inequalities and poverty, plural legal systems and cultural norms that can constitute formidable obstacles to realising rights. They suggest that these sites of struggle can create new possibilities and meanings – and a politics of rights animated by demands for social and gender justice.

This book was first published as a special issue of *Third World Quarterly*.

Andrea Cornwall is a Fellow at the Institute of Development Studies at the University of Sussex.

Maxine Molyneux is Professor of Sociology at the Institute for the Study of the Americas, University of London.

THE POLITICS OF RIGHTS:

Dilemmas for Feminist Praxis

Edited by
Andrea Cornwall and Maxine Molyneux

Routledge
Taylor & Francis Group

LONDON AND NEW YORK

First published 2008 by Routledge
2 Park Square, Milton Park, Abingdon, Oxon, OX14 4RN

Simultaneously published in the USA and Canada
by Routledge
270 Madison Avenue, New York, NY 10016

Routledge is an imprint of the Taylor & Francis Group, an informa business

Typeset in Times by KnowledgeWorks Global Limited, Southampton, UK
Printed and bound in Great Britain by MPG Books Ltd, Bodmin, Cornwall

British Library Cataloguing in Publication Data
A catalogue record for this book is available from the British Library

ISBN 10: 0-415-43772-5 (hbk)
ISBN 13: 978-0-415-43772-1 (hbk)
ISBN 10: 0-415-45906-0 (pbk)
ISBN 13: 978-0-415-45906-8 (pbk)

Contents

Acknowledgements

This book has grown out of a workshop held at the Institute of Development Studies in September 2005 on 'Feminist Perspectives on Rights-Based Development'. The workshop could not have taken place without the generous financial support of the Swedish Ministry for Foreign Affairs, Sida, Swiss Development Co-operation (SDC) and DFID, under the auspices of the Participation, Power and Change programme at IDS. We are very grateful to Julia Brown, Jenny Edwards and Chris Hunter for ensuring the smooth running of the workshop. For their contributions to editing the chapters that appear here, we'd like to express our thanks to Kirsty Milward and Rachel Cooper. We also thank the Institute for the Study of the Americas for funding the attendance of three participants from Latin America. Lastly, we'd like to thank all the workshop participants for their contributions to the lively and insightful discussions out of which this volume took shape. We are grateful to Shahid Qadir at *Third World Quarterly* for the original publication of this collection as a special issue.

Notes on Contributors

Andrea Cornwall is Fellow at the Institute of Development Studies at the University of Sussex. Her current research focuses on the politics of women's engagement in new democratic spaces, and she has written widely on issues of gender, participation and sexual and reproductive health. Her recent publications include *Readings in Gender in Africa* (as editor, 2005) and *Realizing Rights: Transforming Approaches to Sexual and Reproductive Wellbeing* (co-editor, 2002).

Maxine Molyneux is Professor of Sociology at the Institute for the Study of the Americas, University of London. Her recent books include: *Gender Justice, Development and Rights* (with Shahra Razavi) (2002); *Doing the Rights Thing: Rights-based Development and Latin American NGOs* (with Sian Lazar) (2003); *Women's Movements in International Perspective: Latin America and Beyond* (2000); *The Hidden Histories of Gender and the State in Latin America* (with E. Dore), (2000) and *Gender and the Politics of Rights and Democracy in Latin America* (with N. Craske) Palgrave 2001. Her research paper Change and Continuity in Social Protection in Latin America: Mothers at the Service of the State? was published by UNRISD in 2007.

Celestine Nyamu-Musembi is a Kenyan lawyer with a background in legal anthropology. She is currently a Fellow at the Institute of Development Studies, University of Sussex, and researches on land relations and gender equity in resource control, accountability of formal and informal institutions of justice and governance at the local level, rights-based approaches to development, and integrating participatory approaches into rights advocacy.

Georgina Waylen is Senior Lecturer in politics at the University of Sheffield. Her research has focused primarily on gender and politics, particularly transitions to democracy, and gender, governance and globalisation. Her books include *Gender in Third World Politics* (1996), *Gender, Politics and the State* (as co-editor, 1998), *Towards a Gendered Political Economy* (co-editor, 2000), *Engendering Transitions* (forthcoming) and *Analysing and Transforming Global Governance: Feminist Perspectives* (co-editor, forthcoming).

Shahra Razavi is Research Coordinator at UNRISD (United Nations Research Institute for Social Development). She specializes in the gender dimensions of social development, with a particular focus on livelihoods and social policies. Her recent books include *Gender and Social Policy in a Global*

Context: Uncovering the Gendered Structure of 'the Social', edited with Shireen Hassim (2006); *Agrarian Change, Gender and Land Rights*, special issue of *Journal of Agrarian Change* (2003); *Gender Justice, Development and Rights*, edited with Maxine Molyneux (2002); and *Gendered Poverty and Well-being*, special issue of *Development and Change* (1999).

Pratiksha Baxi is Assistant Professor at the Centre for the Study of Law and Governance, Jawaharlal Nehru University, New Delhi. Her most recent publications include, 'Medicalisation of consent and falsity: the figure of the habituated woman in the Indian rape law', in K Kannabiran (ed), *The Violence of Normal Times: Essays on Women's Lived Realities*, and *Adjudicating the Riot: Communal Violence, Crowds and Public Tranquility*, Domains, in D Mehta (eds), *Domains*, forthcoming.

Shirin M Rai is Professor of Politics in the Department of Politics and International Studies, University of Warwick. She is the author of *Gender and Political Economy of Development: From Nationalism to Globalisation* (2002) and the editor of *National Machineries for the Advancement of Women: Mainstreaming Gender, Democratising the State?*. She has also written an article on 'Gendering global governance' for the *International Feminist Journal of Politics* (2004).

Shaheen Sardar Ali is Professor of Law at the University of Warwick. She is the author of *Gender and Human Rights in Islam and International Law: Equal Before Allah, Unequal Before Man?* (2000). Her journal articles include 'Freedom of religion versus equality in international human rights law: conflicting norms or hierarchical human rights? (A case study of Pakistan)', *Nordic Journal for Human Rights* (2003) and 'The concept of Jihad in Islamic international law', *Journal of Peace and Security Law*.

Reena Patel is Lecturer at Warwick Law School, University of Warwick. She is a founder/co-ordinator of the South Asian Research Network on Gender, Law and Governance (www.sarn-glg.org), a network of activists and researchers working together on gender issues from a regional perspective in South Asia. She is the author of *Hindu Women's Property Rights in Eastern India: Law, Labour and Culture in (Inter)Action* (forthcoming).

Jasmine Gideon is Lecturer in Development Studies at Birkbeck College, London. She is the UK's Development Studies Association co-convenor of the Social Protection Study Group. Her recent publications include 'Integrating gender issues into health policy', *Development and Change* (2006) and 'Consultation or co-option? A case study from the Chilean health sector', *Progress in Development Studies* (2005).

Elisabeth J Croll is Professor of Chinese Anthropology at the School of Oriental and African Studies, University of London. She has written widely on social development and gender issues in historical and contemporary China

viii

and in Asia. For several years, she worked alongside UNICEF in Asia to promote awareness of girls' issues and rights in the region. Her publications include *Endangered Daughters: Discrimination and Development in Asia* (2000).

Nkoyo Toyo is a civil society activist and governance expert working in Nigeria. She is the Director of Gender and Development Action, an NGO working in the areas of Gender, Rights and Governance in Nigeria. She is also a member of many feminist and activist networks; and works with others (e.g. IDS' Development Research Centre (DRC) on Citizenship, Participation and Accountability; and Theatre for Development Centre, Ahmadu Bello University, Zaria, Nigeria) on research around democracy and rights in Nigeria.

Mary Hames is the Director of the Gender Equity Unit, University of the Western Cape. Her recent publications include 'The impact of sexual harassment policies in South African universities: the university of the Western Cape', in J Bennett (ed), *Killing a Virus with Stones? Research on the Implementation of Politics against Sexual Harassment in Southern African Higher Education.*

Sarah Bradshaw is Senior Lecturer in Development Studies at the School of Health and Social Sciences, Middlesex University and works with the Nicaraguan feminist NGO Puntos de Encuentro. Her recent publications include *Socio-economic Impacts of Natural Disasters: A Gender Analysis* (2004) for the United Nations Economic Commission for Latin America and the Caribbean (ECLAC) and *Challenging Women's Poverty: Perspectives on Gender and Poverty Reduction Strategies from Nicaragua and Honduras* (2003), a CIIR-ICD Briefing.

The Politics of Rights—Dilemmas for Feminist Praxis: an introduction

ANDREA CORNWALL & MAXINE MOLYNEUX

Since the late 1990s development institutions have increasingly used the language of rights in their policy and practice. A complex array of legal and quasi-legal rules and a significant body of practice concerning rights now exist among international development agencies, NGOs and government departments. These seek to bring a general human rights focus into the heart of development practice, and also to ensure that the specific, third and fourth generations of rights—those of children, the disabled and indigenous populations among others—are incorporated into development policy.[1] Given that in many parts of the world women experience the consequences of a lack of equal rights to men in continuing gender-based discrimination, unequal and poor pay, high levels of violence and continuing exclusion from political arenas,[2] they arguably have the most to gain from a rights approach to development, and they have certainly been among the most active supporters of campaigns to gain acceptance for this agenda.

Yet, in the present international political climate, and as human rights have become increasingly associated with development agendas implicating states and external agencies, advancing rights agendas appears less straightforwardly 'progressive' to some former supporters than it once did. If this is so with regard to human rights in general, it is perhaps even more the case with regard to women's rights, which have become the site of political and ideological struggles, some of which have international dimensions. To take one particularly vivid example, that of the use made of the appalling treatment of women by the Taliban to garner support for US military action: this was a rhetorical move that angered and demobilised many feminist activists whose work was charged with being annexed to, or at least tainted by, imperial intervention.

How, then, are women's rights advocates positioned today in relation to what has undoubtedly become a more contested field of engagement? Does the emphasis on rights offer those working for gender justice a way to address these challenges? And are rights the best way to make a real difference to women's lives?[3] This book draws together contributions to a workshop organised by the editors, and held at the Institute of Development Studies, in September 2005. The aim was to bring together activists, practitioners and academics with experience of development policy and practice to reflect on the implications for feminist politics of the universalisation of 'rights talk' and practice and specifically on the experience of rights-based development (RBD).[4] Among international NGOs and in some parts of bilateral and intergovernmental agencies, rights-based approaches are viewed positively; they are a badge of legitimacy, of progressive intentions in enclaves within mainstream development agencies, distinguishing those who consider themselves more radical than the mainstream. Beyond the confines of the world of international development agencies, however, rights-based development is a term that may find relatively little resonance—and may even, as Sarah Bradshaw suggests in her contribution to this collection, serve to engender disquiet as yet another donor fad.

This collection seeks to go beyond the analysis of rights-based approaches in the discourse and practice of development agencies to explore the broader politics of rights, and the dilemmas they pose for feminist practice. Contributions reflect on the ambiguities and ambivalences of feminism's recourse to rights, on the globalisation of rights language, and on the relationship between rights and the realities of women in different political and cultural contexts. Highlighting the dissonance between liberal rights talk and the pragmatics of legal pluralism, the power of normative cultural injunctions and the very fragility of women's claims on rights even in contexts where some of the most progressive legislation in the world can be found, we aim to show what closer analysis of struggles for women's rights in different localities in the South might offer debates on the politics of rights in development. What emerges from this collection is the sheer diversity of sites in which women's rights have been advanced (or resisted), and the variety of political interests and legal processes involved.

Taken together, the contributions to this book highlight a series of dilemmas, some of which have proven increasingly divisive amongst feminists. They raise questions about the political legitimacy of a Western-inspired agenda of liberal rights and its fit, or lack of fit, with existing rights regimes and practices in different cultural contexts. And they debate the efficacy of a focus on rights as a way of advancing broader agendas of equality and social justice. In this introduction we set the emergence of 'rights-based development' in context and go on to explore the dilemmas that the politics of rights poses for feminists in this diversity of sites and settings.

Rights then, rights now

More than a decade on from the first iterations of rights-based development[5] it is worth reflecting on the accumulating experience of working with women's rights agendas in the South. It is possible to see this work as an application of feminism's historic demands for equality, present in its modern origins in the French Revolution and associated with demands to end the patriarchal privileges enshrined within liberal, religious and customary laws. As in the West, so in the developing countries, feminists have worked with both a politics of recognition and a politics of redistribution:[6] the former referring to the symbolic injustices of non-recognition or mis-recognition;[7] the latter meaning political–economic distribution. Together these have translated across the world into demands for employment, political representation and access to social provision for women, along with measures to address the harms of non-recognition, ranging from the demeaning of women in public and private life to the androcentric norms that govern law and daily life to the devaluation of women that is expressed in domestic violence, sexual assault and exploitation.

Until the wave of UN conferences of the mid-1990s and the transnational activism that animated them began to make new connections between them, development and human rights had largely been regarded as separate fields of engagement, with the former being concerned with the abuse of power and the latter with economic growth and basic needs satisfaction.[8] Over the course of the 1990s this changed and the normative justification for rights-based development and its 'mainstreaming' into the policy rhetoric of the agencies of the United Nations and government development departments gathered momentum. This was generally welcomed by social movement activists and NGOs, many of whom had been campaigning for years to place development on an ethical basis and who saw the adoption of the rights agenda as a positive step in this direction.[9]

The globalisation of what Fraser has dubbed 'rights talk'[10] was a product of the political circumstances that shaped the last two decades of the past century. The international context at the time favoured advances in human rights. The 1990s represented a high point for liberal internationalism, with a strong global human rights movement, within which feminism played a critical part, and the spread of democratic governance across the world in the wake of the collapse of the USSR and of dictatorships in Latin America, and the end of apartheid in South Africa. The agenda-setting UN conferences gave women's rights advocates and social movements an opportunity to advance feminist agendas in these broadly favourable conditions, and a number of tangible gains were secured. Most states signed up to the

3

proposals for gender equity contained in the 1995 Beijing Platform for Action and Convention on the Elimination of all forms of Discrimination against Women (CEDAW), and this helped to promote positive changes at national level in women's rights and political representation.

The optimism that first accompanied the spread of democracy and rights had already begun to ebb by the end of the 1990s. This trend was soon accelerated as hopes of it delivering on its promise gave way to political disillusion under the shadow of military aggression and growing terrorist violence, environmental deterioration, and fears over the economic and political futures of many developing countries. The US-led invasions of Iraq and Afghanistan sought their justification as much in the name of human rights and democracy as in the claim to further international security. At the very moment in which political liberalism and human rights had achieved some global legitimacy, their credentials in the eyes of many development workers were being undermined.

The 'rise of rights' may now have plateaued,[11] as a new mood of conservatism spreads through the international aid community, spurred by the demands and focus of the new aid modalities and the exigencies of donor harmonisation. The global politics of sexual and reproductive health and rights policy has increasingly become a battleground, as conservative forces have sought to claw back gains that were made in the 1990s. At the national level, democratising reforms that might have lent support to the furtherance of women's rights have stalled in the face of unpopular neoliberal policies which have continued to take a disproportionate toll on women, of growing conservative opposition to feminist demands and of declining governmental support. Women's rights to exercise control over their own bodies and life choices seem, in many settings, ever more precarious, as new configurations of global and local religious forces fuel a conservative backlash.

What it means to take a 'rights-based approach' varies significantly across different kinds of international agencies.[12] The World Bank, for example, has professed that its work is inherently concerned with social and economic rights, while maintaining its claim that to explicitly promote rights would contravene its principles of engagement. For UN agencies the use of international conventions and other agreements, such as the International Covenant on Economic, Social and Cultural Rights (ICESCR), to guide programming are in conformity with their own defined role. Bilateral agencies have tended instead to define 'rights-based' in terms of principles—such as Sida's commitment to mainstreaming 'the rights perspective' throughout their work, or DFID's articulation of an approach that is underpinned by human rights principles such as non-discrimination, participation and obligation.[13] It is among international non-governmental organisations that the most explicit commitment to 'rights-based' develop-ment is found:[14] this too, arguably, relates to these bodies own positionality, and to the shifting role that intermediary organisations of this kind have come to play in today's aid industry. What is, however, striking is the priority that a number of these organisations—Action Aid, in

4

particular, but increasingly also CARE and Oxfam—have come to give *women's* rights.

The descriptor 'rights-based' offers a means of legitimising not only development interventions, but also the actors involved in this work. It provides moral authority and purpose, justifies intervention and gives succour to those concerned with enhancing the capacity of those who have historically been marginalised to claim rights and recognition. Beyond the ethical claims made for rights as embodying essential principles of justice, rights language has gained appeal among international development actors for more prosaic reasons. As Mary Robinson expresses it, rights create the conditions which encourage enhanced accountability through 'higher levels of citizens' empowerment, easier consensus and increased transparency'. A turn to rights, framed in this way, complements mainstream development efforts to promote 'good governance' and 'participation'.[15] Again in Robinson's words, it 'gives moral legitimacy and reinforces social justice principles that already underpin development thinking, providing a more authoritative basis for advocacy'.[16] In an era of the Paris Agenda, where new aid modalities drive increasing levels of aid spending through governments, enhancing citizen voice is amenable to being recast as optimising efficiency, where, as one bilateral donor put it, 'rights and entitlements are equated with a supply and demand model'.[17]

Celestine Nyamu-Musembi's article in this book makes clear that the embrace of rights by the development mainstream needs to be unpacked and subjected to closer inspection. What kinds of rights have been advanced, and why? And which and whose rights have been compromised in the process? Nyamu-Musembi's analysis points to the extent to which rule-of-law reforms have served to advance market-oriented policies, with scant regard for issues of gender equality or social justice. Many would agree that governments tend to be selective in their promotion of rights, and sceptics question the 'right to exploit' awarded to many transnational companies (TNCs) in developing countries. She notes:

> The post-cold war climate in which the reforms have taken place has meant that objectives that are viewed as incompatible with market-oriented legal reform are abandoned or held in abeyance . . . In such a climate, the enactment of laws that enable deployment of state resources to safeguard women's rights, for instance through extending social security benefits to the agricultural sector and export processing zones (EPZs) can and does become less of a priority. Even where governments profess commitment to such goals, for instance through constitutional guarantees of gender equality, this commitment is not reflected in the articulation of priorities or the allocation of funds.

What have these shifts in the international aid architecture and discourses of development offered struggles for the realisation of women's rights? Although spurred largely by instrumentalist arguments, a concern with women's economic opportunities and political representation has found its way back onto the agenda of international development via the limited, but tangible, aims of the Millennium Development Declaration and associated Goals. A number of international development agencies has begun to use the language of women's rights where once the fuzzier, more politically compromised, notion of 'gender equality' was all that could be discerned in their policies and prescriptions; 'gender mainstreaming' has, in many of these agencies, fallen into abeyance. Today's talk of 'women's empowerment' has no less of the instrumentalism that has characterised mainstream development's embrace of 'participation'. Yet many activists now feel that the return to a sharper focus on 'women' rather than on the generalities of 'gender' might offer the prospect of returning attention to the issues of power that lay at the heart of the original Gender and Development agenda, and with it, women's rights.

Several articles in this book are concerned with the situated analysis of the politics of framing and claiming women's rights in a diversity of political and cultural contexts, and they highlight a series of issues that reflect—and to some degree reframe—issues that have long been a challenge for feminist engagement. Contests over and struggles for women's rights in changing and diverse political environments present feminism with a series of dilemmas, four of which are posed by our authors from their experience of working with rights, either at the grass roots or in association with development organisations. These are, first, the question of how feminists and feminism are positioned in relation to what is essentially a liberal discourse and politics of rights within settings where other understandings of justice and mechanisms for securing it may prevail. Second, the strategic dilemmas faced by feminists when confronted by the gulf that frequently separates the formal existence of rights regimes and the lived realities of most women for whom rights are far from having acquired much substantive meaning in their lives.

The third dilemma, long present within feminism, is in part a question of strategy and concerns its relationship, as a movement, with the state. Rights work can and does proceed at grassroots level and through transnational network advocacy. But ultimately rights are enshrined in and guaranteed by states, and feminists who work to advance or reform women's rights are necessarily drawn into negotiation with states and parties and must engage in state arenas if they are to be effective. The dilemma that this presents to feminism is: what are the conditions under which such negotiation with states is possible, and at what risk to feminism's independence and overall objectives?

The last of our four dilemmas has grown with the very successes associated with feminism, namely the increased presence of women in political spaces, and the greater attention that is being paid by states to issues that directly concern women. Many of those now seeking to define women's issues are indifferent or openly antagonistic to feminism's agendas. Where and how can alliances be made in these circumstances? If politics is the art of compromise, then what accommodations if any are feminists required to make in particular contexts?

Liberalism and some feminist discontents

Our first feminist dilemma centres on a tension inherent in the articulation of human rights: that between a universalising rights regime founded in liberalism and alternative legal and normative frameworks underpinned by particularities of religion and 'custom'. UN legal frameworks recognise cultural rights, and the International Labour Organisation's (ILO) convention 169 recognises the principle of legal pluralism—one that has been incorporated into basic law in parts of Latin America and elsewhere. However, the tensions between different legal principles, and the disjunctions and frictions that arise in relation to them, are particularly acute in relation to women's rights. This is not only because of assumptions inherent in liberalism about the autonomous sovereign subject of rights, which has formed an important strand in the critique of 'Western' liberal feminism. It also gains new dimensions in the elision of the discursive properties of liberal rights with political projects that are much more particularistic in intent, yet garland themselves with the legitimacy of liberal rights to gain political purchase.

Feminists working to advance women's rights through state reform agendas are confronted with difficult choices in settings where a relatively powerful and pervasive state institutionalises its own interpretations of women's rights and may itself be implicated in their violation. Such conditions are apparent where attenuated and ineffective statutory institutions meet the resurgence of religious and 'community' judicial institutions in a context of plural legal frameworks. Several chapters in this collection explore the complexities that arise from these syncretic legal systems and how they have to be taken into account by those working to advance women's equality. Syncretism takes many forms and is not simply to be understood as an adaptation that is made in the transition from 'tradition' to 'modernity' or from pre-capitalist to capitalist social relations. Rather it is a characteristic of many modern settings, a result of political struggles and of differing versions of the good society.

Shahra Razavi's chapter on contemporary Iran underscores this point. As she shows, the idea that there is a clash over two discrete and clearly identifiable political–legal systems, one modern and Western, the other traditional and Islamic, mis-represents what is in reality a new configuration, the result of a far more fluid and pluralised set of interpretations and legal forms recombining elements of each across different legal terrains. The Iranian state enunciates the rhetoric of democracy and human rights, along with an absolutist discourse of obedience to a theocratic state and law. Meanwhile democratic Islamists in opposition currents work with a particular interpretation of the sacred texts to argue for an Islamic Enlightenment reading of the Koran. Such complex political-discursive conditions, symptomatic of modernity with elements of a reinvented 'traditionalism', provide women's advocates with an array of difficult strategic options and allies, and in the Iranian case, Razavi argues, not ones that seem likely to deliver very much to women.

In their analysis of the uses of law to regulate women's sexuality in India and Pakistan, Pratiksha Baxi, Shirin Rai and Shaheen Sardar Ali draw on findings from ethnographic studies to highlight the 'interpretive contestations' that take place around the definition and judgement of 'honour crimes'. Through the analysis of appellate judgements they provide a fascinating account of the ways in which claims and counter-claims come to be located in a rich field of meanings in which other contests come to be played out: between tradition and modernity, 'communitarian "justicing"' and the interplay of, as they put it, 'the governance of communities and the governance of polities'. They draw attention to the use of human rights language in these judgements, which, they argue, represents the conjunction of 'the embedding of law in the politics of honour and the new-found honour of human rights languages and rhetorics'. The use of human rights discourse invoking Pakistan's international obligations to uphold women's rights to reframe notions of what constitutes an 'Islamic public' resonates with Razavi's account of reformist strategising in Iran.

What Baxi *et al*'s rich treatment of appellate judgements reminds us is that rights, after all, are not in themselves inherently transformative: it shows that it is *how* rights come to be framed and claimed that defines their potential. Feminist ambivalence about the capacity of states to deliver on women's rights highlights not only the issue of access to justice, but also the ways in which competing judicial frameworks may come into play in defining the contours of claims and judgements. Baxi *et al* note the extent to which administering justice in India and Pakistan may come to rely on 'localised notions of sovereignty, often in contravention to constitutional law or even the rule of law'. They draw attention to the 'competing spheres of legal subjection' in which the prosecution of 'honour crimes' may be sought.

Reena Patel's treatment of Hindu women's property rights in India sets rights claims in the context of plural normative systems and the restrictions these may place on women's opportunities to make viable the rights they have. Patel's historical and cultural contextualisation of Hindu law raises the question of whether statutory laws offer a powerful enough instrument for change if they fail to take account of the mediating influence of normative frameworks embedded in historically contingent relations and practices in shaping legal judgement. She asks: 'Insofar as rural women continue to be located within social, economic, political and cultural structures founded on precepts derived from religion, can a presumption to the contrary by law be valid? Can law presume the non-existence of the normative force of religion and yet be reflective of and pertaining to women's lives?'.

The answer may be an uncomfortable one for feminists to contemplate, but Patel's reflections are also a reminder that the law is not the only means of social regulation, nor does it exist in isolation from society. It is to some degree reflexive, and shapes, and is shaped by, social, political and cultural practices in sometimes conflicting ways. Legal reform, as is often said, does not immediately transform social relations, and feminist activists often work most effectively within a broader remit to help disempowered women gain some economic and social leverage within their localities. As in Iran, so in

India, feminists navigate difficult political and social terrains which can be sites of resistance or of transformation depending on the success of their practices, and the availability of mechanisms which allow them to challenge resistant power holders and compel accountability.

Rights and realities

Our second feminist dilemma is one that is not unique to feminism: it is a familiar dilemma, and one that often serves as the basis for a critique of the optimism of development talk about rights.[18] It is the gulf that exists between elegant laws and the indignities of women's everyday realities, and between being accorded a right and being in any position at all to make use of it.

In some parts of the world recent decades have been exceptional for the sheer quantity and range of gender-related legal and public policy reforms, especially where democratisation has been accompanied by new, progressive constitutions. Keck and Sikkink have identified a 'cascade effect' whereby the adoption of international conventions by states has led to changing national laws and this in turn has influenced policy and practice.[19] Constitutions were key sites in this process of mediation and in the post-1980s wave of democratisation electoral politics enabled some feminist demands to be mainstreamed within the process of constitutional reform.[20] The relatively positive results achieved led, as Georgina Waylen argues in her chapter, to a growing feminist interest in 'constitutional engineering', spurred by a recognition of the need to go beyond the earlier campaigns for quotas and the establishment of women's machineries. Waylen shows that, in the cases of Latin America and South Africa, women's movements were effective in securing an impressive range of new rights for women in the workplace, in the family and sometimes even in the more difficult area of sexual and reproductive matters. In Waylen's comparison of Latin America with South Africa the critical variables shaping these positive outcomes were governmental will (represented by popular democratically elected parties) and the strength of women's movements. Yet, even if they are broadly supportive, all too often governments fail to deliver resources to match their commitments.

Constitutional reform has clearly offered a window of opportunity to feminists and in generating new legal instruments and processes has in theory at least extended access to justice. In South Africa Mary Hames notes how constitutional mechanisms came to be complemented by subsidiary legislation and by the creation of a series of new legal mechanisms through which rights claims could be pursued. Yet, even as such gains must be celebrated, questions arise about the extent to which they can lead to meaningful change without serious efforts to address the persistent problems of poverty and inequality.

Some governments patently fail to deliver justice or protection to women, despite fine words and rhetorical commitments, as is manifestly the case in Ciudad Juarez in Mexico, where there have been shamefully few successful prosecutions for the murder of hundreds of young women and minimal protective measures have been put in place to enhance women's security.[21] As for the strength of women's movements, in many parts of the world, this is waning, as feminist issues fail to galvanise young women as once they did. Many women's movements depend upon long-serving and dedicated activists who have had to invest a great deal of energy in a process that is difficult to sustain over a long period and where the gains might appear slight. Social movements have also undergone a process of 'NGOisation' which has often been accompanied by some loss of activism as a result of a greater compliance with donors' agendas for funding purposes.[22]

Concerns over the professionalisation of NGOs and civil society organisations (CSOs) have added to this unease. Here, it is argued, personnel are now more engaged with service provision, project and policy work than with advancing more challenging and imaginative agendas.[23] Some feminists, indeed, link this to the dominance of the UN framework, which they see as placing an exaggerated emphasis on rights.[24] Others fear that the national feminist agenda is being displaced by the international one, the latter defined as a 'de-radicalised UN agenda' and attributed to the 'excessive' influence of international co-operation on women's movements that are dependent on it for funding. Critics further maintain that the focus on national and international policy arenas 'has distanced them [activists] from the grass-roots, from the needs and concerns of local women'.[25] These concerns are often justified but it must also be said that feminist NGOs remain among the most active and influential forces behind rights campaigns, and have been important in translating international and national rights into on-the-ground practice, as in legal literacy and reproductive health initiatives. In some cases NGOs are the sole public defenders of women's rights; the recent campaign in Kyrgyzstan against criminalising abortion was conducted by feminist NGOs in a country without a single female representative in parliament.[26]

Based on her experience of working with a Nicaraguan-based feminist NGO, Puntos de Encuentro, Sarah Bradshaw finds an ambivalent attitude towards working with the language of rights. On the one hand, she suggests, rights talk serves to unify disparate organisations to undertake collective actions to advance women's claims. On the other hand, invoking rights clearly has divisive potential, particularly evident in the case of reproductive and sexual rights. For Puntos de Encuentro, rights *per se* were felt to be less effective in dealing with issues of power and inequality *within* the organisations engaged in development work. For these, feminist discourse was considered more effective than the emphasis on rights and, as they put it, 'needed no translation'. Rights had, they felt, been 'stolen' by donors, but feminism had not been co-opted and had retained its radical force.

While such variations in attitude are common in debates over the usefulness or otherwise of rights, it is clear that the political and social context within which activists are working accounts for much of this variability. What is radical in one context, challenging embedded institutional and social authority, is less so in another, and strategies have to be elaborated accordingly. Which rights matter, and how best to advance them, are often settled less in theory than in the quotidian practice, limits and material/political constraints that women's advocates encounter in their varying locations. But, if rights are pursued in different ways and in different arenas, who or what has the responsibility for ensuring that rights on paper are effective in practice?

Feminisms and the state

Liberal rights discourse implies not only an individual rights-bearing subject, but also specifies a relationship with the state as provider and guarantor of rights. The state therefore becomes the focus of feminist advocacy, and changes in legislation and statutory institutions its object. Our third feminist dilemma arises in the relationship between feminisms and the state. Whether to work within, alongside or outside the state has long divided feminists, and doubts are constantly being raised over the nature and value of this involvement, especially as rights have been absorbed into policy and governments have taken over the rhetoric of women's rights. While this is undoubtedly a sign of success, it is also accompanied by political risks. The troubled relationship between feminisms and the state is a key theme in the contributions to this collection. They reveal the inherent ambivalence and multifaceted dimensions of this relationship, and indicate the limits of a recourse to the state and its institutions for feminist strategy.

A key issue has been that of whether women's organisations and individuals should collaborate with states that are themselves far from achieving desirable levels of democratic institutionalisation and transparency. There is a widespread concern over the 'co-option' of women's movements by governments whose espousal of gender equity programmes has more to do with gaining international funding or political clients than with a desire to emancipate women from oppression.[27] More generally, governments tend to be selective in their adoption of women's issues, or worse, to cynically reinterpret them to suit their own purposes, ones which sometimes diverge radically from feminist principles. While official rhetoric proclaims gender sensitivity, the practice in effect often serves to perpetuate male bias. Feminism also runs the political risk of appearing to support coercive policies, or policies that are actually detrimental to women, as evident, for example, in the transformation of feminist demands for women's control over reproduction into birth control policies that offer little real choice of contraceptive method and may be harmful to women. Mary Hames' account of South Africa's 'moral regeneration' programme serves as a vivid reminder of the contradictions in the ways in which the state takes up 'women's issues'.

The move towards decentralisation in many parts of the world has brought new political opportunities, but few financial resources; new democratic spaces have opened up, but are all too often sites for the same old exclusionary practices women have experienced in other political arenas.[28] Feminists increasingly question whether so much effort should be dedicated to working in these arenas when the tangible results appear so meagre. Quotas and equal opportunities declarations may have enhanced women's political representation, but the global average is still 17% for women parliamentarians. Moreover, women have in many cases lost entitlements to former social rights as a consequence of the market-oriented legal reforms described by Nyamu-Musembi and the pursuit of economic liberalisation that they represent. Economic globalisation and neoliberal policies have had particularly negative effects on state capacity in areas such as social policy. For poorer women in many parts of the world, as Jasmine Gideon's analysis of Chile's neoliberal reforms suggests, new economic opportunities have come at the cost of welfare and labour rights and the right to health.

Global understandings of rights as promoted in UN conventions have moved beyond the classic focus on political and civil rights, often criticised by developing countries, to include social and economic rights. The principle of the 'indivisibility of rights' was affirmed in the 1994 Vienna Conference. Yet, as Gideon suggests, and as a number of our contributors confirm, translating commitments made in the international arena—such as the ISESCR, which forms the basis for Gideon's analysis—into viable legislation and policies at the national level can commit states to exceeding their capacity to deliver. It is here that the feminist dilemmas outlined earlier in our discussion come to be entangled with dissonance between the universalising normative framework of human rights discourse, the particularities of cultural constructions of those who form its objects, and the complexity of interrelationships between implementing institutions. A case in point is that of the rights of the girl child, the focus of the contributions of Elizabeth Croll and Nkoyo Toyo.

Elizabeth Croll expresses doubts as to how far the widespread adoption of UNICEF's girl child platform has translated into effective national programmes or local projects in support of girls in East, South and Southeast Asia. Interestingly, even in a region where human rights are sometimes counterposed to 'Asian values', there is widespread government and civil society support for children's rights, including girls' rights, and there are some hopeful indications that new initiatives are emerging from these quarters with more far-reaching agendas. Yet the predominant emphasis has been on education; little attention has been paid to the rights and needs of the girl child either in rhetoric or in policy. Croll criticises this narrow concentration on one dimension of girls' vulnerability, noting that, even though discrimination against girls is increasing rather than decreasing in these regions, 'it has been an uphill struggle to . . . gain support for . . . [attention to] survival, health and . . . exploitation or violence, all of which are surely prerequisites for moving through the life cycle, let alone success-ful education'. She goes on to suggest that the focus on the girl child should be changed to one in which girls' rights are clearly foregrounded as a more holistic way to confront these deeper issues of discrimination and neglect.

Nigerian activist Nkoyo Toyo's analysis of the controversy surrounding the translation of the Convention on the Rights of the Child (CRC) into domestic legislation in Nigeria reveals some of these complexities. Toyo homes in on the contests arising around the provision in this legislation for a minimum age of marriage. While the Nigerian Constitution prohibits discrimination on the grounds of sex, this provision does not extend to marriage, inheritance, divorce and other elements of family life, which in Nigeria's plural legal system may fall under the domain of Islamic personal law. Further, the Nigerian Constitution recognises cultural and religious rights alongside fundamental human rights. Toyo's account reminds us that the state is no monolith; progressive national-level legislation can be roundly resisted by state-level governments and made unimplementable. Feminists are, after all, not the only social actors seeking alliances with the state—and, in this context, are only some of those who claim to speak for and about 'women'. This, as we go on to examine, creates dilemmas and tensions for the pursuit of 'women's rights'.

Which women? Whose rights?

Our fourth feminist dilemma is also of ancient lineage, but one that has gained new potency in relation to today's rights struggles. It is the question of *whose* notions of womanhood come to be embodied in the processes of framing and claiming rights. Feminists may well have grasped the potential in rights for enhancing recognition of women's demands and have pressed for greater female participation in deliberation and decision making. Yet, as a number of the contributors to this collection makes clear, what women themselves and those who represent them demand has brought its own challenges.[29]

'Women's issues' have come to be taken up by a diverse set of organised interests, each of whom claim to be acting in the interests of women and of the good society. Anti-feminist interests have gained ground in many countries as religious conservatives have mobilised around arguments for a re-moralisation of society, in which idealised representations of a 'traditional' home and child-centred womanhood are key signifiers. Mary Hames explores some of the contradictions that emerge in countries such as South Africa, where the dissonance between the 'moral regeneration' agenda pursued by senior political leaders supported by the archaic conservatism of the country's legal institutions, and South Africa's celebratedly progressive legal frameworks is becoming increasingly evident. The recent trial and acquittal of former South African Deputy President Jacob Zuma, Hames notes, epitomises this dissonance, and represents a significant setback for the pursuit of women's rights in this context.

Women may be entering politics in larger numbers, but may make use of their visibility to reinforce conservative norms and to restrict women's rights. In a number of regions, highly conservative religious institutions have been markedly more active than feminist organisations in preparing women for engagement in the political arena, grooming new leaders and offering women political opportunities that are unmatched by other alternatives.[30] In others, the active pursuit of feminist agendas by those women who make it into political office may be tantamount to political suicide; the means of entry into

13

politics may in itself preclude those with an evident commitment to gender equality.[31] Shahra Razavi shows, in the context of Iran, how conservative women parliamentarians were active in militant opposition to all human rights conventions, including the Convention on the Rights of the Child. Coupling calls for further segregation and even execution of sex workers with measures that would allow women to 'better attend to their familial duties', such as early retirement and extended maternity leave, such politicians invoke ideals of womanhood that, Razavi notes, revert to those of the early 1980s.

The politics of contradictions, fissures and frictions among those who speak for 'women' plays out in the intensification of contests over the content of women's rights. Nkoyo Toyo evokes some of these 'differences within' in her account of competing positions and positionalities in debates about women's rights among elite political wives, Islamic and Christian defenders of their version of the moral order, and feminist activists seeking gender justice. As Toyo reminds us, where competing rights claims clash with contested notions of womanhood itself, interpretations of their normative content are becoming an ever more intense site for feminist struggle. Female solidarity can never be taken as given and is often difficult to secure across the full range of women's human and reproductive rights.

Conclusions

The globalisation of rights and the appearance of RBD as a policy instrument have proceeded in tandem over recent years, offering women's advocates some potential to seek improvements in women's status and entitlements. But, as the contributions in this collection show, the realities are complex, the strategies variable, and the outcomes not straightforwardly positive. In pluri-legal settings women's rights are subject to varying interpretations, and fought over by different political and social forces which seek to promote their agendas through claims made in the name of women or the good society. Rights claims are also a site of division among women, whose increasingly visible public presence has provided feminism with both friends and foes.

The increasing visibility of women in public life and the pluralisation of opportunities for women's political participation is, then, no guarantee of support for women's rights. It is precisely in relation to gender-specific issues such as sexual and reproductive rights that feminism has met unprecedented challenges—including from women themselves. Old dilemmas and divides among women have been exacerbated by these fractures, and require feminists to navigate new political terrains and confront new hazards. The dilemmas we draw attention to here frame differences that are compounded by the harsh political realities in which efforts to advance women's rights need to contend. If these differences complicate any simple attempt at bridging differences between regionally situated feminisms, they hold particularly significant complications for the advance of women's rights.

14

Does this mean that feminists should give up on rights? None of our contributors has suggested this, but many of them express unease at the risks associated with the ways in which rights agendas have been adopted selectively to suit governments or have been annexed to powerful institutions without the democratic guarantees that might allow more consultation and deliberative processes over how they are to be applied. Despite the dynamism of some of the processes inspired by the human rights movement, there remains a wide—and in some cases, widening—gulf between the aspiration and principles and their application in many national settings. Even in places like post-apartheid South Africa, which have established robust legal frameworks enshrining women's rights, these have been only patchily implemented; as Hames' account so poignantly shows, those for whom these rights were envisaged are barely aware of their existence.

While the contributions to this book demonstrate how entrenched the challenge of realising women's rights remains, they also hold other, more hopeful lessons. Struggles to acquire legal rights achieve more than encoding claims in legislation: they foster a sense of entitlement, of the right to have rights, that in itself constitutes an important dimension of rights practice.[32] For all the challenges that this collection highlights, glimmers of hope are evident in the very contests that are so evident in the widely different locales that are the focus of our contributors' analyses. At the micro level, as well as in the contests taking place in national legislatures and international negotiations, women are increasingly visible in their efforts to make their demands heard, making pragmatic use of whatever levers exist to mobilise for change. Plural political identifications serve as rallying points for these demands: as feminists, as mothers, as workers or as those who stand to lose most from the perpetuation of existing inequities. Whether in the strategic use of human rights language in appellate judgements in Pakistan, in the tactics of feminist activists in Nigeria, in the workshops in which South African women come to realise the rights they have, or in the debates in which progressives in Iran contest conservatism, these sites of struggle are in themselves productive of new possibilities and meanings—and of a politics of 'rights' animated by demands for social and gender justice that refuse to be silenced.

Notes

1 For a discussion of rights and development, see P Uvin, *Human Rights and Development*, Bloomfield, IA: Kumarian Press, 2004, which, despite good general discussion, has limited reference to women's rights.

2 For statistical summaries of gender inequalities, see UNIFEM's Report for Beijing + 10 *Progress of World's Women 2000*, New York: UNIFEM and, for an analytic overview, see UNRISD, *Gender Equality: Striving for Justice in an Unequal World*, Geneva: UNRISD, 2005.

3 This is not the place to rehearse the arguments for and against rights. There is an extensive literature on this general issue and on the particularities of women's rights and the implication of 'globalising' women's rights. For some examples, see R Cook (ed), *Human Rights of Women: National and International Perspectives*, Philadelphia, PA: University of Pennsylvania Press, 2004; DP Forsythe, *Human Rights in International Relations*, Cambridge: Cambridge University Press, 2000; M Molyneux & S Razavi (eds), *Gender Justice, Development and Rights*, Oxford: Oxford University Press, 2003; and J Peters & A Wolper (eds), *Women's Rights, Human Rights: International Feminist Perspectives*, London: Routledge, 1996.

4 A joint initiative of the Participation Group at the Institute of Development Studies and the Institute for the Study of the Americas, School for Advanced Studies of London University, this conference was funded by Sida, SDC, DFID and ISA.

5 The UK's DFID was one of the first to promote this idea, which emerged in the second half of the 1990s.

6 N Fraser, 'Redistribution, recognition, and participation: toward an integrated conception of justice', *World Culture Report*, 2, Paris: UNESCO, 2001.

7 C Taylor, K Anthony Appiah, A Gutmann, J Habermas, S Rockefeller, M Walzer & S Wolf, *Multiculturalism: Examining the Politics of Recognition*, Princeton, NJ: Princeton University Press, 1994.

8 K Tomasevski, 'The World Bank and human rights', in M Nowak & T Swinehart (eds), *Kehl am Rhein: Engel Yearbook on HR in DCs 1989*, Kehl am Rhein: Engel, 1989, pp 113–114.

9 See, for example, J Kerr, E Sprenger & A Symington (eds), *The Future of Women's Rights: Global Visions and Strategies*, London: Zed Books, 2004. This enthusiasm contrasted with the critique of human rights from sections of the left and other quarters as a form of Western imperial intervention. See also, for discussion of this position, S Žižek, 'Against human rights', *New Left Review*, 34, 2005, pp 115–131. T Woodiwiss, *Human Rights*, New York: Routledge, 2005 provides a nuanced treatment of the issues.

10 N Fraser, 'Women, welfare and the politics of needs interpretation', in Fraser (ed), *Unruly Practices*, Cambridge: Polity Press, 1989.

11 R Eyben, 'The rise of rights: rights-based approaches to international development', *IDS Policy Briefing*, 17 (May), Brighton: Institute of Development Studies, 2003.

12 A Cornwall & C Nyamu-Musembi, 'Putting the "rights-based approach" to development into perspective', *Third World Quarterly*, 25 (8), pp 1415–1437, 2004; and Uvin, *Human Rights and Development*.

13 DFID, *Human Rights for Poor People*, Target Strategy Paper, London: Department for International Development, 2000; and Sida, *Perspectives on Poverty*, Stockholm: Sida, 2002.

14 See Gready and Ensor's recent collection, which focuses on international NGO (INGO) experiences with 'rights-based approaches'. P Gready & J Ensor, *Reinventing Development? Translating Rights-based Approaches from Theory into Practice*, London: Zed Books, 2005.

15 J Gaventa, 'Introduction: exploring citizenship, participation and accountability', *IDS Bulletin*, 33 (2), 2002, pp 1–11.

16 M Robinson, 'What rights can add to good development practice?', in P Alston & M Robinson (eds), *Human Rights and Development: Towards Mutual Reinforcement*, New York: Oxford University Press, 2005, p 29.

17 Workshop proceedings. The source is anonymised to preserve confidentiality.

18 See, for example, the work of Ian Scoones and others on sustainable livelihoods in Southern Africa. I Scoones & W Wolmer, 'Livelihoods in crisis? New perspectives on governance and rural development in Southern Africa', *IDS Bulletin*, 34 (3), 2003.

19 M Keck & K Sikkink, *Activists Beyond Borders: Advocacy Networks in International Politics*, Ithaca, NY: Cornell University Press, 1998.

20 See for example, on Latin America, M Htun, *Sex and the State: Abortion, Divorce and the Family under Latin American Dictatorships and Democracies*, Cambridge: Cambridge University Press, 2003; and N Craske & M Molyneux (eds), *Gender and the Politics of Rights and Democracy in Latin America*, London: Palgrave, 2002. On South Africa, see S Hassim, 'Representation, participation and democratic effectiveness: feminist challenges to representative democracy in South Africa', in A-M Goetz & S Hassim (eds), *No Shortcuts to Power: African Women in Politics and Policy Making*, London: Zed Books, 2003; and A Gouws, *(Un)thinking Citizenship: Feminist Debates in Contemporary South Africa*, Cape Town: University of Cape Town Press, 2005.

21 A Ortiz-Ortega, 'Femicide and the politics of "justice" in Mexico', paper presented to the Feminist Perspectives on Rights-Based Development conference, Institute of Development Studies, 26–27 September 2005.

22 SE Alvarez, 'Advocating feminism: the Latin American feminist NGO "boom"', *International Feminist Journal Of Politics*, 1 (2), 1999, pp 181–209; and I Jad, 'The NGO-isation of Arab women's movements', *IDS Bulletin*, 35 (4), 2004, pp 34–42.

23 The four-country study carried out by Molyneux and Lazar reached similar conclusions. M Molyneux & S Lazar, *Doing the Rights Thing: Rights-Based Development and Latin American NGOs*, London: ITDG Publishing, 2003.

24 S Bracke, 'Different worlds are possible: feminist yearnings for shared futures', in Kerr *et al*, *The Future of Women's Rights*.

25 S Álvarez, 'Latin American feminisms "go global": trends of the 1990s and challenges for the new millennium', in S Álvarez, E Dagnino & A Escobar (eds) *Cultures of Politics/Politics of Cultures:*

Revisioning Latin American Social Movements, Boulder, CO: Westview, 1998, p 315; and Molyneux & Lazar, *Doing the Rights Thing*.

26 See Women Living Under Muslim Laws website, at www.wluml.org.

27 A-M Goetz, 'Women's political effectiveness: a conceptual framework', in Goetz & Hassim, *No Shortcuts to Power*.

28 R Mohanty, 'Institutional dynamics and participatory spaces: the making and unmaking of participation in local forest management in India', *IDS Bulletin*, 35 (2), pp 26–32; and A Cornwall & A-M Goetz, 'Democratizing democracy: feminist perspectives', *Democratization*, 12 (5), 2005, pp 783–800.

29 For discussions of commonalities and differences among women, see, for example, JR Jakobsen, *Working Alliances and the Politics of Difference: Diversity and Feminist Ethics*, Bloomington, IN: University of Indiana Press, 1998.

30 S Batliwala & D Dhanraj, 'Gender myths that instrumentalise women: a view from the Indian frontline', *IDS Bulletin*, 35 (4), 2004, pp 11–18; and C Nyamu-Musembi, personal communication.

31 Goetz, 'Women's political effectiveness'.

32 C Nyamu-Musembi, 'Towards an actor-orientated perspective on human rights', *IDS Working Paper*, 169, Brighton: Institute of Development Studies; and R Petchesky, *Negotiating Reproductive Rights*, London: Zed Books, 1998.

Ruling out Gender Equality? The Post-Cold War rule of law agenda in Sub-Saharan Africa

CELESTINE NYAMU-MUSEMBI

The post-cold war era has been referred to as a time of 'rule of law revival'.[1] The rule of law (ROL) is seen as indispensable to establishing a market economy and democratic rule, the two prongs of the neoliberal project. In sub-Saharan Africa reforms associated with the political change that occurred in the immediate post-cold war era have been justified in terms of these twin goals.[2] Some of the reform initiatives were generated directly by domestic agendas, but there has been significant involvement of multilateral and bilateral actors in legal and institutional reforms in sub-Saharan Africa, not least in setting the overall tone and focus of the reforms.

The overwhelming emphasis and investment has been in creating a suitable legal and institutional environment for the market.[3] There has been an emphasis on harmonising national laws with international 'best practice' so as to create a suitable foreign investment climate.[4] Some attention has been paid to the democratic rule prong, for instance through reform of electoral laws, courts and the establishment of national human rights commissions. The bulk of legal reforms, however, have focused on revising laws on commercial transactions and improving judicial efficiency in the resolution of business disputes.

In this same period the region has seen a significant rise in the profile and impact of movements concerned with gender equality and women's empowerment. The key concerns they have articulated can be grouped into the following broad categories:

- Progressive constitutional reform to end sex discrimination and guarantee women equal rights in all spheres, including family relations. In some sub-Saharan African countries family relations are governed by personal laws based on custom and religion, which are exempt from constitutional scrutiny of their discriminatory effect.
- Ending institutionalised gender bias and corruption in the functioning of justice institutions, including informal and quasi-formal institutions.
- Stronger guarantees of women's economic security through reforms to property laws, primarily those concerning land.
- Reform of labour relations laws to end gender discrimination in the formal sector, but also to extend labour and social security regulations to poorly regulated sectors such as farming, informal businesses and export processing zones (EPZs), which are often dominated by women.

Juxtaposing these priorities with an exploration of what the ROL reforms have focused on, this paper's central question is: has the post-cold war ROL agenda in sub-Saharan Africa enhanced or impeded gender equality?

This chapter is divided into three main sections. The first gives an overview of the ROL reform programme in sub-Saharan Africa. The second discusses the priorities that have been articulated by gender justice advocates in the region, and then evaluates the reform initiatives taken by governments and donors in order to highlight specific gender gaps in the ROL agenda. The concluding section observes that the overall climate in which the reforms are being promoted threatens to delegitimise the pursuit of any goals seen as incompatible with the core agenda of creating efficiently functioning legal institutions for the market. Although this core agenda may arguably produce benefits that trickle down to all citizens in the long run, in the absence of explicit commitment to social justice and redistribution, there have been few gains for gender equality.

Setting the scene: overview of the rule-of-law agenda in sub-Saharan Africa

On the whole rule of law projects have been donor-funded and donor driven. Funding for justice sector reforms in sub-Saharan Africa grew from $17.7 million in 1994 to $110 million in 2002.[5] The World Bank and a few bilateral programmes have played a highly significant role in shaping the agenda. Overall the World Bank's lending under the theme of rule of law is tiny compared with other themes. The trends in funding are summarised in Table 1.

TABLE 1. World Bank lending to African borrowers under 'rule of law' 1994–2003 (US$ millions, annual average)

	1994–97	*1998–99*	*2000*	*2001*	*2002*	*2003*
Rule of law	38.2	21.0	26.7	34.0	22.5	34.5
Total lending	2390.6	2463.2	2159.1	3369.6	3793.5	3737.2
Percentage	1.6%	0.8%	1.2%	1%	0.6%	0.9%

Souce: Compiled based on http://www.worldbank.org/annualreport/2003/table/5-1.htm.

In 2004 ROL lending accounted for only three per cent of total World Bank – International Development Agency lending.[6] However, the total figure spent by the Bank on ROL activities is probably higher than these figures reflect, for two reasons. First, these figures do not include assistance classified as technical or advisory. Second, they do not reflect funding for sector-specific reforms, such as 'financial and private sector development' which also includes a component for related legal and institutional reforms. Thus, in order to get a full picture, one would need more information beyond the figures reflected as covering rule of law activities. It is also important to note that the influence of institutions such as the World Bank is not felt only through the funding they provide. It is also exerted in the ideas they promote through their policies and research, and through conditionality requirements, so that measures taken at the national level will reflect World Bank requirements without this being explicitly stated.

The information available from bilateral agencies would suggest that, with a few exceptions, they have not been key players in ROL projects in sub-Saharan Africa. Bilateral agencies with a substantial involvement in ROL activities include the US Agency for International Development (USAID), the UK Department for International Development (DFID), and the Danish International Development Agency (Danida). USAID projects in legal and institutional reform have focused on Latin America, the former Soviet republics and Eastern Europe.[7] USAID activities in Africa focus on developing US–Africa business linkages through the US Congress's African Growth and Opportunity Act (AGOA).[8] Because of its position as the largest market for garment industries in most African countries' EPZs, the USA has major influence over trade and related legal reforms in the region.

DFID's 'safety, security and access to justice' (SSAJ) programme addresses the priority areas of security of property and protection of assets, access to legal protection, and effective justice institutions.[9] DFID is involved in funding law and order sector-wide reforms in Kenya, Uganda and Tanzania, and has SSAJ programmes in Ghana, Malawi, Lesotho, Nigeria, Sierra Leone and South Africa.[10] Danida provides substantial funding for judicial reform in Uganda under its 'Strengthening the Judiciary Project' launched in 1995.[11] Besides specific projects, donors have also been giving direct budget support and therefore some legal and institutional reforms may not necessarily be attributed to specific donors. The focus of ROL reforms has been, and continues to be, primarily commercial.[12] They have been motivated by 'concern for the creation of a stable business environment in which investment for productive purposes may expand and prosper'.[13] Reforms so far have targeted laws dealing with debt recovery, banking, insurance, taxation, property relations (land tenure reform, intellectual property), corporate governance and freedom of information.[14]

These reforms have largely been 'top-down', with a focus on government institutions and little investment in equipping people to access the justice system.[15] Neither have the reforms been subjected to public debate and scrutiny for their attention to goals such as gender equality, or any other social justice goal for that matter. Since the main areas of law addressed by the reforms are perceived as technical matters there is little involvement of the public.[16]

The ROL agenda's commitment to social justice, let alone gender equity, is doubtful. The key regional financial institution, the African Development ment Bank, makes no reference to legal discrimination on the basis of gender, or to using law to challenge discriminatory exclusion of women. There is a vague reference to such problems but only in relation to access to education.[17] The World Bank's lending for the law and justice sector has not paid attention to gender equality. Such attention is to be found only in the Bank's research work. A 1994 World Bank report sums up the Bank's law-related work in sub-Saharan Africa as dealing with the strengthening of legal institutions related to property rights and contracts, with training of court officials and improvement of court infrastructure, and with training for legal draftsmen, with only a research component going to the role of women in development.[18] The Bank's Africa Division in 1992 issued a series of three working papers focusing on gender and law.[19] The papers highlighted shortcomings in substantive areas of law, such as access to and control of property, labour regulation and access to work-related benefits (such as health coverage), and access to capital (through credit). They also analysed weaknesses in the administration of law. It seems that this analysis has resulted only in relatively small regional initiatives, mostly funded through the Institutional Development Fund, rather than in programmatic work integrated into the mainstream of the World Bank's lending activities.[20] One example of such regional initiatives is the continent-wide Africa Gender and Law Programme. The programme's coverage has been mostly in francophone Africa, with some projects in East Africa, such as support for Rwanda's comprehensive Gender Legal Action Plan.[21]

Gender justice priorities versus the legal reform agenda's priorities

The priorities articulated by gender justice advocates were outlined briefly in the introduction. This section elaborates on them and then evaluates the reform initiatives undertaken by governments and lenders in order to highlight ways in which the reforms fall short in addressing gender inequality.

Enactment and full implementation of progressive constitutional reforms

Thanks to a confluence of domestic pressure and political conditionality imposed largely by bilateral funders, the post-cold war ROL agenda has included reforms aimed at enabling political competition and expanding civil and political rights. This confluence came about as part of the post-cold war euphoria over the 'second wave' of democratisation in sub-Saharan Africa, even though domestic struggles had begun much earlier. These 'rights and democratic rule' reforms are manifest in new constitutions, in the establishment of human rights commissions, in revision of electoral laws and in the repeal of laws that outlawed political dissent. These reforms have developed alongside the reforms oriented toward the creation of a business-friendly legal environment.[22]

On the whole movements for gender equality have been adept at using the 'rights and democratic rule' prong of the ROL agenda to make significant gains in securing rights for women, for instance through favourable constitutional change. Successful mobilisation by women's movements has been one of the key features of recent constitution making in Eritrea (1997), Ghana (1992), Malawi (1994), South Africa (1996) and Uganda (1995). While the gaining of constitutional rights is a significant advance in the struggle for gender equality, more difficult has been the translation of these gains into detailed legislation in substantive areas such as family and property law, and into positive practices at the level of institutions, both formal and informal.

The gender equality movement has sought extension of constitutional scrutiny to personal laws (based on religion and custom) governing family relations. In several countries personal laws are exempt from the constitution's prohibition of discrimination.[23] The mere existence of religious and customary norms does not in itself threaten gender equality. Such norms do need to be given recognition in a pluralistic social context where it is evident that they play a primary role in regulating and giving social–cultural meaning to interpersonal relations. However, there is a serious threat when exemption clauses deny citizens the right to seek redress through the national legal system for unjust treatment justified on the basis of their communities' custom or religion.[24]

Clearly, even though constitutional rights is one area in which gender justice advocates in sub-Saharan Africa have made gains, problems persist. They range from the absence of an adequate constitutional framework in some countries to time lag and resistance to the translation of recently won constitutional rights into concrete areas of law, particularly property and family (as in Eritrea, Ghana, Malawi, South Africa, and Uganda). In all cases the application of gender equality principles in both formal and informal judicial and administrative institutions remains a problem.

Ending institutionalised gender bias in the administration of justice

Formal justice institutions. Institutionalised gender bias has long been a subject of discussion, along with practices such as corruption and ineptitude, which impede people's access to justice institutions. Empirical research in six southern African countries by Women and Law in Southern Africa (WLSA) documents the problems. In addition to problems that affect all users of formal courts, namely language and complex procedures, geographical inaccessibility, cost and protracted delays, WLSA research highlights problems specific to women:[25]

- women's relatively lower literacy levels, which aggravate the problems of language and complexity;
- court buildings not adequately equipped to meet women's needs, especially those of mothers with babies;
- relative under-funding of family courts, the majority of whose users are women pursuing maintenance and custody claims;
- absence of legal aid services in family matters which affects women more;
- under-representation of women in higher courts—women have slightly higher representation in the magistracy, but overall the gender make-up of the judiciary does not reflect that of the general population.[26]

These issues have not been addressed, as the ROL reforms have not focused on enabling people's access to justice institutions, let alone targeted the barriers experienced by specific marginalised groups. In addition, reform activities such as computerisation of registries, setting up alternative dispute resolution to reduce congestion in the court system, and even building court premises have often started with (and sometimes stopped with) the commercial division.[27] A 1997 overview of judicial reform projects supported by the World Bank revealed an overwhelming emphasis on strengthening debt recovery systems, training judges in commercial law and the speedy handling of business disputes, and setting up commercial arbitration.[28]

Informal justice institutions. Informal justice institutions play a significant role in dispute resolution, especially with regard to family matters and predominantly in rural areas. The interaction of formal law and societal norms is a crucial site for generating and enforcing norms on gender relations. The view has long been expressed by feminist legal scholars that, in order to fully understand the impact of formal laws on gender relations, one must examine how people interact with those laws in all spheres, how other regulatory social orders influence their operation, and what the consequences are for men and women in different circumstances.[29] Informal justice institutions are the primary local sites in which 'abstract ideas of rights and justice are given meaning and content and translated into different outcomes for different people'.[30]

The definition of 'informal justice institutions' goes beyond 'traditional' forums. It includes a wide range of systems that can be thought of as being at different points on a continuum. At one end are community-based systems that have little or no relationship with formal state structures; examples include intra- and inter-family mediation. At the other end of the continuum are quasi-judicial forums that are sponsored by or created by the state, but empowered to apply norms such as customary law that are seen as generated outside the state structure.[31]

There are acknowledged advantages to these forums, among them their accessibility, affordability, ability to take into account the broader social context of a dispute, and in some circumstances their ability to deliver decisions based on a sense of justice and equity, where a court would have rigidly applied the law and produced an unjust result.[32] However, problems arise to varying degrees with respect to lack of accountability, absence of an adequate interface with formal justice institutions, gender imbalance in their staffing, and embedded biases rooted in the decision makers' understanding of gender roles and authority.[33]

ROL reforms in a handful of countries have engaged with informal justice institutions. Uganda has integrated its Local Council Courts (LCC) into the judiciary's lower rungs with a right of appeal to higher courts. Each LCC must have at least three women.[34] Tanzania similarly requires that three of the seven members of the village land councils established under the 1999 Village Land Act must be women. In South Africa the constitution gives power to traditional authorities, but at the same time holds them accountable to constitutional principles (such as gender equality) to the same level as any public body. In addition, the South African Law Commission launched a project for the review of customary law and for its harmonisation with the spirit of the post-apartheid constitution.[35] Following public consultations the commission has recommended minimum standards for the operation of community dispute resolution structures. Examples include reasonable representation of women, non-compulsion in participation, and recognition of the fact that unsatisfied parties still retain their rights as citizens to pursue the dispute in any other forum of their choice.[36]

Examples of donors' interest in informal institutions are few and far between. Danida's judicial support for Uganda emphasises the interface between LCCs and higher courts.[37] DFID incorporated guidelines on working with 'non-state justice and security systems' into its policy statement on Safety, Security and Access to Justice,[38] but there is little evidence of its operationalisation. The World Bank is in the initial stages of a programme known as Justice for the Poor, which has an emphasis on community-based systems. Implementation has been going on for about two years in Indonesia, but in the sub-Saharan Africa region the programme has not taken off yet.[39]

Stronger guarantees of women's economic security through reforms to property laws

Reforms to property laws have focused on land, since it is the key resource in the predominantly rural economies. Reform of the legal arrangements governing land (land tenure) has a long history in some sub-Saharan countries. In Kenya, for instance, it dates back to the 1950s. Other countries have seen recent activity coinciding with the post-cold war ROL agenda. These include Cote d'Ivoire, Ethiopia, Ghana, Malawi, Mozambique, Namibia, Niger, South Africa, Tanzania, Uganda and Zimbabwe.[40] Financing for these land law reforms has come from international institutions as well as national budgets, many of which have a substantial donor-funded component. Gender justice advocates have drawn attention to concerns such as:

- land title formalisation programmes that have resulted in registration of family holdings exclusively in the name of the 'male head of household';[41]
- failure to address gender inequities rationalised as customary;
- persistent under-representation or complete lack of representation of women in old and newly created institutions administering land and other key resources;
- complexity and bureaucratic confusion in land systems.

Until the early 1990s the dominant view in governments and in key institutions that funded title formalisation programmes reflected a 'title orthodoxy': strengthening the security of property rights was synonymous with replacing indigenous/customary tenure with formal (often individual) title, and this was the way to create incentives for investment and to stimulate markets in land. Even when the resilience of customary tenure arrangements was acknowledged, the transition to full land titling was seen as inevitable.[42]

However, since the mid-1990s, in response to criticism,[43] there has been a shift in institutional thinking to argue for a more incremental approach, and also one that seeks to build on customary sources of security rather than displace them.[44] This shift celebrates the flexibility and adaptability of customary tenure and the important role it plays at the local level in guaranteeing secure access to land.[45] It has influenced Ghana's 1999 national land policy, which emphasises decentralised, community-based land tenure management systems in conjunction with traditional authority.[46] The shift has also influenced Tanzania's recent Village Land Act of 1999, which recognises the category of 'village land' under the control of village land councils applying customary law.

Nevertheless, the institutional discourses favouring this 're-turn' to the customary have had little to say about the anticipated impact on women's land rights.[47]

The pendulum seems to be swinging back to title orthodoxy once more, spurred on by recent interest in the work of Hernando de Soto, who emphasises the need for formal registration to convert poor people's assets from 'dead capital' into 'live capital'.[48] Lately commentators have relied on his work to speak of title in glowing terms and with renewed enthusiasm, as if the earlier critiques dislodging the 'title = security = productivity' argument never happened.[49] The negative gendered impact of formal title once more goes unquestioned.

The experience of land law reform illustrates that, in a sphere so obviously governed by plural normative orders (ie the overlap between formal law and customary norms), law reformers have got it wrong by making two mistakes. Initially they were fixated on the supposed benefits of formal title and refused to see the continued relevance of customary norms governing land relations. They therefore failed to acknowledge that title was by no means a guarantee of security for all, certainly not for the majority of women and other family members for whom title in the name of the 'male head of household' spelled the erosion of their customary rights to land.[50] Then, belatedly, law reformers recognised the centrality of customary tenure but celebrated its benefits (eg flexibility) without critical analysis of the power relations that shape it. On both counts opportunities to question gender inequalities have been missed.

Recent reforms to property law in some countries have attempted to address gender inequality. In Tanzania the National Land Policy of 1997 stipulates that women should be able to acquire land in their own right, by purchase and/or allocation. Inheritance may be governed by custom, but should not contradict the constitution and natural justice.[51] Both the Land Act and the Village Land Act of 1999 recognise co-ownership for spouses (although it is not made mandatory), and also stipulate that women are able to own land independently. A spouse's consent is required for mortgages, leases and sales, a condition that applies equally to husbands and wives. The new laws also call upon institutions such as the village councils not to discriminate against women. A 2004 amendment to Uganda's Land Act guarantees security of occupancy of family land, which protects the interests of spouses equally. So far there is not enough written on the practical experience of implementing these changes in the law to assess what impact they have had on gender justice concerns.

One crucial observation made by gender justice advocates is that official discussion of gender and land tenure is often disconnected from discussion of broader processes of economic restructuring, for instance those affecting the financial services industry. Yet women's ability to access credit is connected to their ability to demonstrate secure interests in valuable land that they can put up as collateral. Financial sector reforms have not been co-ordinated with reform of land and family laws, yet, from a gender analysis perspective, the connection is obvious. A study of financial sector reforms intended to benefit small and medium-scale enterprises in Uganda highlights the gender-differentiated impact of the reforms.[52] The study argues that the reforms reinforce lenders' biases against lending to people with 'undesirable' collateral (eg women, most of whom do not hold titles to land). The new legislative framework and new government policies on financial services make several assumptions that do not hold true for most women entrepreneurs. For example, it is assumed that all borrowers own titled land in large urban centres, have the resources to hire experts to write business plans and feasibility studies, and have established long-term relationships with banks.[53] Little wonder, then, that the bulk of lending since the new policies were introduced has gone to the small and medium-scale manufacturing sector and not the agricultural and retail marketing sectors where women entrepreneurs are concentrated.

ROL reforms have failed to make a contribution to securing women's property rights and alleviating economic vulnerability.

Extending labour regulation and social security to EPZs and informal sectors

The introduction of export-oriented production through EPZs), particularly in the garment sector, has opened up employment opportunities for women since the 1990s. However, this period has also been characterised by erosion of the legal rights of workers in general. EPZs and large-scale agribusiness have come to epitomise that erosion.[54] Studies of the legal environment governing EPZs—whose workforce is largely female—are recent and few. Although there is an overwhelming perception that EPZs are exempt from key legal requirements, such as unionisation of workers and factory inspections by health and safety officials, it is difficult to find any specific laws granting these exemptions. It is an issue that is defined by ambiguities. Law making has taken the form of sub-legislative devices such as ministerial orders and policy directives, thus by-passing the scrutiny of parliamentary processes. This lack of transparency has generated un-certainty about the applicability of the general law on labour relations to EPZs. A study on EPZs in Zimbabwe pointed out a glaring contradiction between the 1995 law setting up EPZs and pre-existing labour legislation. On the one hand, the 1995 law contained a clause explicitly exempting EPZ enterprises from the Labour Relations Act. On the other hand, another clause gave power to the government's EPZ Authority to enact subsidiary rules setting out conditions of service, termination and disciplinary proceedings between workers and employers in EPZs. The EPZ authority had not made the rules, resulting in ambiguity and leaving most workers unprotected: out of 10 EPZ companies in the study, only five claimed to be applying the Labour Relations Act.[55]

Similar ambiguity prevails in Kenya, where changes to labour laws since economic liberalisation began in the late 1980s and early 1990s have been effected through ministerial orders and sector-specific policy directives. For instance, exemption of EPZs from the requirements of the Employment Act in Kenya was effected through a ministerial order, rather than an amendment to the Act. It is not clear who has regulatory authority over labour relations in EPZs. The 1990 law that sets up EPZs focuses on spelling out the functions of the EPZ Authority and on licensing procedures and benefits available to investors. The labour regulation function is not expressly included in the EPZ Authority's mandate. The authority has nonetheless established a labour relations office, but that office lacks statutory powers and proper linkages to Ministry of Labour officials.[56] Although enterprises are supposed to file annual returns to the EPZ Authority, with respect to staff they are only required to specify numbers of local and expatriate employees and their ranks. No follow-up action is taken other than forwarding the information to the Central Bureau of Statistics.[57] A recent report by a task force reviewing labour laws recommends that EPZs should no longer be exempt, and that the provisions of the Employment Act are to be applied strictly to their operations.[58]

As a result of this general legal uncertainty, several arbitrary practices are prevalent within EPZs that heavily compromise the rights of workers, a majority of whom are women.[59] Gender justice advocates have also raised concerns about extending the application of labour regulations to informal work, such as paid domestic service.[60] Comprehensive social security reform to cover informal and rural sectors dominated by women is also on the gender justice agenda, but not on the ROL reform agenda. An African Development Bank (ADB) report on Africa and the millennium development goals talks in passing about gender-sensitive budgeting, and the need to commit resources to production sectors where women are concentrated.[61] However, there is no mention of reforms to the social security system to extend benefits to rural-based and informal sectors where women are concentrated.

Conclusion

A juxtaposition of the ROL reform priorities with the priorities articulated by gender justice advocates shows a disconnection. The ROL reforms have no agenda for social justice and alleviation of inequality; certainly not gender inequality. The post-cold war climate in which the reforms have taken place has meant that objectives that are viewed as incompatible with market-oriented legal reform are abandoned or held in abeyance 'even if this means that goals such as equality and redistribution must be sidelined in the process'.[62] In such a climate, the enactment of laws that enable deployment of state resources to safeguard women's rights, for instance through extending social security benefits to the agricultural sector and EPZs can and does become less of a priority. Even where governments profess commitment to such goals, for instance through constitutional guarantees of gender equality, this commitment is not reflected in the articulation of priorities or the allocation of funds. This overview concludes that the reforms have been top-down, focused only on formal institutions, and that primacy has been given to commercial interests. Such reforms may arguably produce benefits that trickle down to all citizens in the long run but, in the absence of an explicit commitment to a social justice agenda, it is unlikely that this will happen, and even less likely that the reforms will contribute to gender equality. This state of affairs in sub-Saharan Africa is a reflection of a global post-cold war reality whereby any moral consensus on the rightness of equality and redistribution as social goals is being gradually eroded.[63] While sub-Saharan African governments in general are not known for their receptivity to arguments for gender equality, this global post-cold war climate has provided a dominant discourse that legitimises the lack of attention paid to gender inequality and to social justice broadly.

Notes

1 T Carothers, 'Rule of law revival', *Foreign Affairs*, 77 (2), pp 95–107 uses the term 'revival' because there has not been this level of interest in understanding the role of law in economic development, or this level of activity in law-related reform by development agencies, since the 1960s and 1970s 'law and development' movement.

2 The specific country examples used in this paper are drawn primarily from the East African region, with references to Ghana, Malawi, Nigeria, Zimbabwe and South Africa, and reference to general trends in the francophone region.

3 I Shihata, *Complementary Reform: Essays on Legal, Judicial, and other Institutional Reforms supported by the World Bank*, The Hague: Kluwer Law International, 1997; World Bank, *Sub-Saharan Africa: From Crisis to Sustainable Growth—A Long-Term Perspective Study*, Washington, DC: World Bank, 1989; and World Bank, *Governance: The World Bank's Experience*, Washington, DC: World Bank, 1994.

4 J Faundez, 'Legal reform in developing and transition countries: making haste slowly', *Law, Social Justice and Global Development*, 2000, electronic journal, Warwick University School of Law, at http://www2.warwick.ac.uk/fac/soc/law/elj/lgd/2000_1/faundez/, accessed 28 June 2006; K Pistor, 'The standardization of law and its effect on developing economies', *American Journal of Comparative Law*, 50, 2002, p 101; Shihata, *Complementary Reform*, p 22; and USAID, 'Program Highlights', 2004, at http://www.usaid.gov/policy/budget/cbj2004/highlights.html, accessed 28 June 2006.

5 L-H Piron, 'Donor assistance to justice sector reform in Africa: living up to the new agenda?', *Justice Initiatives*, Open Society Justice Initiative, February 2005, at http://www.afrimap.org/english/images/report/file427a275e61740.pdf, accessed 30 June 2006.

6 See http://www.worldbank.org/annualreport/2004/lending.html, accessed 28 June 2006. Note, however, that when funding activities are categorised by sectors, law-related activities are reflected in the broader sector of 'law, justice and public administration', which pushes the percentage to 25%. This is because the figure includes all central government administrative costs for all projects in the relevant period.

7 See http://www.usaid.gov/our_work/democracy_and_governance/technical_areas/rule_of_law, accessed 28 June 2006.

8 See http://www.usaid.gov/policy/budget/cbj2004/highlights.html, accessed 28 June 2006.

9 See http://www.grc-dfid.org.uk/grc/docs/TSP.pdf, accessed 28 June 2006.

10 Information on DFID's programmes and projects in safety, security and access to justice is available at a restricted-access website: http://www.grc-dfid.org.uk/grc/keycaps/ssaj.html.

11 Nordic Consulting Group (NCG), *Strategic Plan for the Uganda Judiciary: 2002/3–2007/8*, Kampala, Uganda: NCG, 2002.

12 R Islam, 'Institutional reform and the judiciary: which way forward?', *Policy Research Working Paper*, 3134, Washington, DC: World Bank, 2003; and World Bank, *Annual Report*, Washington, DC: World Bank, 2004, at http://www.worldbank.org/annualreport/2004/legal_systems.html, accessed 28 June 2006.

13 I Shihata, *Complementary Reform*, p 90.

14 *Ibid*, pp 75–83; and World Bank, *Annual Report*.

15 See World Bank Group, *Projects and Operations*, 2005, at http://web.worldbank.org/external/projects/main?pagePK=217672&piPK=95916&theSitePK=40941&menuPK=223661&category=majortheme&majortheme=3, accessed 28 June 2006. No African country had a project funded under 'access to law and justice'. See also T Carothers, *Aiding Democracy Abroad: The Learning Curve*, Washington, DC: Carnegie Endowment for International Peace, 1999, pp 161–162; and S Golub, 'Beyond rule of law orthodoxy: the legal empowerment alternative', *Working Paper*, 41, Rule of Law Series, Washington, DC: Carnegie Endowment for International Peace, 2003.

16 T Carothers, *Aiding Democracy Abroad*, pp 161–162.

17 African Development Bank (ADB), *Achieving the Millennium Development Goals in Africa: Progress, Prospects and Policy Implications*, Global Poverty Report, June 2002, at http://lnweb18.worldbank.org/afr/afr.nsf/0/aa2093d2b04ddbd885256be30058f71c/$FILE/mdg-africa.pdf, accessed 28 June 2006.

18 World Bank, *Governance*, p 27.

19 D Martin & FO Hashi, 'Law as an institutional barrier to the economic empowerment of women', *Working Paper*, 2, Washington, DC: Technical Department, Africa Region, World Bank, 2002; Martin & Hashi, 'Gender, the evolution of legal institutions and economic development in sub-Saharan Africa', Working Paper, 3, Washington, DC: Technical Dept, Africa Region, World Bank, 2002; and Martin & Hashi, 'Women in development: the legal issues in sub-Saharan African today', *Working Paper*, 4, Washington, DC: Technical Dept, Africa Region, World Bank, 2002.

20 This is acknowledged with respect to the Eastern African Gender and Law Programme in a foreword by James W Adams (Country Director for Tanzania and Uganda) to G Gopal, 'Gender-related legal

reform and access to economic resources in Eastern Africa', *World Bank Discussion Paper*, 405, Washington, DC: World Bank, 1999.

21 Email communication from Therese Nibarere, World Bank, Rwanda Country Office, 23 March 2004. The bank has also supported dialogue in six Latin American countries on the application of international conventions on gender equality (via video conference). See World Bank, *Annual Report*; World Bank Group, *Gender and Law in Francophone sub-Saharan Africa: The Role of the World Bank*, Washington, DC: World Bank, 2000, at http://www.worldbank.org/afr/findings/english/find155.htm, accessed 28 June 2006; and World Bank Group, 'Access of women to legal and judicial services in sub-Saharan Africa', report of the Workshop of Lomé, 27–30 November 2000, 2001, at http://siteresources.worldbank.org/EXTAFRREGTOPGENDER/Resources/AccessWomenLegal_en.pdf, accessed 28 June 2006.

22 Some commentators suggest that this co-existence has been an uneasy one, fraught with contradictions. See, for example, J Gathii, 'Empowering the weak while protecting the powerful: a critique of good governance proposals', SJD dissertation, Harvard Law School, 1999.

23 Examples include Benin, Kenya, Lesotho, Niger, Swaziland, Zambia and Zimbabwe.

24 Y Mokgoro, 'Traditional authority and democracy in the interim South African constitution', *Review of Constitutional Studies*, 3 (1), 1996, pp 1–28; C Nyamu, 'How should human rights and development respond to cultural legitimization of gender hierarchy in developing countries?', *Harvard International Law Journal*, 41 (2), 2000, pp 381–418; and C Nyamu-Musembi, 'Are local norms and processes fences or pathways? The example of women's property rights in rural Kenya', in A An-Na'im (ed), *Cultural Transformation and Human Rights in Africa*, London: Zed Books, 2002, pp 126–150.

25 See also the list of WLSA publications at http://www.wlsa.co.zw/publications.htm, accessed 28 June 2006. And see WLSA, *In the Shadow of the Law: Women and Justice Delivery in Zimbabwe*, Harare: WLSA Trust, 2000; and WLSA, *In Search of Justice: Women and the Administration of Justice in Malawi*, Blantyre: Dzuka Publishing, 2000.

26 For instance, WLSA's study in Zimbabwe found that, out of 197 magistrates nation-wide in 1999, only 58 (29.4%) were women (based on figures provided by the office of the Chief Magistrate). At that time the Supreme Court had five judges, only one of whom was a woman, and out of 18 High Court judges, only three were female. WLSA, *In the Shadow of the Law*, p 138.

27 C Nyamu-Musembi, 'For or against gender equality? Evaluating the post-cold war 'rule of law' reforms in sub-Saharan Africa', *UNRISD Occasional Paper*, 7, August 2005.

28 I Shihata, *Complementary Reform*, pp 20–22, 39–44.

29 TS Dahl, *Women's Law: An Introduction to Feminist Jurisprudence*, Oslo: Norwegian University Press, 1987; A Griffiths, *In the Shadow of Marriage: Gender and Justice in an African Community*, Chicago, IL: University of Chicago Press, 1997; A Hellum, *Women's Human Rights and Legal Pluralism in Africa: Mixed Norms and Identities in Infertility Management in Zimbabwe*, Tano Aschehoug: Mond Books, 1999; C Smart, *Feminism and the Power of Law*, London: Routledge, 1989; and WLSA, *In the Shadow of the Law*.

30 Nyamu-Musembi, 'Are local norms and processes fences or pathways?', p 128.

31 C Nyamu-Musembi, 'Review of experience in engaging with 'non-state' justice systems in East Africa', study commissioned by DFID Governance Division, 2003, at http://www.ids.ac.uk/ids/law/justicewkshp.html, accessed 28 June 2006.

32 J-J Barya & J Oloka-Onyango, *Popular Justice and Resistance Committee Courts in Uganda*, Kampala: Center for Basic Research, 1994; C Nyamu-Musembi, 'Are local norms and processes fences or pathways?'; and Penal Reform International, 'Access to justice in sub-Saharan Africa: the role of traditional and informal justice systems', 2000, at www.penalreform.org.

33 C Nyamu-Musembi, 'Are local norms and processes fences or pathways?'.

34 L Khadiagala, 'The failure of popular justice in Uganda: local councils and women's property rights', *Development and Change*, 32, 2001, p 64.

35 See South African Law Commission Discussion Papers, 74, 76, 82, 93 and 95, at http://wwwserver.law.wits.ac.za/salc/discussn/discussn.html, accessed 2 June 2005.

36 See South African Law Commission, 'Community dispute resolution structures', Discussion Paper, 87, 1999, at http://wwwserver.law.wits.ac.za/salc/discussn/discussn.html.

37 NCG, *Strategic Plan for the Ugandan Judiciary*.

38 Available at www.dfid.gov.uk, accessed 28 June 2006.

39 See http://www.justiceforthepoor.or.id/, accessed 28 June 2006; and World Bank, *Annual Report*.

40 A Whitehead & D Tsikata, 'Policy discourses on women's land rights in sub-Saharan Africa: the implications of the re-turn to the customary', *Journal of Agrarian Change*, 3 (1), 2003, pp 67–112; and N Kanji, L Cotula, T Hilhorst, C Toulmin & W Witten, *Research Report 1: Can Land Registration serve Poor and Marginalized Groups? Summary Report*, London: IIED, 2005.

41 S Lastarria-Cornhiel, 'Impact of privatization on gender and property rights in Africa', *World Development*, 25, 1997, pp 1317–1333; R Meinzen-Dick, L Brown, H Sims Feldstein & A Quisumbing,

'Gender and property rights: overview', *World Development*, 25, 1997, pp 1299–1302; C Nyamu, 'How should human rights and development respond to cultural legitimization of gender hierarchy in developing countries?'; and AO Pala, 'Women's access to land and their role in agriculture and decision-making on the farm: experiences of the Joluo of Kenya', *Journal of East African Research and Development*, 13, 1983, pp 69–85.

42 World Bank, *Sub-Saharan Africa*, p 104.

43 TC Pinckney & PK Kimuyu, 'Land tenure reform in East Africa: good, bad or unimportant?', *Journal of African Economies*, 3, 1994, pp 1–28; and J-P Platteau, 'The evolutionary theory of land rights as applied to sub-Saharan Africa: a critical assessment', *Development and Change*, 27, 1996, pp 29–86.

44 J Bruce & S Migot-Adhola (eds), *Searching for Land Tenure Security in Africa*, Dubuque, IA: Kendall/ Hunt Publishing Company, 1994.

45 However, critics have pointed out that even this celebration of customary tenure's flexibility was self-serving, in that flexibility was valued for the possibility that communal systems had the potential to spontaneously evolve towards individual control and would therefore no longer present obstacles to titling programmes but might in fact complement them. For chapters that make this observation, see K Firmin-Sellers & P Sellers, 'Expected failures and unexpected successes of land titling in Africa', *World Development*, 27, 1999, pp 1115–1128; and P McAuslan, 'Making law work: restructuring land relations in Africa', *Development and Change*, 29 (3), 1998, pp 525–552.

46 K Kasanga, 'Land administration reforms and social differentiation: a case study of Ghana's Lands Commission', *IDS Bulletin*, 32 (1), 2001, pp 57–64; and LA Wily & D Hammond, *Land Security and the Poor in Ghana: Is there a Way Forward?*, Land Sector Scoping Study commissioned by DFID-Ghana's Rural Livelihoods Programme, 2001, at http://www.oxfam.org.uk/what_we_do/issues/livelihoods/landrights/downloads/ghanasec.rtf, accessed 28 June 2006.

47 Whitehead & Tsikata, 'Policy discourses on women's land rights in sub-Saharan Africa', p 79.

48 H de Soto, *The Mystery of Capital: Why Capitalism Triumphs in the West and Fails Everywhere Else*, New York: Basic Books, 2001; de Soto, 'The mystery of capital', Carnegie Council on Ethics and International Affairs, 21st Annual Morgenthau Memorial Lecture on Ethics and Foreign Policy, New York, 8 May 2002.

49 See, for example, *The Economist*, 'Breathing life into dead capital: why secure property rights matter', 17 January 2004, pp 10–11.

50 Kenya's experience illustrates this erosion of customary land rights. When disputes have arisen between the title holder and family members claiming rights under customary law, Kenyan courts have often ruled that formal title extinguishes all other interests in the land, except 'overriding interests' enumerated in section 30 of the Registered Land Act. Among the interests deemed extinguished are interests based on customary law, such as interests of sons in ancestral land (*Esiroyo v Esiroyo*, 1973, *East Africa Law Reports*, 388) and the interests of wives that allow them to live on and use family land by virtue of marriage (*Wanjohi & Wanjohi v Official Receiver and Interim Liquidator (Continental Credit Finance Ltd)*, Civil Application NAI No 140 of 1988, reproduced in *The Nairobi Law Monthly*, 14, February 1989, p 42).

51 CM Peter, *Human Rights in Tanzania: Selected Cases and Materials*, Cologne: Koppe, 1997; and D Tsikata, 'Securing women's interests within land tenure reforms: recent debates in Tanzania', *Journal of Agrarian Change*, 3 (1), 2003, pp 149–183.

52 The authors of the study, who run the Women's Credit Desk at the Bank of Uganda, have undertaken advocacy work with NGOs, rural women and policy makers aimed both at demystifying the workings of the banking industry and encouraging dialogue towards policies that are more favourable. E Kiiza, W Rwe-Beyanga & A Kamya, 'Accounting for gender: improving Ugandan credit policies, processes and programs', in D Tsikata & J Kerr (eds), *Demanding Dignity: Women Confronting Economic Reforms in Africa*, Ottawa and Penang: The North–South Institute and Third World Network-Africa, 2000, pp 47–56.

53 E Kiiza, 'Accounting for gender'.

54 M Mbilinyi, 'Struggles over patriarchal structural adjustment in Tanzania', *Focus on Gender*, 1 (3), 1993, pp 26–29; and M Mbilinyi, 'The restructuring of agriculture in Tanzania: gender and structural adjustment', *IDS Seminar Series*, Dar Es Salaam: Institute of Development Studies, 1994.

55 E Gwaunza, T Nzira & V Chitanda, 'The socio-economic and legal implications of EPZs in Zimbabwe: some emerging gender concerns', in Tsikata & Kerr, *Demanding Dignity*, pp 145–164.

56 Kenya Human Rights Commission (KHRC), *Manufacture of Poverty: The Untold Story of EPZs in Kenya*, Nairobi: KHRC, 2004, p 21.

57 *Ibid*, p 21.

58 At the same time, the proposed changes introduce new measures that appear to limit workers' rights. Workers would be required to give seven days notice of a strike, and employers have a right to challenge the legality of the strike before a proposed National Labour Court, opening up the possibility

of protracted legal delays that could render strike action void. See L Barasa, 'Workers' right to strike challenged', *Daily Nation*, 30 April 2004, at www.nationmedia.com, accessed 28 June 2006.

59 Gwaunza 'The socio-economic and legal implications of EPZs in Zimbabwe'; and KHRC, *Manufacture of Poverty*.

60 R Lung'aho, 'The gender issues in domestic labour: focus on Uasin Gishu District, Kenya', *Working Paper*, 73, Kampala: Centre for Basic Research, 2001; and A Namara, 'The invisible workers: paid domestic work in Kampala City, Uganda', *Working Paper*, 74, Kampala: Centre for Basic Research, 2001.

61 ADB, *Achieving the Millennium Development Goals in Africa*.

62 K Rittich, 'Feminism after the state: the rise of the market and the future of women's rights', in I Merali & V Oosterveld (eds), *Giving Meaning to Economic, Social and Cultural Rights*, Philadelphia, PA: University of Pennsylvania Press, 2001, p 95; and Y Fall, 'Promoting sustainable human development rights for women in Africa', *Third World Resurgence*, 94, 1998, at http://www.twnside.org.sg/title/africa-cn.htm, accessed 28 June 2006.

63 K Rittich, 'Feminism after the state'.

Constitutional Engineering: what opportunities for the enhancement of gender rights?

GEORGINA WAYLEN

Until recently the majority of feminist and mainstream scholars and policy makers—including many of those who have explored the most effective institutional strategies to improve gender rights—have paid relatively little attention to the potential impact of constitutional design on gender rights. But in the last couple of years this situation has changed. First, the whole issue of constitutional design has gained prominence, particularly as institutional engineering is now a key part of the efforts to 'build democracy after conflict' (or to impose it from the outside), most notably recently in Iraq and Afghanistan. The process of constitutional design has also changed over the past two decades.[1] No longer is the primary emphasis on the kind of elite decision making behind closed doors that typified the design of both the US and many post-colonial constitutions. The actual *process* of constitution making is now regarded as crucially important and it is one that should be open and involve democratic participation by all sections of society.[2]

Second, some feminists have also begun to consider constitutions and constitutional change. Indeed, as constitutions lie at the core of the institutional structure and legal system of a state and define the relationships between the state and its citizens as well as among the citizens themselves, they play an important role in codifying gender rights.

Feminist theorists have moved away from liberal individualist conceptions of constitutions and rights towards understanding constitutions as way of creating frameworks that can embed rights broadly defined.[3] Scholars and participants have also analysed a series of feminist interventions into processes of constitutional change and their aftermath. Protecting and enhancing gender rights has been put on the agenda of some recent constitution-making efforts. Some cases have been in long-standing democracies—of which the best-known examples are the introduction of the Charter of Rights and Freedoms in Canada and the experience of devolution in the UK (particularly in Scotland but also in Wales and Northern Ireland).[4] But there are also examples from some of the 'third wave' transitions to democracy. The best-known case is South Africa where a number of studies have looked at the constitutional negotiations that took place in the first half of the 1990s. And even if some analysts believe that the opportunities for women's participation offered by participatory forms of constitution-making have received little comment, the current emphasis on the importance of process, inclusion and participation in constitution building would appear to open up spaces for greater participation by women and, as a result, to increase the potential to achieve favourable gender outcomes.[5] Many scholars and policy makers are therefore taking constitutional change more seriously as a potential strategy to enhance gender rights.

Given the contemporary significance accorded to constitution-making from all quarters, now is a good time to take stock and explore the conditions that are necessary in order for the design of a new constitution to include measures to protect and enhance gender rights. In this chapter I will assess first the potential gains and limitations of using constitutional change as a strategy for enhancing gender rights. Second, I will assess under what conditions and in what contexts a strategy to use constitutional change can be more or less effective. In addition, I also hope to widen the debate from the two institutional concerns that have dominated feminist discussions on the state/political arena in recent years, namely the emphasis on quotas as a mechanism to enhance women's descriptive representation, and on national women's machineries and gender mainstreaming as mechanisms to enhance women's substantive representation. This focus has been too narrow, as somewhat unrealistic hopes have been invested in quotas as the solution to problems of women's political representation and in national women's machineries and gender mainstreaming as the solution to the problem of the under-representation of both women and gender concerns in policy-making processes. Using Louise Chappell's schema to distinguish the three key institutional arenas, feminists have often focused on the electoral arena (namely women's representation and strategies to improve it—primarily quotas) and the state/bureaucratic arena (national women's machineries), and on the relationship between feminist activists and these two arenas. As a result they have not paid significant attention to the third arena: the constitutional/legal arena.[6] Therefore, although the increased attention recently paid by feminist political scientists to institutions is to be welcomed, to date it has not been sufficiently comprehensive.[7]

In this chapter I will look at an important but relatively under-explored area—the gender implications of the constitutional changes that have taken place as part of recent 'third wave' transitions to democracy—to further our understanding of its potential as a tool to enhance gender rights. Some feminist political scientists have already tried to answer the question of under what circumstances transitions to democracy can result in positive gender outcomes—as transitions are so often seen as failing women.[8] South Africa is one of the case studies often considered to have resulted in more positive gender outcomes than many, if not all, other well known transitions. In answer to the question of why should this be the case, a complex set of factors is important. No single one is decisive, but the role that feminists played in the transition in general, but also in the constitutional negotiations that resulted in a constitution that had gender equality enshrined within it, is a significant part of the picture.

In order to assess the extent to which the process of constitutional design in transitions to democracy can offer opportunities to enhance gender rights, I will examine some cases that demonstrate a range of outcomes, not just those that can be deemed to be relatively 'successful'. Evidence from four 'third wave' transitions—Argentina, Brazil, South Africa and Poland (including a brief consideration of the impact of accession to the EU on transition countries)—will form the bulk of the empirical material (drawn from my larger study of gender and transitions to democracy).[9] I will focus primarily on the processes of constitutional change rather than on their outcomes and subsequent attempts to operationalise any new rights. But I hope that the conclusions that emerge will help to shed some light on other experiences. And I will briefly discuss two more recent experiences—the processes of constitution drafting in Iraq and in the EU. It appears that, in order for constitutional change to be an effective strategy to enhance gender rights, it is necessary not only to have a favourable political opportunity structure but also to have women activists who are able to play a key role both inside and outside institutional arenas. Even then constitutional change can only be one part of a multi-pronged strategy to enhance gender rights.

Constitutional change and transitions to democracy

The design of a new constitution has been an important part of a number of recent transitions to democracy, taking place either as part of negotiations that decided the nature of the new political system or in the period after the inauguration of competitive electoral politics. However, the extent to which the design of a new constitution offered the opportunity to create an enabling framework for the realisation of improved gender rights varied considerably in the four cases we are looking at. In Brazil and South Africa, because a number of women activists' demands were included in the final constitutions, they have been seen as a positive advance for gender rights. In Argentina, although the new constitution of 1994 did not incorporate the demands of activists to the same extent, an alliance of women actors defeated attempts to incorporate a right-to-life clause supported by the president. In contrast, organised women actors played no significant role in the design of the constitution introduced in Poland after the collapse of state socialism. I will consider the Brazilian, Argentine and South African cases in turn to isolate the key factors that influenced how far gender outcomes were positive before briefly contrasting them with the Polish case. In Argentina (and to a lesser extent in Brazil) the drafting of the new constitution took place after the initial return to civilian rule and therefore was not an integral part of the early stages of the transition. In contrast, in South Africa the drafting of the new constitution was a fundamental part of the negotiations and of the process of transition in general.

In Brazil the process of constitutional design was part of a gradual transition to democracy in which the military controlled a long drawn-out process of liberalisation. After the first direct election of a civilian president, Jose Sarney, in 1985, the new Congress to be elected in 1986 was to form a constituent assembly charged with writing the new constitution. According to Jacqueline Pitanguy, the president of the newly established Brazilian National Council on Women's Rights (CNDM), between 1986 and 1989, 'the feminist movement seized on the occasion as a unique opportunity to enlarge women's citizenship rights and promote gender equality'.[10] The CNDM played a key role in this process. It acted as an effective *de facto* women's lobby and co-ordinator for the women's movement, holding conferences, seminars and public forums all over Brazil where proposals for the constitution were formulated, culminating in a Letter (*Carta*) from Women to the Constituent Assembly. The *Carta* included a range of proposals, such as changes in labour legislation, family law, day-care and other improvements in women's rights like the explicit recognition of equality between men and women.[11] It was endorsed by a broad spectrum of women's groups. The CNDM also served as an effective women's lobby at all stages of the drafting of the charter document. It exerted pressure on legislators and liaised between women's movements and 26 female legislators in parliament (sometimes known as the 'lipstick lobby' (*a bancada do batom*)) to press for the inclusion of women's demands.

As a result of all these activities and alliances, many of the women's movement's demands were included in the final constitution. Indeed, Pitanguy claims that the campaign was a success and that 80% of demands, ranging from the recognition of women's sexual and reproductive rights as well as equal rights both within the family and outside of it to 120 days paid maternity leave, were accepted. However, a number of issues were very controversial. Reproductive rights were a key battleground. The issue was raised by feminists who campaigned for the decriminalisation of abortion, but the pro-life lobby (comprising the Christian right, made up of Catholics and Evangelical Christians) also engaged in some very active lobbying in favour of a pro-life amendment.[12] In the end the CNDM, in a strategic move, withdrew its decriminalisation amendment on condition that the pro-life amendment was also withdrawn. Despite the successes, the overall verdict on the constitution is mixed. Alvarez claims that it was those issues that seriously threatened to alter existing gender power relations, such as abortion rights, that were excluded from the final draft.[13] Finally, the constitution itself became a huge and unwieldy document that was very difficult to implement in a context where legal rights on paper did not always correspond to the rights enjoyed in practice. Their exercise also frequently required both further legislation and additional government expenditure. So, for example, the completion of the family equality agenda also required the reform of Brazil's civil code, which has proved difficult to achieve.[14] It was therefore more difficult than many hoped to use the constitution as an enabling framework and the basis for further gains in gender rights in the short term. But it is also important to consider how far the potential gender gains in reproductive rights and protection from domestic violence put forward under the Lula administration 15 years later were facilitated by the 1988 constitution.

In Argentina a new constitution was not introduced until 1994, just over 10 years after the return to civilian rule. The remit of the constitutional convention was relatively narrow, as many important features of the new constitution had already been agreed in a pact between the populist Peronist President Menem and the leader of the main opposition party, Raul Alfonsin.[15] The constitution was designed by a constituent assembly elected in 1993. And, although it was dominated by the two main political parties, no one party was in control and members were elected according to the newly introduced quota law, which stipulated that one-third of candidates on party lists should be women. As a result 26.2% of the assembly members were women, who did organise across party lines on some issues. The process of designing the constitution itself was not subject to the kinds of focused campaign organised strategically by key feminist actors that was seen in the Brazilian case. None the less women did organise inside and outside the constituent assembly to form alliances to safeguard gender rights and to ensure that gender concerns were included in the document. After pressure from women members the quota law was strengthened, allowing third parties such as the Consejo Nacional de la Mujer (CNM) to make electoral challenges and the Convention on the Elimination of All Forms of Discrimination Against Women (CEDAW) was also enshrined in the constitution.[16]

Perhaps the biggest challenge was the defensive organising to prevent the insertion of a 'pro-life' anti-abortion clause initiated by Carlos Menem, after he had lost his initial enthusiasm for women's rights evident early in his presidency and become more closely aligned with the Catholic Church. Outside the assembly 109 women's organisations came together as 'Mujeres Autoconvocadas por el Derecho a Elegir la Libertad' (MADEL) and campaigned against the clause, organising demonstrations and lobbying assembly members.[17] The Argentine national women's machinery, the CNM, also made its opposition to the president's pro-life position public, and campaigned against the clause, leading to the sacking of its feminist-leaning head by Menem. Inside the assembly itself women members, including some from the governing Peronist party, organised together against the clause and as a result it was not included in the final constitution.[18] Organised women were therefore able to have some impact over the process of constitution drafting.

The new South African constitution that was ratified in 1996 after a lengthy period of negotiation and design, has been seen as one of the most successful in terms of both process and outcome. As a result of the long-standing efforts of women activists during and before the transition, it was designed with gender equality enshrined within it and, in comparison to the Brazilian example, it has proved a relatively more effective enabling framework. Two key characteristics of the South African transition made involvement in the constitution writing process central for women activists and a key area for contestation. First, it was a pacted transition in which negotiations between the government and the opposition before the first democratic election would design the interim constitution as well as the future political system. Second, within the opposition, a 'charterist' strand that emphasised the importance of equal rights for all citizens enshrined within law was very important and feminists were able to extend that 'charterist' discourse to gender.[19] Women activists, both within the left-leaning opposition African National Congress (ANC) and outside of it, had recognised for some time the importance of ensuring that gender equality was part of any future constitution. As a result of long-standing activism within the organisation, in 1988 the ANC Constitutional Guidelines had incorporated the demands of women, even if only in very narrow and formal terms.[20] Indeed, even the failings of these constitutional guidelines were subsequently discussed at an in-house ANC workshop on 'Women and the Constitution' held in Lusaka in 1989.[21] Both ANC women in exile and women activists based in South Africa had then agreed at a conference held in 1990 on the need for strategic intervention in the transition process to ensure that their concerns were incorporated into the future constitution.

As a result, concerted efforts were made by women to intervene in those processes. An umbrella women's organisation, the Women's National Coalition (WNC) was set up to influence the transition process and build a women's movement. After an outcry at their absence, women were included in all the negotiating teams, and cross-party organising took place among the women from different political parties participating in the negotiations. A triple alliance of women activists, academics and politicians facilitated by the WNC organised to influence the political process, including the writing of the constitution. The WNC protested about the exclusion of the principle of 'non-sexism' from the first draft of the constitutional principles. In the end women parliamentarians in the constituent assembly won the argument for its inclusion when the interim constitution was presented in 1994.[22] The need for an equality clause in the interim constitution was also accepted early on in the negotiations. However, the biggest area of contention was around the issue of customary law and whether it should be subject to the equality clause. Traditional leaders wanted customary law excluded to safeguard forms of inheritance, property and marriage that maintained their hereditary power. The WNC, and within it the Rural Women's Movement, lobbied and argued vociferously that to exclude customary law would be, according to Catherine Albertyn, to exclude the most oppressed and marginalised groups, namely rural black women.[23] Unsuccessful attempts were made to broker a compromise between these two opposing positions. It was not until the last minute of the second phase of the negotiations, named the Multi-Party Negotiating Process (MPNP) that the traditional leaders lost and customary law was made subject to the equality clause. Partly as a result of the attempts to negotiate a solution, the creation of two new institutions was envisaged: a Council of Traditional Leaders and a Commission for Gender Equality (CGE), the latter being mandated to promote gender equality and make recommendations to parliament about any law affecting the status of women.[24]

The resulting interim constitution contained a commitment to gender equality within a framework of rights. The final constitution agreed by the first parliament, which began sitting as a constituent assembly in 1994, has been called one of the most advanced liberal democratic instruments in the world.[25] It not only contained a commitment to socioeconomic rights but also included gender equality as one of the founding principles of the new state as well as strong and substantive equality protection and the provision for an independent constitutional body to promote gender equality.[26] ANC women had also ensured that the final constitution contained some more specific clauses on domestic violence and reproductive rights. Indeed, the achievement of a subsequent improvement in reproductive rights was facilitated by both this and the existence of the constitution as an enabling framework.[27] But at the same time as it has acted as an important enabling framework for extending gender rights, the constitution has also been subject to the inherent limitations involved in trying to translate formal rights, whether socioeconomic or gender-based, into lived rights in the context of mass poverty, high levels of HIV/AIDS and huge inequality.

The three cases described above have made clear that a central factor in determining how far gender rights were enshrined in these new constitutions was the extent to which key feminists lobbied and were active in the process of constitutional design, raising gender concerns and fighting for inclusion. The openness of the institutional context was also central, as was the receptivity of other key actors to gender concerns, together with the strength of any opposition to improving gender rights. In all three cases women organised together from both insider and outsider positions to form strategic alliances. Although the extent to which gender rights were enhanced in each of the constitutions varied, in all three cases alliances of activists were able to protect existing gender rights. We saw in South Africa that traditional leaders failed to get customary law excluded and in Brazil and Argentina activists were able to prevent the inclusion of a 'right-to-life' clause in the new constitutions. There are few other cases where women's organising in any form has had a significant impact on the shape of a new constitution as part of a transition to democracy.

If we look, for example, at the somewhat different transition from state socialism that took place in Poland after 1989, we see that organised women did not have a significant impact over either the transition itself or the subsequent design of a new constitution. However, in contrast to the pre-existing constitutional set-ups in Argentina, Brazil and South Africa, under state socialism some significant rights for women were already enshrined on paper at least. But these had been granted from above rather than gained as a result of women's activism and in practice did not deliver gender equity. After the collapse of state socialism there were few women organising as women in a position to have a significant impact on the process of constitution making either to protect or enhance gender rights, although some newly formed women's NGOs, such as the Women's Rights Centre, did make submissions. As a result, although the final Polish constitution of 1997 included a clause guaranteeing the equality of men and women, this was hard to realise or enforce as it was not backed up by specific legislation or civil codes and was even directly contradicted by legislation in some fields, such as labour law. Indeed, the new constitution actually included some retrenchment of gender rights. In common with many other cases, a right-to-life clause was one of the most controversial areas. The Catholic Church, whose influence and credibility was high after playing an important oppositional role under state socialism, campaigned successfully for the inclusion of a clause that more clearly included protection for the unborn foetus and consolidated other measures that had already been implemented to restrict women's access to abortion.[28]

But there is one final factor we must consider in the Polish case: adoption of constitutional/legal change as part of the externally driven process of EU accession. Post-socialist Poland saw its future as lying within the European Union and from the late 1990s it began to make the requisite preparations, including the full implementation of the *acquis communautaire* (the totality of EU legislation) for accession in 2004. In the short term therefore perhaps the most potentially far-reaching changes in legal rights for women on the statute books in many post-socialist countries could come from the alterations to their legal frameworks that prospective entrants to the EU made in order to bring their countries into line with EU laws. All the EU legislation pertaining to gender equality was adopted, as well as gender mainstreaming as a strategy.[29] But primary emphasis was given to employment and social policy. Poland started negotiations to join the EU in 1998 and planned to incorporate the *acquis communautaire* between 2001 and 2002. Every year the progress of the harmonisation process (in economic, social and judicial arenas) was monitored. In the area of labour legislation Poland therefore had to implement directives on equal treatment, equal pay, parental leave, part-time work and pensions. For example, maternity leave was increased from 16 to 26 weeks and some maternal benefits were revised to apply to men as well as women. Poland also introduced the notion of indirect discrimination. All these changes could have potentially far-reaching effects.

However, there is also some pessimism as a number of factors lessen their potential impact. Some sceptics argue that, on the EU side, it was the economic chapter that had primacy in the negotiations and there was less concern about the implementation of the social dimensions (which include gender equality).[30] For example, virtually nothing was done about domestic violence. Heinen and Portet claim that, on the Polish side, three factors weaken the impact of the integration process.[31] The first is ideological. Polish information on European integration emphasised how little would change. A leaflet on the equal opportunities chapter spelt out that most of the measures were not compulsory. It argued that Poland would be able to maintain its own values and traditions, citing Ireland as a model. Heinen and Portet argue that, as a result, Poland paid only lipservice to the integration of many of the European directives, adopting them only as a formality. Second, Poland does not have an effective institutional means of control and a system of penalties to ensure that the directives can effectively be implemented. A similar situation can be discerned in the Czech Republic. Positive changes were made to the Labour Code in January 2001 that centred around notions of equality and no discrimination. But until the end of the first half of 2003 no cases had been brought.[32] Finally, although the implementation of the equal opportunities policy is based on gender mainstreaming, it relies on the presence of other gender equality programmes that do not exist in Poland or other post-socialist polities.

Although other commentators share this negative view, Heinen and Portet admit that at the same time the integration process is having a positive impact, as some feminists see it as a way to consolidate a more progressive legal framework around notions of equal treatment.[33] The EU and its standards can therefore provide an important reference point that can be used by feminists and women's NGOs, giving them both legitimacy and financial support for their activities. Thus the changes introduced as a result of the externally driven process of EU accession do have the potential to play a more important role in the future.

Implications for the analysis of gender and constitutional design

We have seen that new constitutions can protect and also enhance gender rights but this is by no means inevitable and indeed will only happen under certain conditions. The political opportunity structure during the constitution-building process must be a favourable one. The process whereby the constitution is designed must therefore be a relatively open, democratic and transparent one in which interventions by feminists are possible. Some of the longer-drawn out and negotiated transitions to democracy have offered these possibilities, particularly when the constitution-making process has been fundamental to the transition itself. Crucially key participants, such as political parties, within these processes have to be open to gender concerns and prepared to take them on board. This is often more likely if women activists have already made gender issues a legitimate part of the opposition. As a result, in some transitions to democracy women activists pressing gender concerns from both within and outside the processes of constitution writing have been able to form alliances with other sympathetic insiders within legislatures, political parties, governments and national women's machineries. Without the presence of all these factors, it is unlikely that gender rights will be enhanced or that existing rights are being protected in new constitutions.

We can use this framework to examine briefly two other contemporary cases where new constitutions have been drawn up and where there is some reason to believe that gender rights might be incorporated: Iraq and the EU. This is because, in the Iraqi case, the occupying powers had the promotion of gender rights as one of their stated aims and, in the EU case, gender equality was already enshrined as an aim within the EU itself. However, in both cases, we can see that aspects of the political opportunity structure and the process of constitution building itself were unfavourable to the incorporation of gender rights. In Iraq the design of a new constitution was central to the creation of a new political system after the overthrow of Saddam Hussein by the USA and its allies in 2003. It was created according to a process and strict timetable set out by the US-led provisional government, culminating in a referendum in October 2005 after the constitution was finalised in August 2005. Despite some efforts to make the process transparent and accountable, a number of factors—in addition to the poor security situation and tight timetable—prevented it from being open to those organised women who were campaigning for the inclusion of gender rights.[34]

First, there were few sympathetic insiders involved in the constitution-building process because the composition of the constitutional committee reflected the dominance of Shia and other religious Islamic groups in the January 2005 elections. About half of its 55 members came from the Shiite United Iraqi Alliance (UIA). Gender rights were not accepted by any important group (except the USA, which also viewed them as 'tradeable' and less important than other concerns). Only eight women were included in the constitutional committee and five of these were representatives of UIA, two were Kurdish representatives and only one was a secular woman.[35] Around half the women representatives were therefore in favour of a constitution in which Islam was a fundamental source of law that would override secular codes.[36] Women's organisations found it difficult to intervene in a process that was dominated by 'traditional' male leaders and, despite organising some demonstrations in favour of women's rights, were not able to exert significant influence over the constitution-building process.

After much dispute over the role of *sharia* law, particularly in the area of personal status law, the final Iraqi constitution contains some important ambiguities. Article 14 states that Iraqis are equal before the law 'without discrimination because of sex' at the same time as it states that laws cannot be passed that contradict the 'established rulings' of Islam and that Iraqis are 'free in their personal status according to their religions, sects beliefs or choices'. As a result the access that most women have to divorce, as well as their rights to inherit property, could be fundamentally compromised.[37] But the exact position will require further clarification either by the new legislature or by rulings from the Supreme Court and neither body looks like it will support the enhancement of gender rights. However, despite efforts by conservatives to remove it, the 25% quota enshrined in the Interim Constitution was maintained and one-third of the candidates for each party competing in the December 2005 elections had to be women. But, again, most of the elected women represent religious parties and are unlikely to go against their party's policies. Perhaps not surprisingly, at the time of writing it appears that the Iraqi constitution will not enhance gender rights. Indeed, it does not even protect those rights that were in place when Saddam Hussein's regime was in power or were enshrined in the interim constitution and there is therefore a danger that pre-existing rights will be lost.

The (failed) EU constitution was designed in a process that included few women and from which many women's organisations felt marginalised and excluded. Although gender equality was entrenched within it, some commentators have argued that the relatively unfavourable political opportunity structure prevented organised women from achieving all they had hoped for.[38] The actual process of formulating the constitution was more democratic and participatory than is usual for the EU, as the proceedings were made public and civil society organisations were able to give feedback. But, at the same time, the participants in the convention were not directly elected and, although the EU has a commitment to gender equality and gender mainstreaming, including in decision making, this did not translate into the presence of significant numbers of women in the convention.[39] In February 2003 only 18 of the 105 members (17%) were women but there were even fewer at the top of the convention hierarchy. No women were among the triumverate presidency and by June 2003 the number of women on the nine-person Praesidium had fallen from two to one (9%).[40] And only one of the 11 working groups was chaired by a woman. Attempts by organised women both inside and outside the EU institutions to influence the constitutional process also had less impact than was hoped for. Proposals from the President of the Committee of Women's Rights of the European Parliament to compensate for the under-representation of women and ensure that the outcome of the convention was more gender friendly were not acted on.[41] Gender advocacy coalitions like the European Women's Lobby, consisting of civil society groups, gender 'experts' and the European Parliament's Committee on Women's Rights actively lobbied the convention, but failed to get it to include more far-reaching equality and non-discrimination provisions in the constitution. Overall civil society actors, because their role was a passive rather than an active one that could influence policy and process, had little impact. Therefore, although some gender rights were constituted within the EU constitution, they were not as robust or as comprehensive as women activists, parliamentarians and commentators would have liked.

Constitutional building processes are therefore not a universal panacea that will enhance gender rights. They offer some opportunities but are only one strategy among others, and a limited one, despite their potential as a significant instrument/strategy to enhance and protect gender rights. This is not, however, a strategy that will be available in all circumstances.

These conclusions reinforce the importance of using a broad strategic repertoire that combines using feminist electoral and bureaucratic strategies, together with constitutional/legal strategies wherever they are possible. But, like the other arenas, the constitutional/legal arena will not always be favourable and open to feminists in all contexts.

Furthermore, the process of achieving 'gender friendly' constitutions is only a starting point. The creation of an enabling framework, particularly in some of the less institutionalised polities that have emerged from some transitions, is not enough on its own. The ability to operationalise these paper rights depends on a number of other important factors. For example, other laws are often needed to make policy on specific issues. Policies on paper have to be implemented and enforced, which requires not only the political will, but also the capacity—in terms of both resources and capabilities. And women themselves have to be able to access those rights and take advantage of new policies that emerge from them. This ability can be enhanced by a culture of rights and a judicial system that facilitates legal challenges, for example through the presence of feminist judges and sufficient resources for all to make challenges. But there is also hope that, once rights are in place and enshrined in law, even where they have been introduced as a result of external factors, with no immediate discernible impact, they can be used in the future as a legal basis to achieve some tangible improvements in 'lived' gender rights.

Notes

1 For an exposition of these ideas, see Vivien Hart, 'Democratic constitution making', *Special Report*, 107, Washington DC: United States Institute of Peace, July 2003.
2 See, for example, Institute for Democracy and Electoral Assistance's (IDEA) international programme on constitution-building processes launched in 2004, at www.idea.int/conflict/cbp.
3 See the discussion of this in A Bartholemew, 'Group differentiated cultural rights, constitutionalism and feminism' and Alexandra Dobrowolsky, 'Women, constitutionalism and contestation: some tentative conclusions', in Alexandra Dobrowolsky & Vivien Hart (eds), *Women Making Constitutions: New Politics and Comparative Perspectives*, Basingstoke: Palgrave, 2003.
4 The best known book-length exploration of this topic is Dobrowolsky & Hart, *Women Making Constitutions*. For the UK experience, see the case studies by F Mackay, F Myers & A Brown, 'Towards a new politics? Women and constitutional change in Scotland'; C Harvey, 'The politics of human rights and gender equality in Northern Ireland'; B Hinds, 'Mainstreaming equality in Northern Ireland'; and P Chaney, 'Increased rights and representation: women and the post-devolution equality agenda in Wales', all in *ibid*.
5 Hart, 'Democratic constitution making', p 10.
6 L Chappell, *Gendering Government: Feminist Engagement with the State in Australia and Canada*, Vancouver: University of British Columbia Press, 2002.
7 But there are some signs that a new and welcome trend towards 'feminist institutionalism' is developing.
8 See, for example, G Waylen, *Engendering Transitions*, Oxford: Oxford University Press, forthcoming.
9 *Ibid*.
10 J Pitanguy, 'Bridging the local and global: feminism in Brazil and the international human rights agenda', *Social Research*, 69 (3), 2002, p 810.
11 For a full discussion of this process, see S Alvarez, *Engendering Democracy in Brazil*, Princeton, NJ: Princeton University Press, 1990, p 251; and M Htun, *Sexing the State*, Cambridge: Cambridge University Press, 2003, p 125.
12 Alvarez, *Engendering Democracy in Brazil*, p 254.
13 *Ibid*, p 252.
14 M Htun, 'The puzzle of women's rights in Brazil', *Social Research*, 69 (3), 2002, pp 733–751; and M Htun, *Sexing the State*, p 127.

15 G Negretto, 'Constitution-making and institutional design: the reform of presidentialism in the Argentine constitution of 1994', paper presented at LASA, Chicago, 1998.

16 G Waylen, 'Gender and democratic politics: a comparative analysis of consolidation in Chile and Argentina', *Journal of Latin American Studies*, 32, 2000, pp 765–793.

17 V Guzman, 'Democratic governance and gender: possible linkages', *Serie Mujer y Desarollo*, 48, Santiago: ECLAC, 2004, p 19.

18 Interview with Maria del Carmen Feijoo, feminist academic and member of the 1993 Constituent Assembly, Buenos Aires, 25 May 1996.

19 Charterism had its early expression in the Freedom Charter drawn up in 1955 by the rights-based Congress Alliance, which laid out the conditions for a non-racial South Africa based on a discourse of equal citizenship for all. For more discussion of this, see G Waylen, 'Women's mobilization and gender outcomes in transitions to democracy: the case of South Africa', *Comparative Political Studies*, May 2007, forthcoming.

20 C Albertyn, 'Women and the transition to democracy in South Africa', in F Kaganas & C Murray (eds), *Gender and the New South African Legal Order*, Cape Town: Juta, 1994, p 47.

21 Interview with Mavivi Manzini, 30 July 2003, Johannesburg.

22 S Hassim, '"A conspiracy of women": the women's movement in South Africa's transition to democracy', *Social Research*, 69 (Fall), 2002, p 718.

23 C Albertyn, 'Women and the transition to democracy in South Africa', p 59.

24 C Albertyn *et al*, *Engendering the Political Agenda: A South African Case Study*, Johannesburg: Centre for Applied Legal Studies, University of Witswatersrand, 1999, p 93.

25 R Southall, 'The state of democracy in South Africa', *Journal of Commonwealth and Comparative Politics*, 38 (Autumn), 2000, p 147.

26 C Albertyn, 'Towards substantive representation: women and politics in South Africa', in Dobrowolsky & Hart, *Women Making Constitutions*, p 104.

27 C Albertyn *et al*, *Engendering the Political Agenda*.

28 See Eastern European Constitutional Review, Women's Rights Centre and EU documentation on discrimination in Poland, Google search, '1997 Polish Constitution'.

29 C Bretherton, 'Gender mainstreaming and EU enlargement: swimming against the tide?', *Journal of European Public Policy*, 8 (1), 2001, pp 60–81.

30 E Matynia, 'Provincializing global feminism: the Polish case', *Social Research*, 70 (2), 2003, p 513.

31 J Heinen & S Portet 'Political and social citizenship: an examination of the case of Poland', in M Molyneux & S Razavi (eds), *Gender Justice, Development and Rights*, Oxford: Oxford University Press, 2002.

32 WIDE Information Sheet, 'Gender equality and EU accession: the situation in the Czech Republic', at www.eurosur.org./wide.

33 Bretherton, 'Gender mainstreaming and EU enlargement', p 68.

34 Transcript of a talk by Manal Omar, 'Women's rights in a new Iraq: the constitution and the future', Council for Foreign Relations, New York, 11 May 2005, at www.cfr.org/publication/8114/womens_rights_in_a_new_iraq.html.

35 I Coleman, 'Women, Islam and the new Iraq', *Foreign Affairs*, January/February, 2006, p 73.

36 Interview with Yanar Mohammed, Director of the Organization of Women's Freedom, on the Democracy Now Website, at www.democracynow.org, accessed 25 August 2005.

37 Coleman, 'Women, Islam and the new Iraq'.

38 R Guerrina, 'Constitutional politics in Europe: continuing trends in the politics of gender', *Identities: Journal for Politics, Gender and Culture*, forthcoming.

39 E Lombardo, 'Integrating or setting the agenda? Gender mainstreaming and the European constitution-making process', *Social Politics*, Fall 2005, pp 412–432.

40 S Millns, 'Mainstreaming gender equality in the EU's constitutional future', paper presented to the ECPR Conference, Budapest, September 2005.

41 Lombardo, 'Integrating or setting the agenda?', p 425.

Islamic Politics, Human Rights and Women's Claims for Equality in Iran

SHAHRA RAZAVI

The demise of cold war politics and the ascendance of liberalism during the 1990s gave human rights agendas unprecedented impetus and legitimacy. In the light of subsequent events—the attacks of 9/11, increasing concerns about 'security', and pervasive militarisation—the prospects for human rights look much less promising. Cold war hostilities seem to have been replaced by a purported 'clash of civilisations' that posits a historical divide between Christian and Muslim cultures. The latter is construed as monolithic, fanatic and despotic, hostile to human rights in general and highly oppressive of women in particular. The barbaric treatment of women by Islamic regimes, such as the Taliban in Afghanistan, and terrorist acts by radical elements within and beyond European countries with sizeable migrant populations, have reinforced suspicion among the general Western public of the Muslim world, seeing it as uniformly hostile to 'Western' values such as human rights, democracy and gender equality.

The tendency in public and media discourses to see Islamic politics as homogeneous, often subsumed under the 'fundamentalist' label, conceals a wide diversity of ideas and movements. The Iraqi sociologist, Sami Zubaida, for example, identifies three broad tendencies within political Islam, which are neither static nor homogeneous.[1] They include what he calls 'conservative Islam', often associated with authoritarian states; radical and militant variants, typically pursued by students and militant youth;[2] and the more reformist and modernist orientations which seek to Islamise state and society, but in the context of economic development, social reform and democratisation.

This chapter focuses on the diverse currents that feed into the latter orientation in Iran's Islamic Republic. Iran—a country where the 'prophetic' role assumed by religious authorities in opposition to a secular state was transformed into a 'priestly' one as these authorities' authority was institutionalised within politics—continues to provide interesting insights into the limits and contradictions of merging religion with the state.[3] While activists in other countries may see Iran's Islamic Republic as a model to emulate, within the country itself the political role of religious authorities is a highly contested one. The need for change is being voiced not only by secular forces, but also by the 'true believers' from within the heart of the Islamic establishment. These advocates of 'reform' (*eslahat*) have included male lay intellectuals, some notable clerical authorities, and a number of feminists with an Islamic orientation.

In the first part of this chapter I argue that these disparate streams of reformist thinking constitute a genuinely local effort—which is not to say hermetically sealed, or immune from global influences—to move Islamic politics out of the cul-de-sac of traditional Islam by endorsing modernist and universal values of human rights and democracy. Gender equality figures centrally only in some strands of this thinking, for example within feminist Islamism of course, but it is also found in the 'dynamic jurisprudence' that is being propagated by some religious scholars. For these intellectuals and public figures whose roots go back to the heart of the Islamic establishment— the security forces, the seminaries and state-controlled media—the turn to human rights, democracy and women's rights constitutes a metamorphosis.

In the second part of the chapter I consider the social and political dynamics underlying these tensions. While the reformist movement was always constrained as a political force (even when reformist elements dominated the parliament and the presidency, from 1997 to 2003), it is today all but gone from the centres of power and decision making, as the traditionalists have tightened their grip over political power. While this represents a major set-back for the realisation of human rights, democracy and gender equality, it nevertheless challenges the reformist intellectuals and leaders to cultivate a broad social base, bringing into their fold the largely impoverished middle class, women and youth who constituted the 'vote bank' for President Khatami's reformist platform but whose voices have remained muted in subsequent Iranian politics. To do this, the reformists will need to respond to popular grievances about joblessness, poor public services, spiralling inflation, corruption and social and urban decay, in addition to the human rights violations that they have amply exposed. This will mean a broadening of the reformist agenda and mindset beyond its currently liberal (if not neoliberal) frame. This is a tall order, especially for a movement that continues to operate in the context of a highly authoritarian and repressive state.

The 1979 revolution and the assault on human rights

Despite the popularity of the movement that led to the downfall of the Pahlavi monarchy in 1979, the Islamic regime that replaced it ushered in a period of horrific human rights abuses and executions inside the country, and state sponsored assassinations of political dissidents abroad. Women, who had been singled out by the opposition (both secular and Islamic) as symbols of decadence and consumerism under the monarchy, were to bear the brunt of subsequent social and gender restructuring. In a highly significant move the Family Protection Act, which was the flagship of the state's modernisation programme in the 1960s and 1970s, was scrapped in 1979 and replaced by *shari'a* laws that severely curtailed women's rights in the domain of marriage and the family.[4] Many regressive measures followed, such as the forced imposition of the veil, the expulsion of women from the judiciary, the forced segregation of schools and universities, and heightened violence (such as stoning of those who had committed adultery) against women, both domestic and public.

Under these repressive conditions it became extremely difficult for women activists with a secular orientation (like their male counterparts) to be openly engaged in politics inside the country. Many went into exile and those who remained were silenced. Conditions became more difficult during the popular mobilisation for the eight-year war with Iraq (1980–88). In the absence of an opposition, 'women and young people found themselves carrying the mantel of the opposition', in day-to-day street battles with 'morality police' on the issues of *hejab*, or the veil, and of male/female mixing in public spaces in major cities.[5]

Yet the gender segregation of public spaces had some less unsavoury outcomes. The gender gaps in primary and secondary school enrolment, for example, began to narrow. This could be attributed, in part at least, to the willingness of traditional families to send their daughters to school under an Islamic dispensation. The state itself relied on women's mass mobilisation, especially during the Iran–Iraq war, when women were called upon to fill a wide range of public roles.[6] With the economy in deep recession and with the spectre of mass impoverishment, increasing numbers of women were under pressure to look for paid work, even if much of this was badly remunerated and unprotected.

In brief, despite the draconian policies and the (discriminatory) legal edifice erected by the regime, women were far from invisible in public life.[7] Indeed, they seized the few openings that were available to them with great determination, evident in their intellectual and cultural products (in literature, art, cinema and the like) as well as in their achievements in professional and educational institutions, prompting the comment that 'The Islamic Republic has not opened the gates. Women are jumping over the fences'.[8]

The reformist movement and Islamic feminists: the turn to human rights

With the end of the war and the death of Ayatollah Khomeini in 1989, the monopoly that the 'traditionalists' held on politics began to erode.[9] Traditionalist thinking, highly influential in the early years of the Islamic Republic when women were purged from the public sector and the judiciary, is associated with the conservative clerics who have extended their tentacles deep into the key centres of power and decision making and who are neither democratically elected nor in any way accountable to the larger public. These centres include the Council of Guardians, the Expediency Council, the judiciary and indeed the office of the Supreme Leader, himself who holds vast veto powers. While the constitution allows for an elected president and parliament, ultimate authority is vested in the Supreme Leader and the institutions under his command.[10]

These men hold very rigid views of women's roles and rights based on essentialised gender attributes. It is a mode of thinking that is premised on gender difference, the supposed complementarity of gender roles, and a gender-based hierarchy of social responsibilities and rights. Women are seen as caring and nurturing, but also sexualised beings capable of inflicting chaos and confusion if not sufficiently controlled. The veil and segregation are deemed necessary to tame the dangers of female sexuality and to maintain social order and harmony. It is seen as imperative for women to maintain the 'hearth and the home' while the public world of politics and commerce is purified of their presence. Within marriage, full wifely obedience is required, in return for male protection and provisioning. Much of this thinking, codified through *shari'a* law, was placed on the statute books in the early to mid-1980s.

A second perspective, more pragmatic and moderate in so far as it recognised social realities in Iran and women's tenacious presence in public life, was that of the governments of Prime Minister Moussavi (1982–89) and President Rafsanjani (1989–97) and of the technocrats who have occupied high- and middle-level management positions within the state bureaucracy. Rafsanjani, for example, expressed fairly moderate views about the veil, and Moussavi saw segregation and veiling as necessary to facilitate women's active presence in the public sphere. These were views that appealed to a younger generation of women, from low-income traditionalist backgrounds in particular, who had been active in street demonstrations during the revolution, and who despised any attempt to force them back into domesticity. It was this perspective that eventually became dominant, especially with the onset of the Iran–Iraq war.[11]

A third perspective, itself far from monolithic and the most important for this paper, is that of reformism. Some elements of this trend are engaging in a serious rethinking of Islam with a view to reconciling it with the 'universal', 'legitimate' and 'socially just' discourse of human rights.[12] Such proponents argue for the need to shift the debate from traditional or historical Islam's emphasis on *duties* to the modernist and universal notion of *rights*. As Mohsen Kadivar, an eloquent clerical proponent of human rights puts it,

'In traditional Islam, the human person is not the centre of discussion, let alone her/his rights; rather it is God Almighty that forms the centre of religion, and duties to God constitute the body of *Shari'a*'.[13] Kadivar's highly critical perspective on traditional Islam, which he has carefully developed over the past decade through a series of published papers and public lectures, is strongly premised on human rights thinking. Like many of the other proponents of reform, his critical stance towards traditional Islam and his search for alternatives were directly triggered by political developments in Iran and his disagreements with 'the establishment'. Many of the reform proponents have faced inquisition-style trials and prosecutions, served prison sentences, have been banned from giving public lectures and been 'unfrocked' (ie lost their clerical positions).[14]

The voices of reform: discourses in-the-making

The proponents of the rights-based perspective include a group of lay intellectuals widely referred to as *roshanfekrane dini*, or religious intellectuals, among whom by far the most influential and popular has been Abdolkarim Soroush;[15] some clerical figures and seminary intellectuals who want to reconcile Islam with the discourse of human rights, democracy and gender equality through what is called 'dynamic jurisprudence'; and, finally, a diverse group of Islamic feminists who gained increasing prominence throughout the 1980s and 1990s, both inside and outside the parliament.

One of the novel features of Soroush's thinking, compared with that of other Islamic modernists, comes from his insistence on the distinction between religion and religious knowledge. While he sees the core texts of Islam (the Koran, the *hadiths*) as constituents of a divine and timeless 'religion', the interpretation of these texts, he argues, is thoroughly human and this-worldly, and hence time- and context-bound. As he explains: 'That is why the medieval version of Islam has to be sharply different from the modern version, and that is why the modern versions have to be different from each other according to the context . . . and this is also why religious knowledge . . . not being divine by virtue of its subject matter, is open to [debate and] criticism'. Kuzman refers to Soroush's strand of liberal Islam as 'interpreted Islam' (the other two strands being what he calls 'liberal *shari'a*' and 'silent *shari'a*'), seeing the former as the one that enables pluralism and diversity, not just among religious communities but within Islam itself.[16]

Soroush endorses both human rights and democracy as part of the dominant non-religious knowledge of our time, and hence as necessities of the modern age. Democracy is seen as the most legitimate form of governance and also one that is most likely to produce rational and just policies, because it allows pluralism of power and ensures the accountability of those in positions of power (to the people). More specifically on human rights, his view is that these are embedded in modernist understandings of justice, and 'if they are sacrificed for ideology, the religious government will not be seen as just'.[17]

Several observers have drawn attention to the way in which the lay religious intellectuals have side-stepped the 'woman question' in their work.[18] Despite this ambivalence, there is little doubt that the revisionist approach to Islam that Soroush in particular has pursued provides strategic openings for feminist agendas of gender equality. In fact 'his approach to sacred texts has not only enabled women in *Zanan* [an Islamic feminist monthly magazine published in Tehran] to frame their demands within an Islamic framework, but has also encouraged clerics for whom "gender" has become a problem to address it from within a *feqh* [Islamic jurisprudence] framework'.[19]

Both human rights and gender equality are central to the work of clerical proponents of 'dynamic jurisprudence'. Some of these proponents have even collaborated with Islamic feminists; for example, Mohsen Sa'idzadeh, a mid-ranking cleric who is the most vocal proponent of gender equality, was a regular contributor to *Zanan*, where he tried to develop a coherent theory of women's equal rights within Islamic jurisprudence.[20] Mohsen Kadivar, the ardent advocate of human rights referred to above, sees gender equality as one of the main pillars of a human rights regime and a democratic order.[21] Gender equality and women's autonomy have also been central to the work of other clerics in this group, most notably Abdullah Nuri (Minister of Interior under President Khatami), who has taken a very strong stance on the issue of the veil—a taboo subject for complicated historical reasons—arguing that it should be voluntary and not compulsory.[22]

These clerical proponents contend that the rules of *shari'a* with respect to gender concerns are time- and place-sensitive—hence the label 'dynamic jurisprudence' (*feqh pouya* as opposed to *feqh sonati*, or traditional jurisprudence). Moreover, they argue that, in determining the dictates of Islam, the general principles of humanity and morality must take precedence over 'specific provisions found in various sources of Islamic jurisprudence—provisions which they generally contend were intended for, or are a product of, a different time, place and social context'.[23]

As Sa'idzadeh puts it:

> a substantial number of *hadith* and *feqh* theories obstruct the way to establishing equality between the sexes. A majority of jurists and all *hadith* specialists have sacrificed the Principle of equality in Islam to endorse a set of theories resting on assumptions that are no longer valid but still remain part of *feqh*...equality is such an unequivocal Principle that we cannot set it aside for the sake of a set of *feqh* theories.[24]

As Mir-Hosseini concludes, 'Sa'idzadeh has set himself the task of demolishing these theories, arguing that it should be done from within *feqh* itself and using its own language and mode of argumentation'.[25] He has argued, for example, that the assumptions about each gender's nature that underline the traditional assignment of roles (women as nurturers, males as breadwinners) and the discriminatory provisions in orthodox jurisprudence that follow (women's share of inheritance and remedies in case of murder or assault being half the amount due to men) are all social constructs. He then uses the traditional methods and reasoning of Islamic jurisprudence to argue that gender equality is in fact rooted in the dictates of Islam.[26]

Similar in style and argumentation are the writings of Mohsen Kadivar on human rights and women's rights. These constitute one of the most thorough and extensive analyses of traditional Islamic thinking from the perspective of human rights. In an interview with the magazine *Aftab* entitled 'Human Rights and Religious Intellectualism', he provides an astonishingly forthright and harsh critique of traditional Islam from the perspective of human rights.[27] He begins by setting out the reasons why historical (or traditional) Islam is in conflict with human rights thinking, with detailed references to the existing body of human rights instruments and conventions, including the Convention on the Elimination of All Forms of Discrimination against Women (CEDAW). The six grounds on which he sees major conflicts between historical Islam and human rights thinking are: denial of legal equality between Muslims and non-Muslims (the non-Muslim category includes atheists); denial of legal equality between women and men; denial of legal equality between slaves and free individuals; denial of legal equality in public affairs between common people and religious men; denial of freedom of thought and religion; and the endorsement of harsh punishments and torture.

On gender equality more specifically Kadivar draws attention to the irrationality and injustice (in traditional Islam) of allowing physiological differences to determine legal differences in rights: 'if racial differences and differences in the colour of skin cannot form the basis of differences in rights, why should gender become the basis for such differences? . . . Gender discrimination in rights is contrary to fairness, justice, and rationality'.[28]

His response to the question of whether traditional Islam has the capacity to overcome its fundamental contradictions with human rights is unequivocally negative. What is needed, he argues, 'are innovative interpretations of divine principles in the light of new realities of which human rights thinking is a key component, rather than searching in vain for answers in old *hadiths and even in the Koran itself which includes some verses that are contrary to human rights*'.[29] Human rights thinking must therefore take precedence and inform today's Islam. Finally, Kadivar sees the international efforts by Islamic countries to come to terms with human rights thinking (the most recent being the 1990 Cairo Declaration of the Organization of Islamic Conference) as meek, confusing and largely unsuccessful. While the 1990 Cairo Declaration took a positive stance on the issue of slavery, it failed to address the other five areas of tension outlined above, including the area of gender discrimination, where it effectively endorsed 'women's *shari'a* rights as in conformity with their duties'.[30]

It must also be noted that Kadivar, like many of the other reformists, rejects the argument that human rights thinking is a Western construct suited to Western lifestyles. He sees human rights thinking as a global phenomenon whose value lies in its rationality, justice and fairness, 'and thus to submit to human rights thinking is not to submit to the West, but to submit to rationality and justice'.[31]

While high-profile male public figures like Mohsen Kadivar and the popular Abdollah Nuri have contested traditional Islam's endorsement of gender discrimination and tried to push modernist understandings of Islam in the direction of global human rights thinking, with its emphasis on gender equality, the hard work of redressing some of the most harmful Islamic laws, placed on the statute books in the early years after the Revolution, was carried out through the lobbying efforts of a group of women parliamentarians in the late 1980s and early 1990s (in the Fourth and Fifth Parliament that were still controlled by the conservatives).[32] For example, in 1986 the restrictions on the subjects that women could study were removed; in 1992 divorce laws were amended to curtail men's right to divorce their wives at will and to provide adequate financial compensation in the case of divorce; and in the same year women were also appointed as 'advisory judges'. In February 2000 three newly elected female parliamentarians raised questions about the dress code, when they declared their determination not to wear the full covering (*chador*).

These efforts were in turn being fed by the work of women activists and lawyers who were using women's publications as a forum to air women's concerns about *shari'a* laws and to discuss religious rulings from a gender perspective. The activism that these women were engaging in has been widely referred to as 'Islamic feminism', even though it has included the work of some secular feminists, in particular the eminent feminist lawyer, Mehrangiz Kar (currently in exile). While it would be difficult to offer any precise definition of Islamic feminism, or categorisation of the diverse positions held on the question of gender justice and gender equality, Mir-Hosseini usefully describes it as 'a new consciousness, a new way of thinking, a gender discourse that is "feminist" in its aspirations and demands, yet is "Islamic" in its language and sources of legitimacy'.[33]

In Iran the Islamic feminists emerged from the heart of the establishment. Many of them were connected through kinship and marriage networks to elite politics. In other words, they were the insiders who gradually came to adopt critical positions in response to some of the doctrinaire measures adopted by the new state. A wide range of views and positions is represented by the advocates of women's rights who work within an Islamic discourse. Some simply act as 'cheerleaders' of the Islamic Republic, asserting a highly conservative interpretation of women's rights,[34] while others have candidly criticised the state for failing to meet its obligations to grant women their Koranic rights.[35]

Many of these women have complained through women's journals and other media that women's 'voices are not heard', that they are being 'pushed aside' when it comes to public appointments, and that women are being used 'as extras to build up the crowd to give legitimacy to the demonstrations'.[36] They have repeatedly drawn attention to women's absence and marginalisation in the centres of decision making, even under the presidency of Khatami. They have advocated divorce laws that are based on women's autonomy, choice and economic security, and custody laws that are based on the best interest of the child and the mother. They defend women's public presence, and have focused their efforts on highlighting the rights that Islam accorded to women, both in their domestic roles as mothers and wives, and in the public sphere as workers, political actors and as law-abiding and faithful citizens. Their aim is ultimately to revive the woman-friendly aspects of Islam, which they claim has been overlooked over the centuries by masculinist readings of the holy texts.

An important forum for Islamic women's rights advocacy has been the already mentioned monthly magazine *Zanan* (Women). *Zanan*, like other reformist voices, has had an interesting trajectory. Its publisher and managing director, Shahla Sherkat, began her post-revolutionary career as the director of the government-controlled women's weekly magazine, *Zane-e Rouz*, which essentially promoted the 'post-revolutionary ideal woman...a Muslim woman, wearing a chador and carrying a gun'.[37] Dissatisfied with the old clichés, and keen to attract a more diverse readership, once she was ousted from the editorial group in 1992 as part of a purge intended to calm dissident voices in the early 1990s, she set up *Zanan*.

As Afsaneh Najmabadi has meticulously shown, *Zanan*'s interpretive work on women's rights has been novel, with many of the contributing authors engaging in direct interpretations of canonical texts from the perspective of individual women's lived experiences, demands and desires.[38] '*Zanan*'s discussion of justice, oppression, and disobedience in marriage shifts the ground of these concepts from the marriage contract's definitions of what constitutes justice according to sacred revelation, to what constitutes justice in a woman's lived experience'.[39] For example, in a move that is similar to, and informed by, the feminist debates on the social construction of gender difference, *Zanan* argues that women's and men's positions in God's sight are unrelated to their differences-in-creation, and their respective social responsibilities and rights are also unrelated to these differences. It thus becomes possible to embrace the notion of equality of rights for women and men and to condemn discrimination on any basis as counter to this concept of equality. This approach, as we have seen, is very similar to what the clerical proponents of dynamic jurisprudence have been engaged in (and, as was noted earlier, Sa'idzadeh has extensively contributed to *Zanan*'s work on women's legal rights within Islam).

The other move, boldly pioneered by *Zanan*, has been to affiliate itself explicitly with global and Western feminism and to cite and quote from non-Iranian feminists, as well as from secular Iranian feminists both inside and outside the country. This is a practice that has continued up to the present time, with extensive interviews with secular Iranian feminists appearing as a regular feature. *Zanan* has thus become a forum for women's rights advocates of different persuasions, both secular and religious, to engage in debate and writing—reversing the important 'historical trend within which the West and the East, modernism and Islam, feminism and cultural authenticity, have been constructed as exclusionary categories'.[40]

Pluralism in the print media was catalysed in the more liberal era of Khatami's presidency, when the conservatives lost their absolute control of government and when the liberal Ata'ollah Mohajerani presided as the

Minister of Islamic Culture and Guidance (1997–2000). He facilitated the publication of diverse newspapers and weeklies, as well as permitting greater freedom of expression in the arts, especially cinema. In this period a number of other women's publications followed *Zanan*'s lead, especially *Huqug-e Zanan*, *Jens-e Dovvom* and *Zan* (the latter a daily paper, run by Fa'eze Hashemi, which took a daring stance on several issues, including solidarity with Western feminists and their achievements, before being shut down in late 1999).

Mohajerani was forced to resign in December 2000 and the reformist press has been under constant pressure and censorship. As we noted above, from a historical/local perspective, *Zanan*'s stance has been in many ways radical and transformative, reversing the divide between cultural authenticity/Islam and modernity/feminism, trying to build bridges between different strands of the women's movement over common issues and concerns relating to gender inequality, and connecting with global feminism. But this has not been easy: the magazine has faced constant criticism from conservative quarters and has been under pressure and threat from various sides.[41]

While the global human rights and women's rights conventions (including CEDAW) are implicit in *Zanan*'s legal work, an important component of its work on Islamic law has been about providing new interpretations of canonical texts by women and in tune with women's 'lived experiences', thereby breaking the monopoly of the clergy. As such, the task of pushing for CEDAW fell to the reformist elements within the government. Some observers noted the visible change in the attitude of government officials towards the international human rights order, with some parts of the government increasingly engaging with and taking the international human rights debate more seriously.[42] In the area of women's rights, a discernible shift was seen in the perspective of government bureaucrats, whereby the official focus was shifted from promoting and exporting revolutionary values to uncovering how international and global human rights trends are relevant to Iran's circumstances.[43] For example, since early 2002 the parliament has been seriously debating the ratification of CEDAW. The 'woman's machinery' (Center for Women's Participation, as it is called) was arguing that CEDAW be ratified without reservation—a move that was frozen in September 2003 when the conservative Council of Guardians raised strong objections to CEDAW and harshly criticised the parliamentarians promoting its ratification.

Reformism on trial

Even if we agree that these emerging reformist and feminist voices represent a paradigm shift in Islamic thought, the question of what their political impact has been cannot be ignored. What impact, if any, has this new mode of thinking had within formal political institutions (the ideological apparatus, the state, the parliament) and in the embryonic 'civil society' and social movements that operate in more diffuse forms? While it is important not to belittle the importance of ideas (and discourses) as a catalyst for change, what interests me in particular are their political consequences. For this we need to turn to the influence of reformist ideas on key political actors and institutions, especially in the period between 1997 and 2005, when certain reformist elements had a presence in some parts of the policy establishment.

It is no secret that the short-term political liberalisation associated with the Khatami presidency was only skin-deep. While Khatami was voted into power by an overwhelming majority (more than 70%) of the eligible electorate on a platform for change and greater democratisation, the reformist president and government were weakened by several counter trends. For a start the conservative forces maintained their monopoly over the non-democratic, but highly influential, political, military and economic institutions that continued to yield enormous power. These were the ideological arm of the establishment endorsed by the constitution, which was, as noted earlier, neither elected nor subject to democratic accountability mechanisms; the security apparatus, the Revolutionary Guards and the *Basiji* militias, which were being strengthened throughout this period (possibly in preparation for a final confrontation with the reformist forces); and the highly controversial and unaccountable religious foundations that control major economic assets and significant financial flows. Many of the reformist clerical figures referred to in this paper were prosecuted, imprisoned and defrocked by the judiciary and the special court set up for this purpose (Special Clergy Court) within the lifespan of Khatami's government. Most of Khatami's legislative reforms (on freedom of the press, ratification of CEDAW) were blocked by the conservatives, most notably the Council of Guardians, which takes its lead from the Supreme Leader.

Second, the reformists in power were divided on many critical issues, including the pace and scope of reform. The kind of 'insider-reformism' that gained access to power did not, on the whole, endorse a radical overhaul of 'the establishment' (although some ministers and some parliamentarians may have done so). They were reluctant to push for the full democratisation of the constitution and of the political institutions it sanctioned because they did not see the need for systemic change. Nor did they trust the electorate that had 'opportunistically'[44] voted them into office. In effect, the reformists in power were unable to use their main source of legitimacy and bargaining chip *vis-à-vis* the conservatives—the electorate that brought them into office— because they feared that popular mobilisation could lead to a radicalisation of the reform agenda. This element of distrust between the visible leadership of the reform movement that now held government positions, and the diverse social forces (including many women's rights advocates) that had supported the movement, explains why the reformist leadership was not able to create alternative forms of mobilisation, through social movements for example, fearing that a movement of some sort would develop its own agenda rather than allow the existing leadership to represent its demands and interests.[45]

While the reformists were able to maintain their hold over the parliament for some time, their power has receded further in recent years. In the last parliamentary elections (March 2003) they lost their parliamentary dominance to the conservatives as their candidates were weeded out through the tightly controlled selection process for candidates. The new parliament includes a handful of women (fronted by the conservatives), many of them outspoken in support of the project of asserting a conservative interpretation of 'women's rights'. Reverting back to the early 1980s model of 'Islamic womanhood', they have condemned all international human rights conventions, including the International Convention on the Rights of the Child, which was selectively reproduced in school textbooks. They are militantly opposed to CEDAW. To combat prostitution and moral decay they have voiced the need for the imposition of a strict dress code, the further segregation of all public spaces, and the meting out of hard punishments (execution) for sex workers. In a recent meeting with women employees of the Public Media Service (Seda va Seema), one female parliamentarian emphasised the need for early retirement and extended maternity leaves so that women could better attend to their familial duties.

In June 2005, in what became a controversial blow for the reformists, they lost the presidency, thereby bringing all the centres of power under the sway of conservatives associated with the Supreme Leader and the like-minded clerical figures sitting in the Council of Guardians.[46] While no one predicted the victory of Mahmoud Ahmadinejad, and while there were numerous accusations of fraud, irregularities and of money changing hands (probably decisive for the final outcome), it is also clear that popular resentment towards Ahmadinejad's opponent, Hashemi Rafsanjani, in the run-off played into the hands of the conservative candidate.

Rafsanjani's previous tenure was associated with an agenda of economic liberalisation that ended in hyperinflation, cronyism and a series of horrific political murders that remain unresolved to this day.[47] His seemingly moderate and pragmatic stance on numerous issues, both international (Iran's nuclear capacity, relations with the USA) and domestic (cultural issues like veiling and segregation), was tainted by the fact that his brand of liberalism—neoliberal on economic policies, strongly opposed to political democratisation, and only mildly liberal on cultural issues—is widely discredited for its association with economic polarisation and corruption.

Another reason for the gradual erosion of popular support for the reformists and their eventual defeat in the 2005 presidential elections was their failure to present a credible agenda for combating economic and social deprivation that could respond to popular concerns and anxieties about increasing inequality and insecurity. The more conservative elements in the regime were able to exploit these anxieties with their populist revolutionary rhetoric. Ahmadinejad was widely praised for his humble background (compared with that of Rafsanjani and his family, who have amassed huge wealth) and his concerns for the 'common people'. Social freedoms and the kind of rights-based agenda that the reformists stood for, it is argued, do not meet the urgent needs of low-income households, those who have recently migrated from villages and who struggle hard to make a living on the fringes of urban existence.[48] Inflation is currently running well above the official rate of 15% and Ahmadinejad's economic adviser laments that a third of Iranians in their twenties are unemployed.[49] There is a desperate need for jobs, for reliable public services and for basic urban infrastructure.

It would be dangerous, however, to accept the argument that the average woman or man on the street does not need the kind of liberal rights agenda that the reform movement, especially the women's rights advocates, have been demanding—an argument reminiscent of leftist contempt for 'bourgeois rights'. Women's rights within marriage and the family, for example, which *Zanan* has championed, are likely to affect low-income women even more than the well-to-do, who are more likely to have the means to reach satisfactory settlements (over divorce, child custody, inheritance rights, and so on) outside the court system. It is well known that parents with economic means tend to bail out their daughters and sons from the clutches of the morality police, while it is to the offspring of the less well-to-do that Islamic punishments are meted out (for infringing the dress code, or the rules of segregation, and so on). Moreover, disappointment with the reformists in power, I would argue, does not stem from their championing of civil rights which are allegedly irrelevant for the popular social strata, but because they were largely incapable of substantiating those rights (whether with regard to the freedom of expression, of the press and the media or with respect to women's rights).

A further reason for the final demise of the reformists was the changing global politics, with the US president singling out Iran as a rogue state and as part of the 'axis of evil' in 2002. While this handicapped the reformists, who had offered sympathy and support against al-Qaida over 9/11, it strengthened the hands of the conservatives and their confrontational mentality.[50]

Whether the reform movement, and the feminist currents within it, will be able to recuperate from this defeat and present a programmatic alternative to the old and vacuous revolutionary slogans of social justice that are premised on a deeply patriarchal gender order remains to be seen. The prospects for democratisation are also highly contingent on how the tension over Iran's nuclear capacity is handled by the UN Security Council and by the USA in particular. Confrontation over the nuclear issue is likely to weaken even further the already fragile democratic forces in Iran, while strengthening the hands of the conservatives to push forward their agenda for militarisation and eventual confrontation with the 'infidels'. The agenda for women's rights and gender equality remains contingent on how these broader processes of political change are played out in the months and years to come.

Notes

This paper has benefited from useful comments made by Yusuf Bangura, Terence Gomez and Peter Utting. The usual disclaimers apply.

1 S Zubaida, 'Culture, international politics and Islam: debating continuity and change', in W Brown, S Bromley & S Athreye (eds), *A World of Whose Making? Ordering the International: History, Change and Transformation*, London: Pluto Press/Open University, 2004.

2 O Roy, *Globalized Islam: The Search for a New Ummah*, New York: Columbia University Press, 2004.

3 TG Jelen & C Wilcox, 'Religion: the one, the few and the many', in Jelen & Wilcox (eds), *Religion and Politics in Comparative Perspective: The One, the Few and the Many*, Cambridge: Cambridge University Press, 2002.

4 P Paidar, *Women and the Political Process in Twentieth-Century Iran*, Cambridge: Cambridge University Press, 1995.

5 P Paidar, 'Gender of democracy: the encounter between feminism and reformism in contemporary Iran', *DGHR Paper*, 6, Geneva: UNRISD, 2001, p 5.

6 A Najmabadi, 'Hazards of modernity and morality: women, state and ideology in contemporary Iran', in D Kandiyoti (ed), *Women, Islam and the State*, Philadelphia: Temple University Press, 1991, pp 48–76.

7 A Najmabadi, 'Feminism in an Islamic Republic: years of hardship, years of growth', in Y Yazbeck Haddad & J Esposito (eds), *Islam, Gender, and Social Change*, Oxford: Oxford University Press, 1999, pp 59–84.

8 H Moghissi, *Populism and Feminism in Iran: Women's Struggle in a Male-Defined Revolutionary Movement*, Basingstoke: Macmillan Press, 1994, p 183.

9 Z Mir-Hosseini, *Islam and Gender: The Religious Debate in Contemporary Iran*, Princeton, NJ: Princeton University Press, 1999.

10 The Iranian journalist Akbar Ganji condemns this system as a form of 'sultanism'. S Bakhash, 'Akbar Ganji: letter from Evin Prison', *The New York Review*, 22 September 2005, pp 46–47. As Garton Ash explains, this political system has some similarities with a communist party state: both have parallel hierarchies of ideological and state power, with the former ultimately trumping the latter. T Garton Ash, 'Soldiers of a hidden Imam', *The New York Review*, 3 November 2005, pp 4–8.

11 A Najmabadi, 'Feminism in an Islamic Republic'.

12 M Kadivar, 'Human rights and religious intellectualism', *Aftab*, 27 and 28 (Tir, Mordad and Shahrivar 1382), 2003.

13 *Ibid*, p 107.

14 C Kuzman, 'Critics within: Islamic scholars' protests against the Islamic state in Iran', *International Journal of Politics, Culture and Society*, 15 (2), 2001, pp 341–359; and Z Mir-Hosseini, 'The conservative–reformist conflict over women's rights in Iran', *International Journal of Politics, Culture and Society*, 16 (1), 2002, pp 37–53.

15 Soroush was one of the key ideologues of the Islamic Republic in its formative years, and participated actively in the reorganisation of the universities during the 'cultural revolution' that involved the dismissal of many secular professors. He was gradually disillusioned and then distanced himself from the establishment, before becoming an open and ardent critic. His public lectures have been banned in Iran and he now spends most of his time outside the country. For samples of his work in English, see http://www.drsoroush.com/English, last visited 16 March 2005.

16 C Kuzman, 'Liberal Islam: prospects and challenges', *Middle East Review of International Affairs*, 3 (3), 1999, pp 11–19.

17 P Paidar, 'Gender of democracy', p 21.

18 Mir-Hosseini, *Islam and Gender*.

19 *Ibid*, p 215.

20 The most extensive analysis of Sa'idzadeh's thinking and writing is provided by *ibid*, on whose work I rely here. Sa'idzadeh was recently defrocked.

21 Mohsen Kadivar served a two-year prison sentence but continues to write and give public lectures outside the country. For samples of his writing and lectures in English, see http://www.kadivar.com/English, last visited 16 March 2006.

22 Nuri, cited in Mir-Hosseini, 'The conservative–reformist conflict over women's rights in Iran'. The issue of the veil is a sensitive one: under Reza Shah's modernisation drive, in 1936 the veil was forcibly removed and all women had to appear in public without it. The Islamic Republic, on the other hand, forcibly imposed the veil on women in 1980.

23 S Mokhtari, 'The search for human rights within an Islamic framework in Iran', *The Muslim World*, 94, 2004, p 474.

24 Interviewed in Mir-Hosseini, *Islam and Gender*, p 252.

25 Mir-Hosseini, *Islam and Gender*, p 250.

26 While clerics like Sa'idzadeh would not quote or cite Soroush (since he is regarded as an intellectual lightweight in the seminaries), the influence of his thinking on theirs is very clear.

27 M Kadivar, 'Human rights and religious intellectualism'.

28 *Ibid*, p 109.

29 *Ibid*, p 111, emphasis added.

30 Kadivar, 'Human rights and religious intellectualism'.

31 *Ibid*, p 112.

32 H Afshar, *Islam and Feminisms: An Iranian Case Study*, Women's Studies at York, Basingstoke: Macmillan Press, 1998; and Mir-Hosseini, 'The conservative–reformist conflict over women's rights in Iran'.

33 Z Mir-Hosseini, 'The quest for gender justice: emerging feminist voices in Islam', *Islam 21*, 36, May 2004, p 3.

34 The women's journal *Nida'* (The Call), which is the organ of a quasi-governmental organisation headed by Khomeini's daughter, Zahra Mostafavi, is a good representative of this group.

35 Afshar, *Islam and Feminisms*, ch 2.

36 *Ibid*, pp 42–43.

37 R Eftekhari, '*Zanan*: trials and successes of a feminist magazine in Iran', in R Eftekhari, *Middle Eastern Women on the Move: Openings for and the Constraints on Women's Political Participation in the Middle East*, Woodrow Wilson International Center for Scholars, Middle East Project, 2003, p 16.

38 A Najmabadi, 'Feminism in an Islamic Republic'. The dominant method of reformist interpretations of women's issues has been to use the more woman-friendly sources from an already existing set of texts.

39 *Ibid*, p 68.

40 *Ibid*, p 75.

41 Eftekhari, '*Zanan*'.

42 Mokhtari, 'The search for human rights within an Islamic framework in Iran'.

43 N Todidi, 'International connections of the Iranian women's movement', in NR Keddie & R Matthee (eds), *Iran and the Surrounding World: Interactions in Culture and Cultural Politics*, Seattle, WA: University of Washington Press, 2002. Todidi explains, however, that, despite 'some movement toward moderation, a disturbing continuity was reflected in the . . . opposition to certain egalitarian aspects of the Beijing Platform for Action, placing Iran among the leading conservative Muslim states in alliance with conservative Catholic states led by the Holy See' (p 213).

44 I use the term 'opportunistic' here advisedly, not as a criticism of the electorate but to underline the point that Khatami was able to gain such a majority because he stood against a candidate that represented the conservative establishment. Hence a pro-Khatami vote was first and foremost a vote against the conservatives and for change.

45 F Halliday, 'Iran's revolutionary spasm', at http://www.opendemocracy.net, accessed 2 July 2005.

46 In a fascinating analysis of the 2005 election surprise, F Halliday, argues in *ibid* that the Iranian revolution is moving after 20 years not into a 'reform' phase but into a 'twenty-year spasm'—a second reassertion of militancy and egalitarianism that rejects domestic elites and external pressure alike (as in Russia in the second purge era of the late 1930s, China during the Cultural Revolution of the late 1960s, and Cuba in the 'rectification' campaign of the 1980s).

47 C De Bellaigue, 'New man in Iran', *The New York Review*, 11 August 2005, pp 19–22.

48 *Ibid*.

49 *Ibid*.

50 Halliday, 'Iran's revolutionary spasm'. While the election result and the conservative backlash that it represents had many different social and political reasons behind it, the control and manipulation of the election process by the conservative forces (including, very importantly, the security and intelligence services), which was most probably part of a much broader and more intricate strategy to reassert themselves, should not be underestimated.

Legacies of Common Law: 'crimes of honour' in India and Pakistan

PRATIKSHA BAXI, SHIRIN M RAI &
SHAHEEN SARDAR ALI

The issue of 'crimes of honour' has become prominent in the discourses of law and the state in recent years in South Asia. A mass of literature has documented cases where families and community governance bodies torture, abduct or kill women and men for transgressing the familial codes of honour. The term 'crimes of honour' has been critiqued for retaining the emphasis on male honour and eliding the widespread use of violence not amounting to murder to prevent women from sustaining relationships of their choice.[1] Often we find that non-state legal mechanisms as well as state law are used to frame and regulate women's sexual choices. In India and Pakistan ethnographic studies suggest that caste *panchayats* (village councils), *jirgas* (tribal councils), police officers, lawyers, prosecutors and even trial judges uphold localised notions of sovereignty often in contravention of constitutional law or even of the rule of law.[2] Judicial reasoning then must reckon with custom, how customary practices may abrogate rights of women and how such practices are constituted by the patriarchal politics of shame and honour.

'Honour crimes' evoke competing spheres of legal subjection simultaneously: customary laws, family law, criminal law and international law. A range of laws, such as Islamic criminal laws (the Hudood Ordinances) in Pakistan and Indian laws on murder, rape, abduction and kidnapping, normalise violence against women and men who transgress familial, religious, racial, class and caste-based normativities. In both these countries, legal reform has been sparked off through the initiatives of feminist groups and, although the trajectories of the women's movements have followed different histories, many networks have been set up between women's groups to follow up individual cases and exchange information on the laws of each country.[3]

The exploratory analysis in this chapter suggests that the emergence of new and old publics[4] as sites of murder, assault and rape is fashioned alongside the routine use of courts of law, whereby state law is used to 'recover', discipline and/or punish errant daughters. We look at appellate judgments from India and Pakistan, where state law has been used against *adult* women who exercise their right to choose whom they marry. The comparative framework detailing how the politics of honour is normalised, we hope, will allow us to delineate how women are subjected to competing ideas of rights, legality and justice. A comparative perspective also allows us to examine different ways of reading postcolonial legalities, how the law constitutes the nation-state by naturalising some forms of violence as indigenous and excluding others from the picture of national patriarchies, and the tense relationship of the law to emergent publics which are embedded in the politics of honour. In doing this we reflect upon how a rights-based discourse of modern nation-states forms a complex terrain where citizenship of the state and membership of communities are negotiated and contested through the unfolding of complex legal rituals on both sites.

State and the law in India and Pakistan

In the context of colonial law, Sarkar has argued that it was 'cultural' and not 'political' nationalism that enabled middle class modern women to enter the public sphere, by 'domesticating' the nationalist project within the home.[5] Further, the postcolonial state's insistence upon its secular character was mediated by its need to reassure religious minorities, which led to the recognition of 'personal law', first used by the colonial state, for religious groups. This created a context where the Indian constitution reflects the tensions between dominant (unequal) gender relations on the one hand, and some moves towards substantive equality between men and women on the other.[6]

Sarkar's argument about the effects of the colonial projects of cultural nationalism on political nationalism can, to some extent, also be read in the legal discourse in Pakistan. The genesis of the state of Pakistan exemplifies this plurality of norms, especially with regard to the original constitution. This, in its chapter on Fundamental Rights and Principles of Policy, provides for equality and non-discrimination on the basis, *inter alia*, of sex in a number of its provisions (article 25). In addition to article 25, articles 26, 27,

32, 34 and 37 of the constitution of Pakistan set out affirmative action measures enabling women to achieve meaningful *de facto* equality with men in all spheres of life. However, the Hudood Ordinances, Islamic criminal laws promulgated under General Zia-ul-haq in 1999, construct a discourse of difference between men and women, which situates women as fundamentally unequal within an Islamic public. While the Ordinances are an amalgam of five laws,[7] it is the Offences of Zina Ordinance that has the 'most devastating impact on women'.[8]

In reading the complex and divergent legal histories of India and Pakistan we argue that the use of the state in the normalisation of politics indicates that 'the state has an investment in preserving the hegemonic social order in order to mediate and contain social tensions that destabilize the socio-political frame of society'.[9] The state itself is constitutive of the dominant social relations and is therefore limited in its capacity to mediate social conflict: a patriarchal state is definitionally and politically embedded and circumscribed.[10] Moreover, the traditions of nationalism and national movements create a fractured discourse of modernity that half reflects and half rejects 'tradition'—the postcolonial state encounters consequent strains, which are difficult to contain.[11]

The fractured modernity of postcolonial states means that the pressures of globalisation also refract its responses—cultural heritage is fetishised, when, at the same time, the liberalisation of the economy creates new bridges to the 'modern' political economy. The naming of 'honour crimes' as violence against women as it inflects legal discourses and details the role of the state functionaries, such as the police, allows us to suggest how the two nation-states address this form of gendered violence. Through examining the modes of suffering and circumscribing of citizenships we hope to assess the consequences for women and men and communities of this form of violence in order to keep hegemonic social relations in place. The law is also a site where these hegemonic relationships are reconstituted through the recognition of the right to choice. This gains importance, since talk of 'honour' crimes is becoming a transferable discourse being used in other communities in a cosmic civilisational conflict on the one hand, and as a discourse of 'resistance' to globalisation—the erasure of cultural signifiers and the transformation of cultures—on the other.

Two axes might allow us to explore this complex nature of the interaction between modernity and tradition at the local, national and global levels of governance. The first is that of governance of *polities* (state statutory governance bodies such as *panchayats*, courts and the police). The second axis is the governance of *communities* (caste *panchayats*[12] and *jirgahs*[13]). The regulatory power of both is limited as well as complex. This power comes to be articulated at the intersection of disciplinary power of caste or community discourses of honour with sovereign, or as Foucault would say politico-juridical, discourses of crime and adulthood. The translation of caste or community transgressions into crimes shows us how the politics of honour captures state law, while the suspension of legal action against forced marriages allows the familial to escape legal intervention. The claims to citizenship in the realm of the domestic sphere must be understood in the interstices of the relationship between law, violence and governance.

Along the first axis, that of governance of polities, the naming of 'honour crimes' as a form of violence against women has located the *place* of sanctioned violence in caste *panchayats* in India. Recent campaigns against 'honour crimes' have pointed out that caste *panchayats* are illegal, and that the state must intervene in preventing such bodies from mimicking the state's monopoly over violence.[14] In fact, one High Court even refused to accept that caste *panchayats exist*.[15] The effect of the campaigns against 'crimes of honour' in highlighting the *illegality* of caste *panchayats* and in pointing out the way the caste system prevents and punishes marriages of choice, provides a specific critique of Indian patriarchies. The campaigns against 'crimes of honour' move away from benign descriptions of legal pluralism to grapple with how, for women, pluralistic legal systems may be seen as 'fields of overlapping and intersecting forms of subjection'.[16] These campaigns, with all their complexity, diversity and contradictions, foreground competing notions of governance: at the sites of the domestic, community and polity. As such, they become constitutive of affective and impassioned publics, working to fracture state regulatory forms and their much vaunted hegemonic prowess at the local levels. Although sociologists have suggested that *forms* of adjudication in non-state adjudicatory fora are equally constituted by statecraft,[17] it is the abdication of legal intervention against these bodies that has met with serious criticism by activists.

In recent years the governance of the polity at the local level in India and Pakistan has seen an unfolding discourse of decentralisation that has also been linked to the increased participation of hitherto marginalised groups. The 73rd and 74th constitutional Amendments addressed both these through the expansion of the remit of the *panchayat*'s workings and responsibilities as well as the 33% quota for women representatives and leaders. In Pakistan too the change of government in 1999 from a civilian to a military regime led to reservation of 33% of seats for women in all three tiers (union council, *tehsil* administrative unit and district) of local government and 17% in the national and provincial assemblies and the senate.[18] Even as citizenship of women was thus extended through participation in formal institutions of local governance, the government also augmented the regulatory power of the caste *panchayats*. The relationship between this expanded and more visible institutional framework of local governance and the traditional modes of governance of communities through caste *panchayats* was assumed to be one of state predominance. However, we find that the fracturing of state forms at the local level in the face of other hegemonic discourses and regimes of social power remains unmapped, unexpected and most often contingent on the flows of power in particular moments and spaces.

The second axis along which we explore governance is that of *formal and informal adjudicatory systems* and the overlaps that occur when the axis of governance becomes overgrown with the power play on the ground. The discursive and the institutional lines blur and notions of justice and rights stand appropriated by caste *panchayats* and other non-state adjudicatory forums in the name of religion, caste, culture and history. State structures find this combination very powerful at times and threatening at others—the embeddedness of state power makes it vulnerable to co-option by 'civil society' institutions through personnel and institutions 'sensitive' to cultural demands as well as through hegemonic narratives of statehood. This affects the way in which resistance to public violence can be organised, at times with the state's help and at others in the face of the state's betrayal. Schemes run by the state for the empowerment of women can be undermined when local hegemonic communities oppose this and visit incredible violence upon women, without any intervention by the state to stop it.[19] Victim testimonies are not recorded in police stations, MPs and local politicians refuse to 'get involved' in informal 'decisions' passed by caste *panchayats*, and the spectacle of public violence then becomes the domesticated regulation of the wider family norms—intra-*gotra* (see below) marriage, inter-caste/religion marriage—despite their conflict with state law and constitutional mechanisms.

Community based adjudicatory systems such as caste *panchayats* have existed since medieval times in South Asia. Moog suggests that 'while there may well no longer be any truly 'traditional' panchayats left which are unaffected by the formal legal system, there still are tribunals of a traditional type in many areas'.[20] Activists have pointed out that the source of their regulatory power arises from the solidarity of the *gotra*.[21] Karat points out that caste *panchayats*:

> are all-male groups of self-proclaimed guardians of caste interests and 'honour' which have the support of the richer sections and enjoy political patronage. The most powerful of these caste panchayats are those of the upper and middle caste landowning sections. The caste panchayats function as a parallel judicial structure and elected panchayats are either subordinated to or co-opted by them. It is through these caste panchayats that the most regressive social views are sought to be implemented.[22]

Governance of communities by caste panchayats and jirgahs has allowed the development of non-state parallel systems of adjudication. These include not only resolving disputes between members of the community but also passing pronouncements on matters deemed to be relevant to the 'honour' of the caste and ensuring the execution of such pronouncements. At a seminar organised by the Department of Sociology, Maharshi Dayanand University between academics, activists and the heads of the *khap panchayats* in the state of Haryana in northern India, Sooraj Singh, Pradhan of the Meham Chaubisi *khap* (caste *panchayats* of the same *gotra*, from several villages) stated that the *khap panchayats* were invested with a 'divine right' to adjudicate marriages of choice that transgressed caste normativity. 'We cannot allow love marriages. Sarvakhaps do not recognise court marriages either', he said.[23] These pronouncements are of course gendered articulations of patriarchal privilege. Revenge rapes, burning down of homes of those judged to be transgressors of caste boundaries, lynchings and beatings are all employed by these *panchayats* as means of disciplining the communal body.

What then is the relationship between these newly empowered *gram* (village) *panchayats* and the traditional, informal caste *panchayats*, and how does the state negotiate between the two? It is often found that not only are individual members of the two *panchayats* from the same family, but that, as public bodies, *gram panchayats* are supportive of the caste *panchayat* pronouncements of excommunication and even murder. Similar religious and class-based exclusions are practised in Pakistan. Thus, what seems to occur here is the constant and complex negotiation of decentralised state structures with hegemonic informal governance structures that maintain a stable social geography.

It is in the moments of conflict between these two impulses that we can read the story of the socio-legal responses to violent practices such as 'honour crimes'. The dilemma that the state faces was recently articulated by the Indian Union Panchayati Raj Minister, Mani Shankar Aiyar. He said that informal pronouncements by caste *panchayats* were 'not in conformity with the Constitutional provisions or based on the objectivity of free of caste and creed consideration'.[24] The Rajasthan State Human Rights Commission filed a writ petition in the Jodhpur High Court against the caste *panchayats* in the area. The major political parties have, however, never opposed these non-state governance bodies.[25]

At the local level, where the tragic stories of opposition to romantic love take legal form, we find state officers such as the Inspector-General of Police, Rohtak, Haryana emphasising that 'caste played an important role in village life'. He did not think 'that the state had any business meddling in their [caste *panchayats*'] activities, for democracy "essentially means minimal state intervention"'.[26] Chowdhry rightly points out that the belief that 'social issues must be resolved by caste leaders or caste panchayats and not according to the law of the land, which applies a different criterion of justice' has wide prevalence.[27]

If local governance bodies of both polities and communities have become embedded in the landscapes of regulatory violence, the police and the courts as institutions of governance of polities also become resources to enforce and contest notions of male honour and the custodial investments of parents in their daughters. In the next section, we use insights anchored in our reading of appellate judgements from India and Pakistan in specific cases in courts of appeals to reflect on how law is used to regulate women's sexuality and how 'protest' against the use of state law to enforce norms of kinship and alliance is framed within the categories of law.[28]

Juridical responses: legacies of common law

A review of appellate judgements in both countries indicates that the criminalisation of 'choice' in heterosexual marriage demonstrates how law is embedded in the constitution of publics based on notions of honour and how governance of polities and communities overlaps powerfully to regulate sexuality. This is operationalised through local practices of policing, whereby the police acting in concert with the family detain adult women and fabricate criminal cases against both the woman and her partner. The police may position a woman as an accused and/or abettor to a crime, although technically she is named as a victim. The strategies for challenging the criminalisation of marriages of choice also follow a common route in India and Pakistan. The use of the writ of *habeas corpus*—literally, writ to produce the body in court—is a routinised legal strategy to adjudicate consent and coercion in both jurisdictions, which demonstrates the fractured nature of the postcolonial state in the two countries.

The genealogy of the criminalisation of choice marriages in Pakistan may be traced to two powerful legal norms—the colonial archive as it constituted the pre-Hudood jurisprudence and the postcolonial Islamisation of criminal law. In this paper we examine the Hudood Ordinance to explicate how certain forms of sexual autonomy outside marriage were criminalised and how the law itself produces the conditions whereby consensual relationships are legally transformed into *zina* offences.[29]

Zina crimes are defined as extra marital offences, ie wilful sexual intercourse between a man and a woman without being validly married to each other (such as adultery and 'fornication'). 'Fornication', ie heterosexual intercourse between two consenting unmarried adults, is now a crime. Rape (*Zina- bil- jabr*) is subsumed under other *zina* offences.[30] The Hudood Ordinance is applicable to the body population of Pakistan irrespective of religion, sect or creed.[31] One of its most dismaying aspects is that, in a situation where the prosecution fails to prove a woman's complaint of rape or there is no conviction because of insufficient evidence, the testimony of rape is treated as a confession of adultery. Moreover, pregnancy is treated as proof of adultery: used as 'physical confession'. A consensual sexual relationship in a marriage of choice can be converted into a *zina* offence by establishing that a marriage of choice is invalid or by producing 'proof' of an earlier marriage through forged documentation.[32] In this way the law then produces *unchaste* women, sullies their reputations, imprisons them and makes 'rehabilitation' a near impossibility. The number of women in prison has increased drastically since the promulgation of this law, because sexual intercourse outside marriage has become a cognisable offence. Any aggrieved person (not only an aggrieved party) may register a First Information Report (FIR)[33] with the police and the police can arrest such person/s. Further, bail cannot be assumed; women (and men) who are arrested can simply be left in prison for years without any legal assistance.[34]

While Indian law does not prevent an adult from taking an autonomous decision about whom to marry[35] (except for the prohibited degrees of marriage defined under various personal laws), and does not criminalise premarital sex nor punish women for adultery, the laws of rape, abduction and kidnapping are used against women to deter break-up, and to prevent marriages of choice.[36] In the Indian instance, typically, the father (or the guardian) files criminal charges of abduction, kidnapping and/or rape against an adult daughter, asserting that she is underage.[37] The police 'investigation' into the case may result in further criminal charges pressed against the boy's family. Once the woman is 'recovered,' she may face different forms of violence in the police station. If the woman refuses to support her family, she may be declared insane and sent to a state-run mental asylum. Or criminal charges on the grounds of theft and abetting her own abduction and rape may be brought against her.[38]

Those women who do not submit to familial pressure are sent to state-run women's shelters. Chakravarti points out that although the shelter is constructed as a 'neutral' space between two 'parties' who claim custody over the woman, it is a space fraught with manifold dangers from the natal family, and the ever-present threat of custodial violence within the institution.[39] The practices of incarceration of women, then, are dispersed, just as the techniques of custodial violence vary. For instance, the case that sparked off the 1980 anti-rape campaign in India points to the risks of custodial rape when choice marriages are brought into the ambit of criminal law.[40] Thus they point our attention to the fact that, while thinking of how to rename the ethnographic category of 'honour crimes', we must remember that the category brings together custodial violence with domestic violence and hence raises issues of citizenship in the domestic sphere.

Our reading of appellate judgements in the two jurisdictions suggests that the use of state law—such as the criminal law on rape, abduction, kidnapping and theft, or the writ of *habeas corpus*[41]—against consenting adults is not an uncommon phenomenon. Rather the blurring between elopement and abduction is found in colonial legal discourse.[42] Colonial law inscribed women in circuits of sovereign power, where consent or choice was staged in courtrooms as the 'manoeuvre in the field of govermentality, invoking, prescribing and cancelling out new expectations of normative conduct on the part of both governors and governed'.[43] It is the staging of women's choice in contemporary postcolonial courtrooms through the criminal, constitutional and procedural law that complicates understanding of legal manoeuvres in this field of governmentality today.[44]

Unsurprising remains the fact that state law is used not only to foster but also to counter the criminalisation of choice. The appeals to state law range from petitions to quash the FIR, challenges to illegal detention and pleas for personal liberty under the writ of *habeas corpus,* and filing collusive suits for the restitution of conjugal rights and are a few of the ways by which runaway couples use law in complex economies of power. Indian appellate judgements tell us typically that the husband may seek restitution of conjugal rights *against* his wife. The *collusive* case of restitution of conjugal rights is aimed at gaining legal recognition of the fact that the woman was neither abducted nor forced into marriage. This sets the stage for the woman's *consent* to be certified. The performance of women's agency in court is grounded in the anticipation of police action, ie fear of arrest, illegal detention and custodial violence. Courts of appeal have been fairly responsive to women when such petitions are filed in India.[45]

The contestation within the judiciary over the embeddedness of law in local publics may be read off the recent reversals of the trial court judgments by the Federal Shariat Court in Pakistan. Superior courts now increasingly reject honour killings of women by their natal families. They shun the old excuse of being 'provoked by sight of a female relative in compromising position' for murders.[46] In certain cases, courts have refused to give any benefit whatsoever to the accused of killing on the grounds of his *'ghairat'* (honour). In *Muhammad Siddique vs the State*[47] the court upheld the conviction of a father who had murdered his daughter, her husband and their infant child to teach his daughter a lesson for marrying according to her choice. Passing judgment Justice Jilani said:

> These killings are carried out in an evangelistic spirit. Little do these zealots know that there is nothing religious about it and nothing honourable either. It is male chauvinism and gender bias at their worst. These prejudices are not country specific, region specific or people specific. The roots are rather old and violence against women has been a recurrent phenomenon in human history.[48]

Likewise the appellate judgment, while reversing the sentence of stoning against Zafran Bibi,[49] held that 'the controversy around the applicability of hudood laws in Pakistan is related more to the erroneous applications of these laws in the country, rather than the laws per se'.[50]

These judgments characterise the embedding of law in honour, personal motives or politics as erroneous in order to re-signify a notion of an *Islamic public* constituted through the *correct* application of the hudood laws.[51] A combination of Islamic law, the constitution of Pakistan and international human rights instruments emanating both from the UN human rights regime and comparable documents from Islamic forums is increasingly cited. It seems to us that the appellate judgments, which critique the misuse of Hudood laws or evoke the rule of law, are mediating two forms of public critique. On the one hand, the critique is inflected by public discourse from women's groups and human rights activists that have campaigned against 'crimes of honour' in Pakistan. On the other hand, the judicial address intends to disrupt the stigmatic discourses that congeal the perpetrators of 'honour crimes' in the figure of the Muslim and cite Islam as the source of the legitimisation of violence against women. We argue that, by challenging the trial court judgments, the appellate courts in Pakistan are inflected by these discourses. The notion of Islamic publics based on the rule of law rather than on the effect and violence of the politics of honour marks the density of these judgments.

The importance of women's and human rights activist movements that strive to secure the rights of adult women persecuted by their family cannot be underestimated. *Mst Humaira Mehmood vs the State*[52] narrates the traumatic story of Humaira, a 30-year-old woman who married Mehmood Butt, against the wishes of her parents. Her father was a sitting member of the Provincial Legislature at the time. He filed a case of alleged *zina* and abduction against Mehmood Butt. The father knew, at the time of his complaint, that Humaira and Mehmood were lawfully married but went ahead and filed a case of *zina* implicating his daughter and her husband, as a result of which they had to flee their home to avoid being arrested. The couple, apprehensive of their lives and safety, fled to Karachi and sought refuge in the Edhi Centre.[53] Her brother filed a FIR to the effect that his sister had left home after a row with her mother and that he should be given her 'possession'. The police, contrary to procedural laws, illegally detained Humaira in order to 'restore' her to her natal family from whom she had fled in the first instance. After she was 'recovered', Humaira was forced to stage a 'false' marriage ceremony which was documented on video and later produced in court as proof of a prior marriage to a groom of the family's choice. The staging of a false marriage indicates the technologies of power used to simulate elopement as abduction, and translate marriage as bigamy— a *zina* offence—by forging documentary and visual evidence.

Humaira's detention and wrongful confinement was challenged by the AGHS legal aid cell in Lahore pioneered by Asma Jehangir and Hina Jillani. Shahtaj Qazilbash, the Co-ordinator of AGHS who filed the petition, invoked the writ jurisdiction of the High Court of Lahore under the Constitution of Pakistan (Article 199), praying that the court pass directions to produce Humaira in court. Justice Jillani pronounced a landmark decision:

> I find that the police officials who handled this case passed orders and acted in a manner which betrayed total disregard of law and the land and mandate of their calling. Articles 4 and 25 of the Constitution of the Islamic Republic of Pakistan guarantee that everybody shall be treated strictly in accordance with law. Article 35 of the Constitution provides that the State shall protect the marriage, the family, the mother and the child. As Member of the international Comity of Nations we must respect the International Instruments of Human Rights to which we are a party.

The judge reminded the parties that Pakistan is a Member of the United Nations and is a signatory to the Convention on the Elimination of all Forms of Discrimination against Women. He especially drew attention to Article 16, which enjoins all member states to respect the rights of women to family life on a basis of equality with men. Justice Jillani also refered to Article 5 of the Cairo Declaration on Human Rights in Islam to reinforce his argument of women's human rights within an Islamic framework. He condemned in no uncertain language the practices of policing by the state and the family by holding that, 'If these guards become poachers then no society and no State can have even a semblance of human rights and rule of law'.[54] Common law is aligned with Islamic law to regulate the family as an institution that cannot mimic the state by appropriating legitimacy to detain and take custody of adult women in the domestic realm.

Unlike in Pakistan, Chakravarti argues that the category of 'honour crimes' has become prevalent in public discourse in India rather late.[55] This does not mean that such forms of violence were not reported earlier. Rather, they became a regular way of plotting such narratives of violence during the 1990s. During this period the collapsing of 'crimes of honour' in Islamic ways of life in discourses of right wing governance has had pernicious effects. The right-wing discourse on 'honour crimes' makes the claim that, while such crimes occur frequently in 'Islamic' countries like Pakistan, these are not 'normal' to secular Indian contexts. Hence, honour crimes become a terrain to mark *differences* between different kinds of patriarchies, which then are tied to the concerns of *Hindutva* nationalism. This discourse thereby stabilises the iconography of honour crimes as 'pre-modern', characterising honour crimes as an example of a *pathological* form of patriarchy which is excluded from the recognition and domestication of other forms of national patriarchies brought under review and reform by the state. Women's groups such as AIDWA have criticised the stance taken by the right-wing government, which shows evidence of violence against consenting adults who marry against the customary norms of caste, community or class.[56]

This iconography of the modern and the pre-modern, secular and Islamic, offers us an *internalist* perspective on how to read, in terms of Stanley Fish, the 'interpretive communities' of appellate courts in a comparative framework.[57] We turn to a judgement pronounced by the Allahabad High Court in response to the petition of a young couple seeking the court's help, since they feared that they would killed for violating caste norms by marrying each other. The narrative detailed in the judgement concerns Sujit Kumar, a 30-year-old *Jat* and Rashmi, a 22-year-old who hailed from the Tyagi caste. Rashmi's parents wanted her to marry a person much older than her and when she refused this marriage proposal, her parents threatened to kill her.

This judgment elaborates judicial disapproval of 'honour killings' or 'harassment of people who love each other and want to get married'.[58] The Court takes note of the accounts published in the newspapers to support its observation that 'honour killings' have been permitted by state machinery:

> The barbaric practice of 'honour killings' that is, killing of young women by their relatives or caste or community members for bringing dishonour to the family or caste or community by marrying or wanting to marry a man of another caste, community or whom the family disapproves of, is frequently reported to take place in Pakistan which is a State based on feudal and communal ideology. However, this Court has been shocked to note that in our country also, which boasts of being a secular and liberal country 'honour killings' have been taking place from time to time, and what is deeply disturbing is that the police and other authorities do not seem to take steps to check these disgraceful and barbaric acts. In fact such 'honour killings', far from being honourable are nothing but pre meditated murder.[59]

In relegating communalism and feudalism to the 'other', the judgement makes a fantastic hermeneutic leap, by denaturalising 'honour crimes' as not belonging to the everyday patriarchal practices of a 'secular' nation. The 'horror' of the killing is simultaneously placed alongside another imagery— that of such crimes being located in primordial temporalities and backward spaces in the interior of Pakistan. Distancing itself from its *absolute other*— the state of Pakistan—the Indian nation-state is pictured as 'secular' and 'liberal', where such 'barbaric' and 'disgraceful' acts are found to be intolerable.[60] The juridical discourse on honour crimes then becomes a site for contestations that succeed in *displacing* the place of violence in such spaces of law. One may even argue that the processes of naming specific forms of violence against women as 'honour crimes' itself entails this displacement.

Conclusions

Only a few tentative concluding remarks remain warranted. First, we see in the rise of the visible and violent display of power by forms of communitarian 'justicing' under the auspices of caste *panchayats* and *jirgahs* in India and Pakistan a marker of increasing tension between the governance of communities and the governance of polities through an attempt to regulate decentralised local economies. We suggest that this 'inter-legality', to evoke Santos,[61] stands ruptured through the campaigns against 'crimes of honour'. Second, we see in the overlapping of governance of polities and communities, of refracted responses of state fractions—the courts and the police—an uneasy reflection of the tense relations between tradition and modernity. Constructing the Self and the Other is a complex social negotiation which takes place upon a fractured terrain of social power, with unpredictable, contradictory and unstable outcomes. These boundaries of Self and Other are often defended and policed through demonstrations of violence, which, while not legitimated by all state fractions, is tolerated and even participated in by others. 'Crimes of honour' and of passion then become more than just crimes: this is violence that regulates sexuality within communities, which is seen as 'legitimate' within the community as a means of securing its cultural borders and insuring against transgression of its norms.

Third, and related, our analysis of the universe of appellate judicial discourse is suggestive of both the embedding of law in the politics of honour and the new-found honour of human rights languages and rhetorics. For example, in the case of *Sujit Kumar and others v State of UP*, judicial discourse constructs a secular and modern public in opposition to the feudal and communal Pakistani publics, while placing the onus on the police to protect the couple from the threats of the family. And in the case of *Mst Humaira Mehmood v the State* the court reinscribes a notion of the Islamic public, challenging the idea that an Islamic public is tolerant of 'honour' crimes, while addressing the international obligation of Pakistan as signatory to various UN conventions to uphold the equal rights of women.

The politics of naming 'crimes of honour' enters a specific modality of delineation where certain places come to be seen as 'natural habitats' of this form of violence, even though the displacement of this place of violence through legal discourse is precisely what has been contested by feminist scholars. Moreover, the naming of 'honour crimes' needs to be chronicled to detail its circulation in local, national, diasporic and global spaces, not least to flag the kinds of legal and institutional innovations that these campaigns have achieved. Since the 'legitimating project of procedural legality' remains incomplete without an understanding of how legal regimes are intrinsically entangled with genealogies of dispersion,[62] we must surely examine what kinds of *manoeuvre* of law and sovereignty are fractured in different sites, in the contexts of nationalism, immigration or globalisation. Hence, the circulation of the category of 'honour crimes' is critical to furthering our understanding of how law is embedded in the constitutions of publics.

The diverse legacies of common law forge an anxious articulation with the categories of tradition and modernity, which inhabit spaces between the governance of polities and the governance of communities, and constantly reconstitute the relationship between the local, national and the global. As our discussion on appellate judgements shows, the languages of women's equality and women's rights do not lend themselves to easy translations. The interpreters of legal regimes and the challengers to these negotiate and contend over the meanings attached to laws, their purview and their wider social importance. It is in these interpretative contestations that women's rights, their claims to citizenship in the domestic sphere, and, indeed, the forms of statecraft take shape.

Notes

We would like to thank Prof Upendra Baxi and Uma Chakravarti for providing a close as well as supportive scrutiny of our work. Any shortcomings are, of course, ours alone.

1 U Chakravarti, 'From fathers to husbands: of love, death and marriage in north India', in L Welchman & S Hossain (eds), *'Honour': Crimes, Paradigms and Violence against Women*, London: Zed Books, 2005, pp 308–331.

2 The same is the case in Afghanistan, where experience suggests the Loya Jirgah was invoked to institutionalise a post-Taliban constitutional ordering.

3 See the CIMEL/INTERRIGHTS Project on 'Strategies to Address Crimes of Honour' at http://www.soas.ac.uk/honourcrimes/.

4 Publics can be defined in three distinct ways and spheres. First, 'there must be as many publics as polities, but whenever one is addressed as the public, the others are assumed not to matter...[second], public also has a sense of totality, bounded by the event or by the shared physical space [and third there is] the kind of public that comes into being only in relation to texts and their circulation'. M Warner, 'Publics and counterpublics', *Public Culture*, 14 (1), 2002, pp 49–90.

5 ME John & J Nair (eds), *A Question of Silence? The Sexual Economies of Modern India*, New Delhi: Kali for Women, 1998, p 3822.

6 Z Pathak & R Sunder Rajan, 'Shah Bano', *Signs: Journal of Women in Culture and Society*, 14, 1989, pp 558–582.

7 The Prohibition (Enforcement of Hadd) Order 1979; Offences Against Property (Enforcement of Hudood) Ordinance 1979; Offences of Zina (Enforcement of Hadd) Ordinance 1979; Offences of Qazf (Enforcement of Hadd) Ordinance 1979; and Execution of Punishment of Whipping Ordinance 1979.

8 F Gardezi, 'Nationalism and state formation: women's struggles and Islamization in Pakistan', in N Hussain, S Mumtaz & R Saigol (eds), *Engendering the Nation-State*, Lahore: Simorgh Women's Resource and Publication Centre, 1997, p 92.

9 K Sangari & S Vaid, *Recasting Women, Essays in Colonial History*, New Delhi: Kali for Women, 1993; and J Stacey, *Socialism and Patriarchy in Communist China*, Princeton, NJ: Princeton University Press, 1983.

10 S Watson & R Pringle, 'Fathers, brothers, and mates: the fraternal state in Australia', in S Watson (ed) *Playing the State, Australian Feminist Interventions*, London: Verso, 1990; C McKinnon, *Toward a Feminist Theory of the State*, Cambridge, MA: Harvard University Press, 1989; C Smart, 'The woman of legal discourse', *Social Legal Studies*, 1 (1), 1991 pp 29–44; and SM Rai & G Lievesley, *Women and the State: International Perspectives*, London: Taylor and Francis, 1996.

11 U Chakravarti, 'Rhetoric and substance of empowerment: women, development and the state', unpublished paper, 1999; P Chatterjee, 'The nationalist resolution of the women's question', in K Sangari & S Vaid, *Recasting Women: Essays in Colonial History*, New Delhi: Kali for Women, 1993, pp 233–253; K Jayawardena, *Feminism and Nationalism in the Third World*, London: Zed Press, 1987.

12 *Panchayats* are councils historically consisting of five members, although that number is by no means sacrosanct. *Gram* (village) *panchayats* are local government bodies and caste *panchayats* are regulatory bodies of caste-, *biradari*- and *gotra*-based communities.

13 *Jirgas* are councils which, like *panchayats*, also assume a state (*sarkari*) form and a tribal and community regulatory form.

14 B Karat, *Survival and Emancipation: Notes from Indian Women's Struggles*, New Delhi: Three Essays Collective, 2005.

15 See A Takhtani, 'A multi-faceted study of society and culture', *Times of India*, 13 April 1997, p 3.

16 Abu-Lugodh, cited in EP Moore, 'Law's patriarchy in India', in M Lazarus-Black & SF Hirsch (eds), *Contested States: Law, Hegemony and Resistance*, New York: Routledge, 1994, p 92.

17 BS Cohn, 'Anthropological notes on disputes and law in India', *American Anthropologist* (special issue on 'Ethnography of Law', ed Laura Nader), 67 (6, Part 2), p 106, noted that, while the intersection of 'lawyer's law' and 'local law-ways' may shape the outcomes of cases heard in courts, equally forms of state law are mimicked while adjudicating disputes in non-state fora. MN Srinivas, 'A caste dispute among washerman of Mysore', *Eastern Anthropologist*, 7, 1954, pp 149–168 for example, describes how in a caste *panchayat* the plaint and rebuttal were written, written evidence was relied upon and the English word 'damages' appeared in the vernacular.

18 SM Rai, F Bari, N Mahtab & B Mohanty, 'South Asia: gender quotas and the politics of empowerment: a comparative study', in D Dahlerup (ed), New York: Routledge, 2006.

19 Chakravarti, 'Rhetoric and substance of empowerment'.

20 RS Moog, 'Conflict and compromise: the politics of Lok Adalats in Varanasi District', *Law and Society Review*, 25 (3), p 550.

21 *Lineage* or patrilineal descent from the same ancestor, which prohibits inter-*gotra* marriage.

22 B Karat, 'Price of honour: caste panchayats as instruments of terror', *Times of India*, Editorial, 14 April 2004, at http://timesofindia.indiatimes.com/articleshow/614604.cms.

23 TK Rajalakshmi, 'Caste injustice', *Frontline*, 22 (1), 23 April–6 May 2005, at http//:www.hinduonnet.com/fline/fl2209/stories/200506001005000.htm.

24 *The Hindu*, 20 October 2004.

25 Indeed, the Indian representative at the UN Social, Humanitarian and Cultural Committee and a BJP member of the Rajya Sabha, SS Ahluwalia, protested vigorously when Kofi Anan included India among the countries where violation of human rights was taking place under the garb of protection of cultural norms.

26 Chakravarti, 'From fathers to husbands'.

27 P Chowdhry, 'Enforcing cultural codes: gender and violence in northern India', in John & Nair, *A Question of Silence?*, p 337.

28 See SE Merry, 'Courts as performances: domestic violence hearings in a Hawai'i family court', in Lazarus-Black & Hirsch, *Contested States*, pp 35–58.

29 The definition of who is a minor or major in the eyes of the law has become quite complex. An adult has been defined in section 1 of the Offence of Zina (Enforcement of Hudood) ordinance 1979 as 'a person who has attained, being a male, the age of eighteen years or being a female, the age of sixteen years, *or has attained puberty*' (emphasis added). This definition has an adverse impact on women, because a girl as young as 12 or 13 (or even younger) who has reached puberty may be considered an adult and punished under the zina laws or the accused may use the consent of such an 'adult' as grounds for seeking acquittal. *Bashir v The State*, Pakistan Legal Decisions, 1986 FSC 196 is a case in point.

30 Asifa Quraishi argues that under the Hudood Ordinance the language that frames *Zina-bil-jabr* does not draw on debates within Islamic law about *Zina* under duress either as '*Hiraba*' (forcible assault upon the people, involving some sort of taking of property) or civil redress for a rape survivor in its law of '*jirah*' (wounds). Rather the definition of the offence of rape (*Zina-bil-jabr*) retains the language of colonial law that was in effect after the independence of Pakistan in the pre-Hudood period. A Quraishi, 'Her honor: an Islamic critique of the rape laws of Pakistan from a woman-sensitive perspective', *Michigan Journal of International Law*, 18, 1997, p 287.

31 For a critique, see S Beulah, 'The state and the minorities in Pakistan . . . but some are more equal than others', in Hussain *et al*, *Engendering the Nation-State*, pp 260–266.

32 A Muslim woman cannot contract marriage with a non-muslim by law in Pakistan. See MA Mannan (ed), *DF Mulla's Principles of Muhammadan Law*, Lahore: Pakistan Legal Decisions Publishers, 1995. The principles of Islamic family law thus supersede the equality provisions of the Constitution of Pakistan.

33 The law has now been amended in so far as the procedure for a FIR and arrest is concerned. Where a complaint is registered under the Zina Ordinance, a senior police officer has to make an inquiry to determine whether there exist, *prima facie*, any grounds for filing the case and, if so, to proceed further. Since this amendment is only very recent, it is too early to evaluate its impact.

34 In 2003 over 7000 women and children were in prison in the 75 jails throughout Pakistan, of which most were charged with the offence of *zina*. In 1982 there were a total of 70 female convicts in Pakistani prisons. *Report of the National Commission on the Status of Women*, Pakistan, 2003.

35 Indian laws do not prevent inter-caste or inter-community marriages of choice between men and women under the following laws. 'Under Section 3 of the Indian Majority Act, 1975...[t]here is no prohibition of inter-caste or inter-community marriage in the law. If a person who is a major wants to get married to a person of another caste or community the parents cannot legally stop him/her. That being so, the Administration must ensure that nobody harasses or ill-treats or kills such people for marrying outside his or her caste, community or class'. *Sujit Kumar and others v State of UP and others*, 2002 (45) ACC 79 at 81.

36 See P Chowdhry, 'Private lives, state intervention: cases of runaway marriage in rural North India', *Modern Asian Studies*, 38 (1), 2004, pp 55–84; and Chakravarti, 'From fathers to husbands'.

37 If the girl is below 16 years she cannot consent to sex and, if she is below 18, she is considered a minor.

38 P Baxi, 'The social and juridical framework of rape in India: case studies in Gujarat', unpublished PhD thesis, Department of Sociology, Delhi School of Economics, University of Delhi, 2005.

39 Chakravarti, 'From fathers to husbands'.

40 Mathura, the young tribal woman who was raped by policemen, was detained in the police station following a complaint by her brother for having eloped with her lover in *Tukaram and Anr v State of Maharashtra*, 1979 AIR 185 SC. See also *Premchand v State of Haryana*, AIR, 1989, p 937.

41 Nasser Hussain argues that the colonial history of the writ of *habeas corpus* must be seen as 'a history of increasing and ultimately complete legal institutionalization', which details 'the disparate ways in which law posits legal subjects, and extends and consolidates state power'. Citing a case published in 1814, Hussain observes that 'the court was even willing to use the writ to intervene in family disputes'. N Hussain, *The Jurisprudence of Emergency: Colonialism and the Rule of Law*, Ann Arbor, MI: University of Michigan Press, 2003, pp 69–70, 85.

42 V Dhagamwar, *Law, Power and Justice: The Protection of Personal Rights in the Indian Penal Code*, Delhi: Sage Publications, 1992.

43 Hussain, *The Jurisprudence of Emergency*, p 85.

44 Indian judgements labour the point that courts act to allow the expression of women's autonomous desires freed from patriarchal constraints. This is performed by giving a woman time to 'cool down', either in the court or the shelter, in conversation with herself, her natal family or a 'lady advocate', during which she composes herself or is persuaded, emboldened, reassured and/or freed of familial pressures.

45 Chakravarti, 'From fathers to husbands'. See *Oroos Fatima alias Nisha and another v Senior Superintendent of Police, Aligarh and another*, Criminal Law Journal, 1, 1993.

46 S Warraich, '"Honour killings" and the law in Pakistan', in Welchman & Hossain, 'Honour', pp 78–110.

47 Pakistan Legal Decisions, 2002 Lah 444.

48 *Ibid*, pp 447–448.

49 Zafran Bibi was convicted of *zina* and sentenced to stoning to death. Her husband had been imprisoned for nine years in a murder case, hence the pregnancy was considered a 'confession' of adultery. She alleged rape but, because of contradictions in her statement, the accused was acquitted while she was found guilty. On appeal the Federal Shariat Court set aside the conviction.

50 Pakistan Legal Decisions, 2002 Federal Shariat Court 1 at p 12 bc.

51 Also see *Zarina Bibi v The State*, Pakistan Criminal Law Journal, 1997, p 313 Federal Shariat Court.

52 Pakistan Legal Decisions, 1999 Lah 494.

53 The Edhi Trust is a national welfare organisation established by Abdus Sattar Edhi in Karachi. It is now the largest welfare organisation in Pakistan, with over 300 centres across the country, providing medical aid, family planning and emergency assistance.

54 However, the illegality of the police is evoked alongside Article 35 of the Constitution, which reinscribes the woman in love within the parameters of reproduction and marriage.

55 Chakravarti, 'From fathers to husbands'.

56 Letter written to the Union Minister for External Affairs (Government of India, New Delhi) on 16 October 2002 on behalf of AIDWA by Brinda Karat.

57 S Fish, *Is There a Text in This Class? The Authority of Interpretive Communities*, Cambridge, MA: Harvard University Press, 1980.

58 *Sujit Kumar and others v State of UP and others*, 2002 (45) ACC 79 at 81.

59 *Ibid*, at 80.

60 *Ibid*.

61 B de Sousa Santos, *Towards a New Common Sense: Law, Science and Politics in the Paradigmatic Transition*, New York: Routledge, 1995.

62 Hussain, *The Jurisprudence of Emergency*, pp 71–72.

Hindu Women's Property Rights in India: a critical appraisal

The framework of rights is important for women's equality and empowerment. However, rights can mean different things in different contexts at
different times. Rights may be understood to reflect agreed political claims or
they may be understood as emanating from and grounded within law. For
most purposes, the framework of law is important to ground rights claims, to
provide an effective structure which further legitimises such claims and to
promote their implementation. The basis of rights as legitimate claims has
important consequences for their ability to bring about change. This paper
addresses the need to critically define the bases and contours of 'rights' as
legal entities. It argues that the idea underlying a particular claim, its
legitimacy and therefore effectiveness within a legal framework must be
critically evaluated. The legitimacy of claims presumptively conferred within
a legal framework must be interrogated in the light of legal, historical,
political and cultural contexts. Such a contextual and critical analysis is
crucial for effective protection of rights claims through law. This requires us
to situate our analysis within the particular historical and political
development of the legal/constitutional framework, particularly in the
context of the postcolonial state. From a feminist perspective this is

particularly critical in laying out and demarcating engagements with the state.

The role of the state, and through it the law, has been significant in feminist struggles in postcolonial contexts, as the state is alternately the propeller of change or the focus of change itself. In the process of staking out women's claims at local, national and international levels legal change has been a primary arena for pressure and negotiation. Within this, the development of wider 'gender-equal' constitutional frameworks and a growing focus on 'women's rights' issues have been pre-eminent. These struggles have often required not only the identification and recognition of issues as discriminatory and unequal to women, but also the challenge of transforming these into 'rights' against which state action or inaction can be monitored.

Taking the case of Hindu women's property rights in India, this chapter analyses legal developments in the Indian context to highlight the short-comings of the right to property, even though this is protected by law. Hindu women have enjoyed independent property rights since 1956, with the passage of the Hindu Succession Act, which granted equal shares to females and males in respect of parental property.[1] Nevertheless, it is widely acknowledged in India that legal rights guaranteed to Hindu women have by and large not been exercised by them.[2] As I explore in this chapter, the conceptualisation of rights to property for women in India is problematic, as both the constitutional and legal frameworks which aim to confer the right to property upon women are framed by religion.

This chapter develops the legal analysis from a contextual and legal pluralist perspective. Arguing that it is necessary to locate particular rights claims in law within wider historical and political processes, it also grounds the critical evaluation of such claims within law from the perspective of women's lived realities. It emphasises the need to move beyond positive law and the enunciation of rights within it, and to take account of women's particular locations and the constitutive realities of their lives. The perspective of legal pluralism enables this, and thus becomes essential to any critical consideration of legal norms and processes.

To the extent that legal rights for women are aimed at generating equality-based distribution strategies and can be powerful structures for supporting these aims, they require critical evaluation in any strategy for change using law. It has become evident in addressing the gendered effects of access that economic relations are embedded in social, political and cultural relations.[3] The issue of women's right to property therefore needs to be located within wider debates regarding gender and access to resources. Within various strategies to address women's place within economic development the issue of increasing women's access to resources has been a significant part of efforts at mainstreaming gender within development policies.[4] To this end, legal strategies have indeed a role to play in removing entrenched inequalities in society which exclude or preclude women's equal access to resources. In this sense, creating non-discriminatory frameworks is the starting point for redressing discrimination on the basis of gender. However, to the extent that the issue of equality needs to be taken beyond generating neutral structures and towards creating structures for the empowerment of women to achieve equality in fact rather than only in principle, we need to continuously query the commitment of the state, its institutions, laws and personnel.

This chapter uses the example of Hindu women's property rights in India to query and critique the supposed commitment of the state to women's equal access to property through enabling legal provisions. In recognising that access to property is often pertinent for the very survival of women, particularly in the contexts of extreme social, economic and political marginalisation, the protection offered by law is held up to scrutiny in the light of such a context of marginalisation and exclusion. The legal provisions relating to women's right to property are analysed in their historical and political context before evaluating the nature of rights claims in the context of plural normative systems which may be binding upon individuals. The article then moves on to consider possibilities for change in the given context, where women's lives are determined by religion, poverty and marginalisation.

Law, rights and political processes

In India women's right to property is framed within separate regimes of religious law. In the case of Hindus, it is constructed as women's claims to land as a 'right', addressed to a 'Hindu woman' located within the 'family' and framed by religious ideology. The construction of women's claims within the family or the private domain is embedded in the liberal framework of law to which considerations of 'Hindu' ideology and identity are added.[5] The incorporation of 'Hindu' structures in the law is founded upon the particular historical processes through which the latter evolved, particularly its engagement with 'tradition' and 'modernity'. The consequent retention of religion and 'Hindu' as a fundamental principle completes the construction of women's claims to land within the law as a private/personal issue.

The constitutional framework

The Indian Constitution, and the legal framework it supports, provides a starting point for analyses of law and state in contemporary, postcolonial India. It is a normative document, explicit in its vision of the society it seeks to foster and embodying the avowed values, aims and objectives of the state after independence. It is also a highly detailed document, one that outlines the means and processes to be adopted in establishing such a society.[6] However, the liberal framework adopted in the constitution sits uncomfortably with simultaneous state-led initiatives to redress the structural and historical inequality of various groups, among them women. These tensions are most clearly borne out in relation to state action, through laws and institutions, in respect of the historically disadvantaged groups whom they are meant to address.[7]

Although the constitution sets out to integrate women into a full, democratic citizenship, through specific provisions to achieve their equality and empowerment,[8] it nevertheless remains limited by its liberal ousting of 'private' spheres from its purview. This is clear in state reluctance to remove religion as the principle for personal (family) law.[9] It may also be seen in the reluctance to put into effect a Uniform Civil Code,[10] although it is a Directive Principle of State Policy, and one which the state had undertaken a specific commitment to pass. Further, the legal reform of Hindu family law shows a clear ambivalence in the state towards a complete overhaul; instead, it retained much of traditional Hindu law relating to the family, while attempting to introduce change on an issue of fundamental significance within traditional Hindu law.[11]

The liberal tradition also bears upon the significant problem of securing substantive rights as opposed to formal rights. In positing a universal, abstract, individual subject, liberalism ignores the realities of the individual and all her attendant characteristics. Gender, class, status, power, age, religion or caste in the context of India are obscured or ignored. A reform agenda that seeks to address gender inequalities through the creation of rights is problematic where women are simply 'brought within' legal provisions without sufficiently taking account of their realities in terms of religion, caste or class.[12] As Pathak and Rajan remark on the state's treatment of the subject in the controversial Shah Bano Case:[13]

> Certainly, the Constitution of India, following Western constitutional models, did envisage [this] unity of the Indian subject within the legal system ... In the ideal, subjects in law are undifferentiated, non-descript, equal and singular.[14]

'Modernity' in Indian law and its engagement with the past

The retention of religion within the liberal and democratic constitutional framework of the post-independent Indian state is tied to the particular historical processes involved in and leading up to that state's formation. Whereas the project of modernity imbues the objectives of the state on the one hand,[15] on the other hand, its evolution as such is founded upon the predominance of its opposite—'tradition'—and the shared primary principle of religion.

The opposition of the 'modern' to the 'traditional' was at the heart of various debates preceding independence. The social reform debates, the impact of European scholarship on India and British administrative policy together gave impetus to the 'modernisation' of India, while the orthodox opposition simultaneously argued for the protection of an idealised 'Indian tradition'. These opposing movements were, however, organised around one shared principle, that of religious sanction. While reformists sought to argue that the 'modern' was indeed in keeping with the true spirit of the Hindu religion and therefore sanctioned by it, the orthodoxy used their interpretation of religion to argue that it did not sanction the changes sought.

British administrative policy and official discourse legitimised religion as the core principle, and the implementation of law and its reform proved to be a predominant arena for these debates. As such, law came to embody the outcomes of debates on specific issues.[16] Lata Mani provides a vivid account of this process in the context of suttee, where time and again court pundits were asked the question 'whether the practice was sanctioned by religious texts'.[17] The same praxis is reflected in the regulation of courtesans,[18] in widow remarriage and age of consent.[19]

In the interplay of reformist agendas and the privileging of religion within colonial discourse women became pre-eminent, but problematic, signifiers as the embodiment of 'tradition'.[20] The existing legal framework reflects the postcolonial state's continued engagement with the debates of the past. While independence brought the adoption of a new constitution, a vast body of law, judicial and administrative, continued as before with minor changes. The constitution explicitly provides for the continuance of laws passed before its inception, subject to certain conditions,[21] and continues to privilege religion and the concept of 'tradition'. The very constitution of 'Hindu law' in legislation and its implementation by the judiciary have significant implications upon the constructions and definitions of 'Hindu' women's rights and entitlements. To the extent that law continues to be structured upon the same principles as before independence, attempts to 'modernise' their status through legislative reform in the postcolonial state lose their transcendental and transformative potential.[22]

Women's rights through the lens of legal pluralism

The preceding section highlights the structural constraints of the existing legal framework within which positive rights are constituted. In the case at hand the creation of the legal 'right' to property for women in India focuses on their religious identity and locates their claim within the family. This section emphasises the need to move beyond positive law and the enunciation of rights within it, and to take account of women's particular locations and the constitutive realities of their lives. The perspective of legal pluralism enables this, and thus becomes essential to any critical consideration of legal norms and processes. Legal pluralism is the broad perspective within which 'law' is understood as being multi-locational, with various centres of power beyond the state to include the family and other social structures. As such, the rules which bind individuals are not only codified law, but customary practices, religious rules and other social norms.

Legal pluralism furthers the analysis of rights within law by accounting for the normative role of religion in women's lives. As Petersen has argued:

> Including sub-state levels of normative systems and structures as a subject of study is both relevant and crucial if the aim is to increase knowledge of the actual legal situation of women in most countries. Such knowledge is necessary to put forward appropriate, relevant and realistic demands for changes in order to bring about actual improvements in the lives of women.[23]

In the context of our discussion a legal pluralist approach pushes us beyond assumptions to a critical examination of the normative effect of 'Hindu' law. It enables us to explore the extent to which 'Hindu' law 'exist[s] as social fact because it receives social observance'.

The recognition that there are regulatory or normative systems other than formal law that affect and control people's lives is central to a legal pluralist approach. The operation of legal rules and the sources of law and legal doctrine must be critically examined to understand the interrelationship between law and women's lives. This means that:

> In addition to conventional legal sources such as case law, statutes, subsidiary legislation, legal theories in textbooks and articles, the practices in fora where the arrangements which directly affect the position of women are made, are also examined. Examples of such fora are the family, the workplace, the church community, the local courts and administrative agencies.[24]

This perspective obtains a wider scope for the consideration of law than from a positivist position, for law is seen as a rule-generating and rule-upholding process that takes place in various locales. A recognition of the plural and non-hierarchical structure of norms that affect women's lives leads to:

> [an] understanding of legal norms—or legal sources—as being engendered by different, overlapping, coexisting, co-operating and/or competing structures... a more profound examination and evaluation of both diverse types of norms and of the different values underlying such different normative systems.[25]

On rural women's rights to land in India, therefore, our analysis must include the consideration of all three: statutory rules, the operation of Hindu religious norms, and the evaluation of norms drawn from women's socio-cultural realities. In their relation to land ownership women are governed by a combination of legal, social and cultural norms, values and institutions. To study the role and impact or effectiveness of one of these, namely statutory norms, is to overlook the essential inter-linkages and impacts of others. It also follows that, in order to embark upon a process of increasing gendered access to resources through law, a more comprehensive understanding of the ways in which the law may or may not facilitate this is essential. This prevents the exclusive emphasis on statutory law and avoids erroneous assumptions of its overriding power, allowing for more informed methods to be adopted. Such methods would take into account the precise interdependence and interconnectedness of cultural values, religious norms, gender ideology and social organisation in order to evaluate the maximum effectiveness of the statutory norm.

Legal pluralism addresses the critique of liberalism by providing the basis for law to shift its focus from the public world to those arenas which are significant in their regulation of individuals. The question of property rights, in particular, is subject to many normative frameworks. For example, the issue of inheritance and succession rights for Hindu women derives directly from the Hindu notion of 'family', as the property in question does not disturb distinctions made in Hindu law between ancestral and personal property. The effect of this is to strengthen and continue the operation of the family and its specific forms in regulating property entitlements. Thus the gender ideology operating here is directly derived from norms and notions related to the 'family'. For a vast majority of women in the world the family/ household is where they carry out their daily activities and by extension where they are most regulated. Women may in different places be subject to different regulatory norms at different times within the family. What is essential is that these must be recognised, analysed and addressed. A legal pluralist perspective is vital to develop a broader conceptualisation of gendered perspectives within law in a variety of contexts.

The starting point for such a perspective is with women's daily experiences as a basis for generating the 'problem' requiring exploration. While Smith is concerned mainly with sociology when she says that this 'provides the starting point for a more adequate sociology',[26] the principle remains true for legal analysis. Understanding women's relationship, if any, to inheritance rights and to ownership through inheritance needs to begin with women's own life experiences within the context of inheritance and in relation to land.

What therefore is the identity of the women in the Hindu small peasant household within their familial and social context? To what extent can such identity accommodate or predicate a particular relationship to land ownership? In what ways does it operate to define and maintain notions of legitimacy of women's right to ownership? In what manner do notions of 'legal' legitimacy rest upon socio-cultural constructs? These questions need to be further examined in developing rights-based approaches to gender equality in land rights.

Gender and access to resources

Feminist perspectives on development have broadened understanding of rights, of legitimacy of claims and of the ways in which access to resources are determined by gender. Gender determines to a significant extent and manner which resources become available, as well as the means by which such access may be defined or legitimised. Gender relations refers to the relations of power between women and men, which are revealed in a range of practices, ideas and representations, including the division of labour, roles and resources between women and men, and the ascribing to them of different abilities, attitudes, desires, personality traits, behavioural patterns, and so on.[27] Taken as largely socially constructed rather than biologically determined, gender relations are both constituted by and help constitute these practices and ideologies in interaction with other structures of social hierarchy such as caste, class and race.

Whereas the notions of 'needs' and 'rights' are primarily accepted as the basis of resource allocation and distribution, the very definition of these notions is argued to be tied to the issue of gender.[28] Gender identities, as they constitute and are constituted by gender relations, determine how the rights and needs of particular individuals are established. This often involves a process of contestation over how a need becomes established as a right, where not only the satisfaction of needs is contested, but also its definition and interpretation. In relation to women and land the contestation is at three levels: to establish the need for women's right to land, to define the parameters of that need, and to translate that need into actual rights in practice.[29] Therefore, in order to understand women's access to land as a resource, it is essential to conceptualise it within the framework of the social relations that determine gender relations and which in turn affect property relations.

Agarwal echoes this in arguing for the recognition of the dialectical link between the material context and the gender ideology in conceptualising gender and access to property. She argues that establishing gendered access to resources requires contestation over matters which are simultaneously material and ideological, acting with and reinforcing one another, where gender ideologies can obstruct women from obtaining property rights.[30] Ideas about gender underlie practices such as female seclusion, which erode women's personal autonomy through the control of women's mobility and sexual freedom.[31] These ideologies and associated practices restrict women's ability both to exercise their existing property claims and to successfully challenge persisting gender inequalities in law, public policy and practice in relation to their claims.[32]

The link between gender relations, as an aspect of social relations, and property brings into focus the need to locate explorations of gendered access to property within the cultural and social systems within which they operate, for 'property is not primarily a relation between people and things, but a relation between people and people—a social relation or a set of social relations'.[33]

Thus it is important to study kinship relations within which property, marriage and labour are embedded, and which control women's control over property, as they reveal very real differences along gender divisions.[34] Since concepts of property are ultimately bound up with concepts of the person, we need to look at how kinship systems help to construct men and women in different ways, as different sorts of persons. Arguing that it is the kinship family system which constructs women in such a way that they are less able to act as fully operative subjects, Whitehead notes:

> A woman's capacity to 'own' things depends on the extent to which she is legally and actually separable from other people, the issue raised is the extent to which forms of conjugal familial and kinship allow her an individual existence so that she can assert rights as an individual against individuals.

The issue raised is the extent to which forms of conjugal, familial and kinship relations allow a woman an independent existence so that she can assert her rights as an individual. Conjugal, familial and kinship systems appear often to operate so as to construct the position of women as subordinate, such that by carrying kinship (or familial or conjugal) status women are less free to act as full subjects in relation to things and people.

This brings out the need to extend the analysis of the law to relations and organisations, and to locate it beyond the public spheres and in the household. The role of kinship, family and household structures as they operate towards constructing women's identity must be addressed. Further, the way in which particular gendered relations of production and distribution within these structures establish norms for legitimacy must be analysed. This will provide the basis for an understanding of how these identities are linked to access to property within the legal framework.

Possibilities for change

The realities of most women's lives in Indian society militate against their willingness to substantiate their claim to parental property through succession. This remains true notwithstanding recent changes to the Hindu Succession Act. Women's identification with their roles as mothers, daughters and sisters, informed by the Hindu religious ideology to which they subscribe, weakens the social legitimacy of such a claim to a significant extent. In most cases women's roles as mothers, sisters and daughters are predicated upon the identification of their interest with their (husband's) family on the one hand, and separation from the natal family on the other. The consequence of this is the preclusion of their individual self-interest, reinforced by the acknowledged non-membership of a Hindu female within her natal family. Further, while there is a separation of women's interest from their natal family, the very separation is predicated upon females' exclusion from independent property ownership and does not lead to an expression of their separate interest in terms of independent property ownership of their share through succession.

Legal provisions for women's equal right to parental property are premised on the existence of the following cultural and social realities of Hindu women in India. First, the identification of a woman's personhood independent of her relations to others in the family. Second, the continuing identity of a woman as a member of her parents' family even after marriage, and in which she can therefore have a legitimate expectation. Third, the willingness of women, as sisters, to jeopardise their relations with brothers and the security they may expect thereby, by competing with brothers for the same interest in land.

With respect to property belonging to the husband, however, even Hindu women identify their interest with that of their (husband's) family. In fact, such interest is often understood and expressed as totally subsumed within that of the family. However, women's interests are conceived as legitimate only in terms of the community of the marital family and the community of interest precludes a legitimate interest for *individual* interests. However, women's awareness of the tenuous nature of their position within the husband's family also forms the basis for the emergence of an alternative understanding, that their independent interests and substantiation of these through property ownership *should* be accorded legitimacy. Thus it is argued that women should be entitled to a share in their husbands' property not only as widows upon the husband's death but during the entire period while the marriage subsists. Although the existing legal and religious normative frameworks do not accord such a right, it is nevertheless possible to *argue* for the legitimacy of such a claim. Indeed, there is a growing recognition of the need for a regime of marital property in India.[35]

It is necessary to recognise the difficulties of law adhering to religious principles while at the same time attempting to reform certain aspects of them, without establishing a basis that is meaningful to the people it addresses.[36] We need to explore other norms and values which simultaneously form part of people's decision making in their everyday lives, but which may not be based upon religious ideology.[37] For example, whereas the 'religious' aspect of parents' relationship to their daughter may be based upon their (religious) duty to secure her marriage, and separation from her subsequent to her marriage, perhaps the content of the 'duty' could be explored by examining the extent to which it could include the provision of basic endowments such as education and health. Or, whereas married women must, of necessity of their religious beliefs, take account of their honour and modesty and be constrained in independent action, we need to explore to what extent their action within a group of women could foster independent action without a violation of their beliefs.[38]

There is clearly legitimacy for women's claim to a share of their husbands' property not only as a widow, or upon separation while he is still alive, but also while the marriage subsists. Here we need to explore the means of establishing women's claim and entitlement to such property without necessitating a formal separation or institution of women's independent ownership. Property could be held jointly by both husband and wife, or singly by the husband alone, with the wife having a recognized charge over it (to the extent of her share) for the purposes of transfer through sale, credit or gift. Where the claim of the creditor, buyer or transferee has to be realised, her independent ownership/title could be effected for such purpose.

The same principle could also be extended to the daughter's share in parental property. This would make unnecessary the active assertion of her claim to her share by the daughter, and perhaps also mitigate the fear of endangering good relations with her family. Given that land is very rarely bought or sold in rural areas, the value of the land is greatest as a source of credit and, arguably, fulfils a significant need in the case of cultivators. In this situation creating a lien over the property, which need not be demarcated in title and ownership until a transfer is to be effected, leads to a greater potential for its use by women. Both daughters and wives could use their (residuary) right to a share in the property far more effectively than when required, as at present, to assert their claim in opposition to sanctioned beliefs and norms by which they live and to which they are subject.

A further arena for rethinking legal regimes and rights is that of females' property traditionally envisaged under Hindu Law. The concept of *stridhana* may have been limited in its traditional form, covering only certain kinds of objects under very specific situations. Nevertheless, it is worth addressing for at least two reasons. First, it is embedded in popular notions of right and legitimacy as females' property, as that which a Hindu female can legitimately claim as hers in the otherwise exclusionary regime of Hindu law. Second, the current practice and spread of dowry reveals prevalent notions of the practice as legitimate among most people, including women. This is based upon the equivalence commonly made between dowry and *stridhana*. Most importantly, however, *stridhana*, or its modern avatar of dowry, also operates *to exclude any further right* of a Hindu female to property, including parental property. We need to bring the concept of *stridhana* back within the fold of women's legitimate claims and rights and to widen that principle of legitimacy to include other forms of property. This requires a rethinking of dowry as a *legitimate* vehicle for transfer of property to the female by her parents and the development of appropriate structures in law.

Although a consideration of these measures may indeed lead us to a consideration of structures and operations outside the realm of formal law, perhaps it can also lead to an acceptance of the limits of law to affect people's lives. Yet the policy framework set out by law is a very powerful framework for inducing change and supporting change in other areas of state policy. The role of law in moving away from setting up religion as the basis of people's actions could lead to an emphasis on, even the encouragement of, addressing other fundamental values by which people live.

Conclusion

The role of law as a guarantor and generator of rights is important. However, where the aim of intervention is the achievement of justice for women and the equal actual enjoyment of their rights, the substance of law in the case of guaranteeing Hindu women the right to property falls substantially short of the aim. To the extent that law is a specialist and particular framework among others in society, such shortcomings may be seen by some to be marginal to the overall project of increasing women's access to property. On the other hand, the role of law as an instrument for change may also be exaggerated because of its power to confer legitimacy and thereby order social relations. For law to effectively enable and contribute to women's empowerment, it is important to be neither over-reliant on it, nor to be ignorant of its potential impact. Beyond this, it is important also to critically evaluate the ways and extent to which law is both constructed by and constructs existing social and gender relations. Only by doing this can we develop strategies for change at relevant points of coherence or disjuncture between rules of law and the overall normative context provided by society.

A critical evaluation of law in terms of its effectiveness may begin and end with an analysis of its internal structure, form and the content of its particular provisions. Taking the inherent logic of statute, decision or other legal instrument, its logical coherence and ultimate validity may be analysed. Loopholes/fallacies within it may be identified from and addressed to the logical structure set up by the law. Such an analysis undoubtedly furnishes us with a critical insight into the potential limitations of law in achieving its objective and exposes gaps in the law's actual form, so as to ultimately raise questions about its content. A formal evaluation of the Hindu Succession Act, for example, brings to light the inconsistencies within its provisions and the possible consequences of these upon its goal of protecting women's equal rights under succession. This in turn enables us to raise issues regarding its ultimate achievement and the fulfilment of its objective and purpose.

Understanding the impact of law calls for an analysis of the social context and reality within which the legal provisions are meant to be applied. By asking of legal provisions what their social implications, causes or effects are, we supplement formal analyses.[39] Contextualising Hindu law in its constitution through colonial engagement and analysing how it operates to reinforce the normative force of religious principles in women's lives helps strengthen arguments for achieving substantive as well as normative justice. Insofar as arguments for substantive equality focus upon the need for a Uniform Civil Code to disengage law from religion, a focus on the formal regime may again be misplaced. To the extent that such a code replaces religion with secular principles as the basis of law, how far would this be a realistic foundation of law? Insofar as rural women continue to be located within social, economic, political and cultural structures founded upon precepts derived from religion, can a presumption to the contrary by law be valid? Can law presume the non-existence of the normative force of religion and yet be reflective of and relevant to women's lives? To what extent can law ignore such realities and yet be effective?

The particular legal framework promoting women's right to land through inheritance and succession reveals the extent to which law in fact reflects ideological standpoints in two respects. First, an evaluation of the statute and judicial decisions on various aspects of Hindu Law establishes that law reaffirms constitutive aspects of Hindu women's roles and identities which exclude their claim to land.[40] Second, insofar as the right to Hindu women's ownership of property is a change introduced by the law, which in fact contravenes their role and position predicated upon their exclusion from property, there appears to be a co-existence of contradictory propositions established by law. In this, the right to ownership is effectively overcome by law's simultaneous reaffirmation of Hindu women's traditionally constituted roles.

Legal structures and embodied entitlements through 'rights' must be analysed from a combined perspective drawing upon legal, development and empowerment objectives. In this discussion of women's claim to land in India, the insights from these perspectives broaden the scope of law's purview so that legal analysis comes closer to encompassing the totality of factors that affect the subjects to whom it is addressed and sharpens our position on rights-based strategies for gender equality.

Notes

1 Imbalances remained in the 1956 act, which have recently been rectified through amendments in 2005. See R Patel, *Hindu Women's Property Rights in Eastern India: Law, Labour and Culture in (Inter)Action*, Aldershot: Ashgate, 2006, forthcoming.

2 See B Agarwal, *A Field of One's Own: Gender and Land Rights in South Asia*, Cambridge: Cambridge University Press, 1994; and U Sharma, 'Women, work and property in north-west India', in H Alavi & J Harris (ed), *Sociology of 'Developing Societies': South Asia*, London: Macmillan, 1989.

3 See D Elson, *Male Bias in the Development Process*, Manchester: Manchester University Press, 1991; and CON Moser, *Gender Planning and Development: Theory, Practice and Training*, London: Routledge, 1993.

4 See I Tinker (ed), *Persistent Inequalities: Women and World Development*, New York: Oxford University Press, 1990; S Wieringa, 'Women's interests and empowerment: gender planning

reconsidered', *Development and Change*, 25 (4), 1994, pp 829–848; N Visvanathan *et al* (eds), *The Women, Gender and Development Reader*, London: Zed Books, 1997; and N Kabeer, *Reversed Realities: Gender Hierarchies in Development Thought*, London: Verso, 1994.

5 R Patel 'Women's right to property under Hindu law: gendered entitlements and traditional obligations', *Indian Socio-Legal Journal* (Special Issue on Legal Pluralism in India), XXXI, 2005, pp 73–94.

6 Nussbaum's development of the capabilities approach in the context of the Indian Constitution acknowledges this normative model, incorporating values to be actively pursued by the state involving 'affirmative material and institutional support, not simply a failure to impede'. As she puts it, fundamental entitlements addressed to lower castes and women are 'not only not incompatible with constitutional guarantees, but are actually in their spirit'. See MC Nussbaum, 'Capabilities as fundamental entitlements: Sen and social justice', *Feminist Economics*, 9 (2–3), 2003, pp 33–59.

7 See M Galanter, *Competing Equalities: Law and the Backward Classes in India*, Berkeley, CA: University of California Press, 1984; and N Menon, 'The impossibility of "justice": female foeticide and feminist discourse on abortion', *Contributions to Indian Sociology*, 29 (1–2), 1995, pp 369–392.

8 Provisions within the Fundamental Rights Chapter and the Directive Principles of State Policy.

9 For an illuminating, thorough and contextual critique of the processes of law and politics in relation to Muslim women in India, see V Narain, *Gender and Community: Muslim Women's Rights in India*, Toronto: University of Toronto Press, 2001.

10 F Agnes, *Law and Gender Inequality*, New Delhi: Oxford University Press, 1999; A Parasher, *Women and Family Law Reform in India: Uniform Civil Code and Gender Equality*, New Delhi: Sage Publications, 1992; Parasher, 'Family law as a means of ensuring gender justice for Indian women', *Indian Journal of Gender Studies*, 4 (2), 1997, pp 199–229; I Jaising (ed), *Justice for Women: Personal Laws, Women's Rights and Law Reform*, Mapusa: The Other India Press, 1996; and RK Agarwala & A Ramanamma, 'Women and the family law', in L Sarkar & B Sivaramayya (eds), *Women and Law: Contemporary Problems*, New Delhi: Vikas Publishing House, 1994.

11 Patel, 'Women's right to property under Hindu law'.

12 Menon, 'The impossibility of "justice"'; R Kapur & R Cossman, *Subversive Sites: Feminist Engagements with Law in India*, New Delhi: Sage Publications, 1996.

13 *Mohammed Ahmed Khan v Shah Bano Khan*, All India Reporter, SC 945, 1985.

14 Z Pathak & S Rajan, 'Shah Bano', *Signs: Journal of Women in Culture and Society*, 14 (3), 1989, pp 558–582.

15 See, for example, the Report of the Hindu Law Committee 1947, on the need for legal reforms to reflect India's place in the international community of nations. Government of India, *Report of the Hindu Law Committee*, New Delhi: Government of India Press, 1947.

16 JDM Derrett, *Religion, Law and the State in India*, London: Faber and Faber, 1968. For a more formal historical account of the British administration in India, see DD Basu, *Commentary on the Constitution of India*, Bombay: Tripathy, 1983; and MP Jain, *Outlines of Indian Legal History*, Bombay: Tripathy, 1966.

17 L Mani, 'Contentious traditions: the debate on sati in colonial India', in K Sangari & S Vaid (eds), *Recasting Women: Essays in Indian Colonial History*, Delhi: Kali for Women, 1990, p 100.

18 See VT Oldenberg, 'Lifestyles as resistance: the case of the courtesans of Lucknow, India', *Feminist Studies*, 16 (2), 1990, pp 259–287; and J Nair 'From Devadasi reform to SITA: reforming sex work in Mysore state, 1892–1937', *Feminism and the Law: NLSIU Journal*, 1, 1993, pp 82–94.

19 See U Chakravarti, *Rewriting History: The Life and Times of Pandita Ramabai*, New Delhi: Kali for Women, 1998.

20 See A Chhachhi, 'Identity politics, secularism and women: a South Asian perspective', in Z Hasan (ed), *Forging Identities: Gender, Communities and the State in India*, New Delhi: Kali for Women, 1994, pp 74–95; P Chatterjee, *Nationalist Thought and the Colonial World: A Derivative Discourse*, London: Zed Books, 1993; and K Sangari & S Vaid (eds), *Recasting Women: Essays in Indian Colonial History*, Delhi: Kali for Women, 1990.

21 Article 13, Constitution of India, 1950.

22 See A Parasher, 'Family law as a means of ensuring gender justice for Indian women', *Indian Journal of Gender Studies*, 4 (2), 1997, pp 199–229.

23 H Petersen, 'Legal pluralism and its relevance for women's law', in R Mehdi & F Shaheed (eds), *Women's Law in Legal Education and Practice in Pakistan*, Copenhagen: New Social Science Monographs, 1997, p 152.

24 W Bentzon *et al*, *Pursuing Grounded Theory in Law: South–North Experiences in Developing Women's Law*, Oslo: Tano Aschehoug, 1998, pp 66–67.

25 Petersen, 'Legal pluralism and its relevance for women's law', p 154.

26 DE Smith, *India as a Secular State*, London: Oxford University Press, p 84.

27 See HL Moore, *A Passion for Difference: Essays in Anthropology and Gender*, Cambridge: Polity Press, 1995.

28 See N Fraser, *Unruly Practices: Power, Discourse and Gender in Contemporary Social Theory*, Cambridge: Polity Press, 1989.

29 See Agarwal, *A Field of One's Own.*

30 *Ibid.*

31 See N Gandhi & N Shah, *The Issues at Stake: Theory and Practice in the Contemporary Women's Movement in India*, New Delhi: Kali for Women, 1992; and A Bagwe, *Of Woman Caste: The Experience of Gender in Rural India*, London: Zed Books, 1995.

32 See T Dyson & M Moore, 'On kinship structure, female autonomy, and demographic behaviour in India', *Population and Development Review*, 9 (1), 1983, pp 35–60; and Agarwal, *A Field of One's Own.*

33 A Whitehead, 'Women and men: kinship and property: some general issues [1]', in R Hirschon (ed), *Women and Property—Women as Property*, London: Croom Helm/New York: St Martin's Press, 1984, p 176.

34 Sharma also gives an insightful analysis on the significance (or not) of dowry as a form of property that has traditionally been accorded to women in Indian society. As she puts it, 'dowry goes *with* the daughter *to* the son-in-law', thereby refuting the claim that dowry may be considered women's property. Sharma, 'Women, work and property in north-west India', p 163.

35 See F Agnes, *Law and Gender Inequality*, New Delhi: Oxford University Press, 1999.

36 See A Bilgrami, 'Secular liberalism and moral psychology of identity', *Economic and Political Weekly*, 4 October 1997, pp 2527–2540; and Smith, *India as a Secular State.*

37 See Gandhi & Shah, *The Issues at Stake*; and R Thapar, 'Secularism and society', *Economic and Political Weekly*, 24 August 1985, pp 1437–1438.

38 See B Agarwal, 'Gender and land rights revisited: exploring new prospects via the state, family and market', *Journal of Agrarian Change*, 3 (1–2), 2003, pp 184–224.

39 See JW Harris, *Legal Philosophies*, London: Butterworths, 1997.

40 See R Patel, *Hindu Women's Property Rights in Eastern India*; and S Basu, 'Cutting to size: property and gendered identity in the Indian higher courts', in RS Rajan (ed), *Signposts: Gender Issues in Post-Independence India*, New Delhi: Kali for Women Press, 1999, pp 248–291.

Accessing Economic and Social Rights under Neoliberalism: gender and rights in Chile

The International Covenant on Economic, Social and Cultural Rights (ICESCR) provides an important framework within which it is possible to consider rights-based approaches to development, particularly from a gender perspective. It has been argued that an emphasis on rights can be used as a vehicle for increasing the accountability of governments to their citizens,[1] and activism around the ICESCR can be used to pressure governments to fulfil the obligations laid out in the covenant. One hundred and fifty-one states have currently ratified the ICESCR and therefore have a duty under international law to do so.[2] The ICESCR, first ratified in 1966, clearly predates current rights-based approaches to development. Indeed, many international development agencies have deliberately distanced their rights-based work from the ICESCR because of its historical association with communism during the cold war era and the pivotal role it played in the struggle fought by many radical Third World states within the UN to establish a New International Economic Order (NIEO) that would result in a global redistribution of resources.[3] While the extent to which this was achieved through the Declaration on the Right to Development in 1986 is subject to debate, present day rights-based approaches advocated by development organisations can often be defined through their lack of reference to the Right to Development and the ICESCR. Nevertheless, the importance of the legal obligations of states that have ratified the ICESCR can not be underestimated and the covenant therefore does provide an essential starting point for looking at these issues.

In recent decades the ascendancy of neoliberalism has presented new challenges in relation to governments' ability to guarantee these rights to all citizens. Neoliberal reform programmes promoting market liberalisation, privatisation and deregulation have been implemented in a wide range of countries in both the North and the South, leading to massive restructuring of economies. Liberalisation of trade and deregulation of labour markets has opened economies to increased foreign investment and has resulted in an expansion of exports in many Southern countries. These developments have brought new prospects for certain sectors of societies—for example, new employment opportunities, especially for women, have arisen as a result of export expansion.[4] Indeed, in some instances this export expansion has been linked to poverty reduction.[5] Nevertheless, many of these new forms of employment are often subject to discrimination and exploitative working conditions and workers are in effect denied access to welfare and labour rights as outlined in the ICESCR. The gender division of labour means that women are more likely to be located in these precarious forms of employment than men.

At the same time there have been huge social and economic costs associated with neoliberalism, particularly for women.[6] Cuts in public expenditure and the privatisation of health, education and welfare services combined with women's increased participation in the paid economy have placed increased pressure on women's 'double burden' resulting in a 'squeeze on care'.[7] Moreover, as an increased number of countries in Latin America, including Chile, experience a shift from health systems based on social insurance, whereby risks are spread across the population, to systems based on individualised private health insurance, concerns have arisen about the ability of large sectors of the population to secure their right to health.

These processes of change raise important questions about the ability of governments to fulfil their obligations as laid out in the ICESCR. To what extent are these processes gendered? And what differential impacts might they have on the rights of women and men? If some citizens are experiencing a greater violation of their economic and social rights than others, what can the ICESCR offer to these marginalised groups? Moreover, in an era where international financial institutions such as the World Bank and the International Monetary Fund play a central role in establishing the agenda for social policy at a national level, how far can citizens really claim their rights if they remain excluded from policy debates? Drawing on the case of Chile, this chapter will seek to address these questions.

The first part of the chapter provides a broad overview of the ICESCR and outlines the processes of operationalising rights as set out in the covenant. It also briefly examines feminist critiques of the ICESCR. The second part of the chapter highlights some of the ways in which groups of women workers are being denied access to many of the rights within the ICESCR, particularly the right to health. Chile is an ideal case study, since it is often considered as the 'neoliberal success story' and provides a model for welfare provision across Latin America. Finally, drawing on the experiences of Chilean NGOs working in the health sector, the analysis will consider how citizens can use the ICESCR to claim their rights, given the limitations of participatory mechanisms in Chile.

The International Covenant on Economic, Social and Cultural Rights

The ICESCR states that men and women have equal right to the enjoyment of all the rights it sets out. These rights include:

- the right to work, including the opportunity to gain a living by work which is freely chosen (Article Six);
- the right to just and favourable conditions of work, including fair and equal remuneration, safe and healthy working conditions and reasonable limitation of working hours (Article Seven);
- the right to form and join trade unions (Article Eight);
- the right to social security (Article Nine);
- the right to an adequate standard of living, including adequate food, clothing and housing (Article Eleven);
- the right to the highest attainable standard of physical and mental health (Article Twelve).

Special mention is made of the family, which should be accorded 'the widest possible protection and assistance', while 'marriage must be entered into with the free consent of intending spouses' (Article Ten).[8]

This covenant is considered to impose three types of obligations on states that are party to it (termed 'states parties'):[9] the obligations to respect, protect and fulfil the rights enumerated in it. The obligations on states parties are qualified in Article Two (i) of the ICESCR. This says that 'Each State Party to the present Covenant undertakes to take steps, individually and through international assistance and co-operation, especially economic and technical, to the maximum of available resources, with a view to achieving progressively the full realisation of the rights recognised in the present Covenant'. Article Two (ii) sets out the principles of equality and non-discrimination in relation to the provision of covenant rights. The implication of the phrases 'to the maximum of available resources' and 'with a view to achieving progressively' is to allow a state to realise its obligations over a(n) (indefinite) period of time. Considerable debate surrounds the question of the nature of states parties' obligations and the broader question of justicability of economic and social rights.[10] The Committee on Economic, Social and Cultural Rights (CESCR) monitors state parties' compliance with the covenant. Decisions made by the CESCR are not legally binding and it lacks the authority to drive any political reform to ensure state parties' commitments to the ICESCR are upheld.

Feminist critiques of the ICESCR

It has been suggested that the ICESCR is of limited use to women given its inherent gender bias. Feminist critiques have focused on a number of limitations.[11] First, the covenant incorporates a limited conceptualisation of human rights as applying only to the public sphere of the market and the state.[12] Women are identified as primarily mothers and dependants of male providers, thus limiting their claims to socioeconomic rights; because male breadwinners are expected to provide for the basic needs of their dependants, women are less able to claim such rights on their own behalf. This has been termed the 'male breadwinner bias'.[13] This view is reflected in the language of the covenant, which, for example, refers to 'the right of everyone to an adequate standard of living for himself and his family' (Article 11). Similarly, critics have argued that many human rights principles are inherently biased against women, since they operate primarily in the public sphere and ignore what takes place in the private sphere, where many abuses of women's rights actually take place.[14]

Furthermore the ICESCR does not touch upon the economic, social and cultural contexts in which most women live, since the crucial economic and social power relationship for many women is not one directly with the state but with individual men, whose authority is supported by patriarchal state structures. It fails to recognise the needs of the many women who do not participate in the paid economy, or participate as unpaid family labour in family businesses and who are thus not covered by the rights conferred on workers who earn wages in the paid economy.[15] For example, although the right of women to paid maternity leave is recognised, this only applies to women who are already integrated into the paid economy as independent earners.

In response to some of these limitations the UN Division for the Advancement of Women (DAW) set up an Expert Group in 1997 in an attempt to consider how to advance women's social and economic rights. To date work is continuing as a number of feminist organisations around the world focus attention on the ICESCR as an arena for activism, both in terms of improving the convention as a normative framework, and in using the reporting mechanism to 'name and shame' governments.[16] Despite the limitations of the ICESCR it can still offer women's organisations important mobilising opportunities since, as Beetham argues, it 'offers internationally authorised discourse to the deprived to legitimate their own struggles for their realisation'.[17]

The challenge of guaranteeing rights

One of the key challenges presented by the ICESCR is that of operationalising the covenant and ensuring that the rights laid out in it are guaranteed to all citizens. Much debate surrounds the question of how states can do this in practice and what the obligations laid out in the covenant really mean. To this end the CESCR was established in 1985, though as stated earlier its role is limited. However, decisions made by the CESCR are not legally binding and it lacks the authority to drive any political reform to ensure state parties' commitments to the CESCR are upheld.

One important area of work of the CESCR is the issuing of General Comments. These provide an authoritative substantive interpretation of the covenant and its application to issues of concern. One such area is that of public services, particularly in the context of the cutting back of public expenditure in the current era of neoliberal reforms. In their proceedings the CESCR have clarified that the concept of 'progressive realisation' in the ICESCR does not permit the perpetuation of economic injustice and disparity. States are required to take steps continuously to improve people's enjoyment of economic, social and cultural rights.[18] Moreover, the principles set out in General Comment Three in theory prohibit a government reducing basic public services if this policy is assessed to be detrimental to the enjoyment of the rights in question. Some commentators are hopeful that they will thus provide states that are party to the treaty with some defence against the imposition of neoliberal economic reforms as conditions of loans from the IMF and World Bank.[19] There is currently an open-ended UN Working Group responsible for looking at the relationship between Structural Adjustment Programmes and Economic, Social and Cultural Rights.[20] However, there is no international court that can hold states (or international financial institutions) accountable for violations of economic, social and cultural rights.

The only international implementation mechanism is via the system of reporting to the CESCR. Those states which have ratified the covenant are expected to submit a report to the ICESCR within two years of ratifying it, and then provide a follow-up report every five years. States are expected to provide detailed information on the degree to which rights are implemented and areas where difficulties have occurred. Government representatives are expected to answer questions about the report to the ICESCR. 'Concluding observations' are issued by the committee regarding compliance with the covenant in the reporting state.[21] These are made public at the end of each session, but are not legally binding. National and international NGOs and community-based organisations (CBOs) are able to submit information to the committee on the extent to which a state has complied with the covenant (so-called 'shadow reports') and they can present their views directly to the committee. It is not, however, possible for individuals or groups who feel that their rights under the covenant have been violated to submit formal complaints to the CESCR.[22]

The case of Chile

Chile ratified the ICESCR in 1972 under the leadership of the Socialist President Salvador Allende. While all human rights were suspended under the military dictatorship of General Pinochet between 1973 and 1990, following the return to more democratic forms of government in 1990 attempts have been made to restore human rights. Indeed, the CESCR have congratulated Chile on the progress that has been made in restoring rights to citizens in their Concluding Observations on Chile's latest Report to the committee in 2004.[23] The committee do raise concerns about a lack of progress in other areas, particularly the lack of an adequate minimum wage, the low level of women working in the paid economy (the rate of female labour force participation is around 42% and is one of the lowest in Latin America), and the inherent gender bias in the reformed pension system.[24]

In addition, the committee raise concerns regarding the inherent gender bias in the private health insurance companies, discussed in more detail later, although no mention is made of the particular difficulties faced by informal workers, as we shall see. A shadow report was also presented to the committee by the Santiago-based feminist human rights NGO, La Morada Women's Development Corporation, in conjunction with human rights experts from the USA.[25] However, the main focus of the shadow report was the violation of women's sexual and reproductive health rights in relation to Article 12. These are clearly a grave cause for concern but will not be specifically discussed here.

Labour market deregulation and the growth of informal work

The ascendancy of neoliberalism across Latin America over the past few decades has presented important new challenges to governments' in guaranteeing social and economic rights to their citizens. While new employment opportunities have developed, thus facilitating citizens' right to work and increasing individual autonomy for many female workers, at the same time there are also new challenges when viewed from a rights perspective. As the discussion of the Chilean case study will show, workers are often subject to discrimination and exploitative working conditions, thus violating their rights to just and favourable working conditions as laid out in the ICESCR. The current gender division of labour in Chile also means that the majority of workers in these precarious forms of employment are women.

An integral part of neoliberal reforms has been a deregulation of labour markets in order to increase foreign investment, for example through lowering labour costs and introducing more flexible forms of working. This has been a prominent feature of reforms in much of Latin America, including Chile, where new labour codes have facilitated the replacement of indefinite contracts with fixed-term contracts, and have promoted the use of temporary, part-time, seasonal and hourly contracts in hiring and permitted restrictions on the right to strike, collective bargaining and the organisation of workers.[26]

As a consequence of such reforms there has been an unprecedented expansion of the informal economy in recent years.[27] An International Labour Organisation (ILO) study estimated that 84 out of every 100 jobs created in Latin America during the 1990s were in the informal economy.[28] In addition there has been a dramatic restructuring of production and distribution in many key industries, characterised by outsourcing or subcontracting through global commodity chains. The textile and clothing industries in Chile have undergone these kinds of transformations and, following processes of restructuring since the early 1980s, much of the actual make up of garments is subcontracted and in many cases garments are eventually made up by home-based workers employed on an informal basis. Although the connection between this growth of informal work and the large numbers of women entering paid employment is still subject to debate,[29] what is clear is that the majority of informal workers, and especially home-based workers, are women.[30] In Chile there are around 80 000 home-based workers, around 66 000 of whom are women, and over half of these women are aged between 25 and 44 years old.[31] Home-based work is work that is done in or around the home for a cash income, although within this broad definition different categories of home-based workers can be identified.[32]

The marketisation of health care

Within the context of the increased marketisation of health care the failure of governments to extend the right to fair and equal remuneration to all workers is an important concern, since access to health care is no longer equally distributed. Health sector reforms in Chile are continuing to move towards replacing the system of social insurance, where risks are shared across the population, to a system of individualised private insurance, where users buy a health plan and make additional co-payments for any extra services they require.

Chile has had a mixed insurance system since the mid-1980s. Workers can choose between the public (FONASA) and private (ISAPRES) sector to contract their mandatory 7% health insurance contributions.[33] Within FONASA entitlements depend upon earnings-related contributions and contributions finance the benefits provided. Around 60% of the population is in FONASA, while the majority of others are either in an ISAPRES or are covered by special social insurance funds, such as those for the armed forces and police.[34] A small percentage of the population is not covered by any health insurance plan.

Critics have warned that the marketisation of the health sector can have important implications for poverty and equality issues.[35] This is becoming manifest in Chile. One example is the problem of 'cream-skimming', which remains an issue within the ISAPRES, whereby those with lower risks are 'creamed' by the private sector, leaving those with higher risks in the public sector, which lacks the resources to adequately care for all those who need it.[36] Even within the ISAPRES the system is highly stratified and many middle-income users often lack sufficient coverage in their plans, especially for more complex health services.

Recent reforms in the health sector have focused on improving access to health care for the lowest income groups and in 2002 the Plan for Universal Care with Explicit Guarantees (AUGE) was introduced. This was intended to improve access to and quality of services for more complex health conditions and 56 conditions were included in the proposals. Health care for these selected conditions will be free to indigents and the lowest income groups, while the remainder of the population have to pay a proportion of the cost, although additional co-payments may be applicable. Since July 2005 treatment for 25 conditions has been guaranteed and the government hopes that treatment for the remaining conditions will be guaranteed by the end of 2007.[37]

While the Plan AUGE received positive support from the CESCR in their Concluding Observations, it has been criticised by health activists, particularly from a gender perspective.[38] In the shadow report submitted by La Morada and colleagues to the CESCR they argue that the 56 health problems included in the AUGE exclude many of the conditions that principally affect women, such as osteoporosis, breast and ovarian cancer and depression. In addition, while the AUGE will in theory improve access for those registered as indigents, the system of co-payments will continue to discriminate against lower income households and therefore women will be disproportionately affected.

Informal work and access to health insurance

Given the nature of informal work—ie that workers have no regular employment contract, wage agreement or regular working hours, and that their work is invisible to others, including policy makers and government agencies, the majority are excluded from non-wage benefits such as health insurance, pensions, paid sick leave and maternity leave.[39] Since women are more likely to be employed in this type of work, this suggests that these processes of exclusion are gendered and that women are less able to access these benefits than men.

The Chilean home-based workers NGO, CECAM, interviewed over 1500 workers, the majority of them female, and found that most of the respondents did not have any sort of health plan.[40] The variable nature of sub-contracted work and salaries makes it difficult for households to make regular contributions required by health insurance plans.[41] In some instances women were registered as a dependant of their husbands, although this points to the issue of 'male breadwinner bias'. However, in the majority of cases the women did not have male partners so had to register as indigents. Indigents are entitled to access basic services, but a number of important exclusions exist. For example, they are not entitled to income subsidies during pregnancy—three months before and two months after the birth of the baby—and they are also excluded from illness-related income subsidies, etc.[42] Many of the women interviewed felt that registering as an indigent lowered their self-esteem and that they were badly treated by health staff because of their low status. The women believed that the health workers saw them as 'lazy women' who stayed at home rather than earning a living. This was not the case but they could not admit to having a job since this would disqualify them from accessing the system.[43] As well as women being denied their rights, this links to broader issues of social exclusion and points to the ways in which many poor people can associate bad experiences of the health care system with their own poverty and powerlessness.[44]

In an extensive study of informal workers conducted by the Centro de Estudios de la Mujer, a feminist research institute based in Santiago, the findings demonstrated that the majority of part-time workers, particularly in the financial and commercial sectors, were women and that they failed to earn regular salaries.[45] Many of the women interviewed were employed to sell financial products and were asked to work fixed hours, but were paid on a commission basis according to the number of financial products they sold. They did not earn additional money for working overtime, but often needed to work beyond the contracted hours in order to meet targets set by the company and earn sufficient income to live off. Similarly, home-based workers in the clothing industry worked long hours that surpassed the normal working week of 48 hours in Chile. In periods of high demand the women often worked through the night and over the weekend in order to supply clothing. Nevertheless, since they were paid on a piece-work basis, they did not receive overtime payments for the additional hours.[46] These conditions clearly disregard the rights laid out in the ICESCR, most notably the right to just and favourable working conditions and fair remuneration. In addition, the majority of part-time workers interviewed lacked formal contracts, working instead according to verbal agreements, and so were not entitled to any form of social protection or health insurance, thus contravening the right to social security.

While special mention is made in the ICESCR of the family, which should be accorded 'the widest possible protection and assistance', it seems that in reality governments are unable to fulfil this obligation, and many households where workers are employed in the informal economy face increasing vulnerability and are unable to protect themselves against risks such as poor health. Studies have shown that in reality such households manage the cost of sickness by extending the threshold of seriousness at which they seek treatment.[47] This implies an absorption into the household of the care and management of such individuals. The prevailing gender division of labour means that it is generally women who absorb this cost.[48]

Gender bias in access to health care

Access to private health insurance in Chile is gendered in a number of ways. First, there is a large gender gap in wages—which in itself contravenes Article Seven of the ICESCR, the right to fair and equal remuneration. Chilean women in all socioeconomic groups earn up to 30% less than men.[49] Research indicates that the gender gap in wages is higher in the informal economy than in the formal economy.[50] The need to overcome this gender gap in wages has been highlighted by the CESCR in their Concluding Observations on Chile's 2004 report to the committee.[51] The CESCR also commented on the need to raise the minimum wage so that workers can achieve a better standard of living.[52]

Women's lower wages have been identified as a key constraint in limiting women's access to the private health insurance companies, the ISAPRES.[53] The cost of health plans is generally higher for women of all age groups than for men of the same age, but for women of reproductive age the cost of a health plan is around three times that for a man.[54] Not surprisingly, ISAPRES members are predominantly men aged between 25 and 49 and in 2001 only 32% of ISAPRES members were female.[55] Yet, as out-of-pocket and other health-related expenditure rises, the implications of this wage gap go beyond limiting women's access to the private sector.

In addition, gender bias in accessing credit means that women may be unable to take out financial loans to pay for health care and this can also affect decisions taken by the ISAPRES companies about whether to accept users who may pose a financial risk. In an extensive study of informal workers carried out by the Centro de Estudios de la Mujer (CEM) a feminist research institute based in Santiago, this emerged as an issue. As one part-time worker in the financial sector explained:

> We are discriminated against and . . . are looked down on. At a bank, if you go and ask for a loan they ask why you are only a sales person. There is an important social cost that you have to bear, there are problems with getting a loan and also problems with joining an ISAPRE. The worst is if you are a woman, and worse still if you are a pregnant woman, a pregnant financial salesperson is the most discriminated against. Banks also discriminate against us because of our variable income.[56]

These constraints clearly raise concerns about women's access to health care and to use the health providers of their choice. Ultimately these processes restrict women's potential to claim their right to enjoy the highest attainable standard of physical and mental health, as stated in the ICESCR. Indeed, the CESCR expressed concern about the inherent gender bias in the ISAPRES in their concluding observations on the Chile Report to the ICESCR, emphasising the need to surmount this.[57] It is also an issue that was highlighted in the shadow report to the ICESCR presented by La Morada.[58]

New occupational health risks

The right of workers to the highest attainable standard of physical and mental health is also challenged by many of the new forms of employment that have developed over the past few decades. While historically men have been more at risk from occupational health hazards, the changing nature of employment has created new and different risks for women. More importantly, since women are less likely than men to have a contract, they are unlikely to be eligible for sick pay and are not covered by Law 16.744, which legislates against work-related illness and accidents. This also means that any occupational health problems that do arise for this sector of the population are not recorded and this has important policy implications.[59]

In the CEM study of informal workers many of the women interviewed reported that long working hours were having negative impacts on their sleeping and eating habits, which clearly have important implications for both physical and mental health and well-being. Women workers, particularly in the commercial and financial sectors, were being asked to work for extensive periods of time to fit in with the demands of the service sector—for example shopping centres regularly open for 24-hour periods, particularly at weekends and over public holidays.[60] While many men are also expected to work long hours, given the relatively rigid gender division of labour in Chile they do not have the additional caring responsibilities that many women have.[61] This 'double burden' means that women often have little time to recuperate after working extended shifts or night shifts. Many of the women interviewed also reported repetitive strain injuries resulting from the nature of their work, such as data inputting, as, in order to earn a decent salary, they had to reach certain targets and were often unable to take breaks if they wanted to complete their work on time.[62]

The expansion of horticultural exports in Chile and other parts of the region has also introduced new health hazards and increased workloads.[63] The high use of pesticides can mean workers face a range of physical and mental health risks, including nausea, birth defects and acute depression.[64] Studies from Chile have shown that there is a high incidence of alcohol and drug consumption (prescription and non-prescription) among temporary fruit pickers (*temporeras*) and high rates of mental illness and higher rates of child malformation have been observed in the areas where fruit growing is concentrated.[65] If, as outlined earlier, depression and mental health problems are excluded from the AUGE, this is a particular cause for concern.

There are around 350 000 fruit workers in Chile, 85% of whom are temporary workers and, of these, 52% are female and only 5% of women have permanent jobs.[66] While around 18.6% of male fruit workers do not have a contract, this rises to 24% for women.[67] Moreover, around half of *temporera* households have no members with permanent stable employment and have per capita household incomes below the poverty line.[68]

Furthermore, there are important urban–rural disparities in the Chilean health system and many rural health services are relatively under-funded. One study has shown that municipalities allocating the highest per capita funds are not the ones with the greatest health needs, and out-patient and in-patient medical care shows considerable geographic variations.[69] Research has shown that rural health care resources are not always allocated in transparent and accountable fashion, whereas this is less likely to occur in urban areas. In addition, it can be problematic attracting and maintaining doctors and health professionals to work in rural health services, particularly those in more remote locations. These issues raise important concerns regarding the specific ability of health services to guarantee the rights of rural users.

Participation in the policy making processes

A final issue that requires consideration is how far and in what form women are able to participate in policy-making arenas. If states are to guarantee an enabling environment for women's enjoyment of their social and economic rights it is essential that all women are included in decision-making processes.

However, the recent shift towards globally applied templates for social policy designed by international financial institutions such as the World Bank often leaves little room for manoeuvre at a national level. Although much emphasis is now placed on citizen participation in the policy process, and governments do have some degree of flexibility in how they implement these global templates, it is not always clear how states are able to simultaneously uphold their obligations to guarantee the social and economic rights laid out in the ICESCR.

There are clear contradictions between the concept of citizen participation as it is presented in much neoliberal thinking and the notion of economic and social rights as conceptualised in the ICESCR. Under neoliberalism the concept of civil society, and by extension the concept of participation, has been transformed. It has taken on new meaning and importance, replacing political society as the key site of political struggle.[70] Political society actors such as trade unions and political parties are replaced by voluntary associations and non-governmental organisations, few of whom are democratically accountable or representative. Power differences and class struggles within civil society are no longer an issue and civil society has become a mere technical tool where citizens can be mobilised to deliver services. Notions of citizenship have been reconfigured as the values, norms and language of market rationality become embedded. This has clear implications for many social and economic rights as they are no longer the responsibility of the state but have become commodities available for purchase by individual citizens in the marketplace.[71] This raises important questions regarding the impact that women's organisations mobilising around rights issues can have.

Concerns around women's health issues were raised by NGOs in their shadow report to the CESCR and women health activists have campaigned around the issue of gender bias in the health sector reforms with mixed results. The top-down nature of the current participatory mechanisms has meant that citizens are unable to hold the state accountable and there has been a lack of transparency in decision making regarding the health sector reforms.[72] Nevertheless, important inroads have been achieved. Gender bias in the health sector has become an issue of public concern widely debated in the national media.

Moreover, the success of women's organisations in other countries and regions suggests that there is some cause for optimism. Groups are constantly identifying new entry points for mobilising around economic and social rights. For example, gender budget initiatives in a number of countries have been a critical tool for NGOs and women's activists to use in promoting women's economic and social rights. As Helena Hofbauer argues, drawing on the case of Mexico, 'budget analysis can help quantify the cost of the provision of specific rights and analyse the resource allocation accordingly'.[73]

If the ICESCR is to do more than offer women's organisations a framework for guaranteeing economic and social rights activism around the covenant it needs to be linked more broadly to the development of alterative economic and social policies such as gender budget initiatives. Citizens need to continue to try and make states more accountable. Mobilisation around the ICESCR offers another tool with which to justify such campaigns.

Notes

1 C Ferguson, cited in A Cornwall & C Nyamu-Musembi, 'Putting the "rights-based approach" to development into practice', *Third World Quarterly*, 25 (8), 2004, pp 1415–1437.
2 http://www.unhchr.ch/pdf/report.pdf, accessed January 2006.
3 Cornwall & Nyamu-Musembi, 'Putting the "right-based approach" to development into practice'.
4 G Standing, 'Global feminisation through flexible labour: a theme revisited', *World Development*, 27 (3), 1999, pp 583–602; and Division for the Advancement of Women (DAW), Department of Economic and Social Affairs, *World Survey on the Role of Women in Development: Globalization, Gender and Work*, New York: United Nations, 1999.
5 N McCulloch & M Ota, 'Export horticulture and poverty in Kenya', *IDS Working Paper*, 174, Brighton: Institute of Development Studies, 2002.
6 P Sparr (ed), *Mortgaging Women's Lives: Feminist Critiques of Structural Adjustment*, London: Zed Press, 1994.
7 UNDP, *Human Development Report*, New York: Oxford University Press, 1999.
8 H Steiner & P Alston, *International Human Rights in Context: Law, Politics, Morals*, Oxford: Clarendon Press, 1996.
9 'States parties' is the term used within human rights treaties to refer to governments who have signed up to the treaties.
10 D Beetham, 'What future for economic and social rights?', *Political Studies*, XLIII, 1995, pp 41–60.
11 D Elson & J Gideon, 'Organising for women's economic and social rights: how useful is the International Covenant on Economic, Social and Cultural Rights?', *Journal of Interdisciplinary Gender Studies*, 8 (1–2), 2004, pp 133–152.
12 B Nuehold, 'Women's economic rights as part of international declarations and conventions', *Women in Development Europe Bulletin*, February 1998, pp 4–11; and V Spike Peterson & L Parisi, 'Are women human? It's not an academic question', in T Evans (ed), *Human Rights Fifty Years On: A Reappraisal*, Manchester: Manchester University Press, 1998.
13 D Elson & N Cagatay, 'Social content of macroeconomic policies', *World Development*, 28 (7), 2000, pp 1347–1364.
14 H Charlesworth, 'What are "women's international human rights"?', in R Cook (ed), *Human Rights of Women: National and International Perspectives*, Philadelphia, PA: University of Pennsylvania Press, 1994.
15 M Williams, 'What are economic and social rights? Women's economic and social rights', *Women in Development Europe Bulletin*, February 1998, pp 12–18.
16 *Ibid*.
17 Beetham, 'What future for economic and social rights'.
18 Centre for Economic and Social Rights, *Economic, Social and Cultural Rights: A Guide to the Legal Framework*, Resources Series 1, New York: Centre for Economic and Social Rights, 2000.
19 AG Pillay, 'The International Covenant on Economic, Social and Cultural Rights', *ESR Review* (Socio-economic Rights Programme, University of the Western Cape), 3 (1), 2002, at http://www.communitylawcentre.org.za/ser/esr2002/2002july_covenant.php#covenant, accessed February 2006.
20 www.unhchr.ch/Huridocda, accessed January 2005.
21 A Chapman, 'A "violations approach" for monitoring the International Covenant on Economic, Social and Cultural Rights', *Human Rights Quarterly*, 18 (1), 1996, pp 23 66.
22 Elson & Gideon, 'Organising for women's economic and social rights'.
23 Comité de Derechos Económicos, Sociales y Culturales, E/C.12/1/Add.105, 1 December 2004, published in *Compilación de Observaciones Finales del Comité de Derechos Económicos, Sociales y Culturales sobre países de América Latina y el Caribe (1989–2004)*, Santiago: UNDP/OHCHR, 2004, at www.ohchr.org/english/bodies/cescr, accessed February 2006.
24 INE (2002) *Mujeres Chilenas: Tendencias en la última década, Censos 1992–2002*, Part 2, Instituto Nacional de Estadisticás, Santiago, at http://www.ine.cl/ine/canales/chile_estadistico/calidad_de_vida/mujeres/mujeres.php, accessed January 2006.
25 Shadow Report on the Third Periodic Report of Chile, Committee on Economic, Social and Cultural Rights, 18 November 2004, presented by La Morada, International Women's Human Rights Law Clinic and the Centre for Reproductive Rights, at http://www.crlp.org/pdf/sr_chile_1104.pdf, accessed February 2006.

26 J Martínez & A Díaz, *Chile, the Great Transformation*, Washington, DC: Brookings Institution and Geneva: UNRISD, 1996, pp 101–129; and UNIFEM, *Progress of the World's Women: Women, Work and Poverty*, New York: UNIFEM, 2005.

27 Other factors have also contributed to this process. See M Carr, MA Chen and J Tate, 'Globalisation and home-based workers', *Feminist Economics*, 6 (3), 2000, pp 123–142 for further discussion of this.

28 R Munck, 'Introduction' to special issue, *Latin American Perspectives*, 31 (4), 2004, pp 3–20.

29 UNIFEM, *Progress of the World's Women*.

30 M Chen, J Sebstad & LO'Connell, 'Counting the invisible workforce: the case of home-based workers', *World Development*, 27 (3), 1999, pp 603–610; and E Prugl, *The Global Construction of Gender: Home-based Work in the Political Economy of the 20th Century*, New York: Columbia University Press, 1999.

31 H Henríquez, V Riquelme, T Gálvez & T Selamé, 'Home work in Chile: past and present results of a national survey', *SEED Working Paper*, 8, Geneva: ILO, 2001.

32 R Pearson, 'Organising home-based workers in the global economy: an action-research approach', *Development in Practice*, 14 (1–2), 2004, pp 136–148.

33 RE Miranda, *La Salud en Chile: Evolución y Perspectivas*, Santiago: Centro de Estudios Públicos, 1994.

34 M Pollack, 'Equidad de género en el sistema de salud chileno', *Serie Financiamiento del Desarollo*, 23, Santiago: CEPAL, 2002.

35 M Mackintosh, 'Health care commercialisation and the embedding of inequality', draft paper prepared for the RUIG/UNRIST project on Globalisation, Health and Inequality, 2003, at www.unrisd.org, accessed August 2004.

36 C Sapelli, 'Risk segmentation and equity in the Chilean mandatory health insurance system', *Social Science and Medicine*, 58 (2), 2004, pp 259–265.

37 http://www.gobiernodechile.cl/plan_auge/que_es_auge.asp, accessed February 2006.

38 A Gómez, 'Health: a human right, a civil right', *Women's Health Journal*, 2, 2002, pp 29–35.

39 Pearson, 'Organising home-based workers in the global economy'.

40 *Ibid*. The NGO responsible for conducting the research in Chile was AnaClara but following internal changes a new organisation, CECAM (Centro de Educación y Capacitación a la Mujer) has now emerged and is responsible for continuing this work.

41 L Benería, 'Shifting the risk: new employment patterns, informalisation and women's work', *International Journal of Politics, Culture and Society*, 15 (1), 2001, pp 27–53.

42 R Bitrán, J Muñoz, P Aguad, M Navarrete & G Ubilla, 'Equity in the financing of social security for health in Chile', *Health Policy*, 50, 2000, pp 171–196.

43 Author's interview with Miriam Ortega Aaraya, CECAM regional co-ordinator, 25 July 2003.

44 P Tibandebage & M Mackintosh, 'The market shaping of capabilities in low income contexts and some implications for social policy: liberalised health care in Tanzania', paper presented to the Conference on Justice and Poverty: Examining Sen's Capability Approach, Von Hugel Institute, Cambridge, 5–7 June 2001.

45 R Todaro & S Yáñez (eds), *El Trabajo se Transforma: Relaciones de Producción y Relaciones de Género*, Santiago: Centro de Estudios de la Mujer, 2004. It is important to differentiate between different types of part-time work that offer different sets of advantages and disadvantages to women and men and not to confuse, for example, flexible working hours for employees with imposed flexibility by firms. Much of the expansion of flexible working in Chile, particularly in the service, financial and agricultural sectors, has been of the latter sort.

46 X Diaz, 'La flexibilización de la jornada laboral', in Todaro & Yáñez, *El Trabajo se Transforma*, pp 123–173.

47 G Bloom & H Standing, 'Pluralism and marketisation in the health sector: meeting health needs in the contexts of social change in low and middle-income countries', *IDS Working Paper*, 136, Brighton: Institute of Development Studies, 2001.

48 R Pearson, 'All change? Men, women and reproductive work in the global economy', *European Journal of Development Research*, 12 (2), 2000, pp 219–237.

49 J Vega, P Bedregal, L Jadue & H Delgado, 'Equidad de género en el acceso a la atención de salud en Chile', *Revista Médica de Chile*, 131 (6), 2003, pp 669–678.

50 Carr *et al*, 'Globalisation and home-based workers'.

51 Comité de Derechos Económicos, Sociales y Culturales, point 36.

52 *Ibid*, point 38.

53 A Ramiréz, *Situación de la Mujer Trabajadora en el Sistema ISAPREs: Economía y Trabajo en Chile*, Santiago: Programa de Economía y Trabajo, Informe Annual No 7, 1997; and OPS/OMS, 'Discriminación de las mujeres en el sistema de instituciones de salud previsional: regulación y perspectiva de género en la reforma', *Equidad y Reforma de la Salud en Chile, Working Paper*, 1, Santiago: OPS/OMS, 2002.

54 Pollack, 'Equidad de género en el sistema de salud chileno'.

55 *Ibid.*
56 Diaz, 'La flexibilización de la jornada laboral'.
57 Comité de Derechos Económicos, Sociales y Culturales, point 56.
58 Shadow Report on the Third Periodic Report of Chile.
59 A Barrientos & S Barrientos, 'Social protection for workers in the informal economy: case study on horticulture', *Social Protection Discussion Paper*, 0216, Washington, DC: World Bank, 2002.
60 Diaz, 'La flexibilización de la jornada laboral'.
61 D Sharim & U Silva, 'Familia y reparto de responsabilidades', *Documento*, 58, Chile: Servico Nacional de la Mujer, 1998.
62 Diaz, 'La flexibilización de la jornada laboral'.
63 S Barrientos, 'The hidden ingredient: female labour in Chilean fruit exports', *Bulletin of Latin American Research*, 16 (1), 1997, pp 71–82.
64 C Dolan, J Humphrey & C Harris-Pascal, 'Horticulture commodity chains: the impact on the UK market of the African fresh vegetable industry', *IDS Working Paper*, 96, Brighton: Institute of Development Studies, 1999.
65 Barrientos, 'The hidden igredient'.
66 *Ibid.*
67 X Díaz & J Medel, 'Salud, género y trabajo: una relación difícil', document prepared for PAHO Mainstreaming Gender Programme, Santiago, 2002.
68 *Ibid.*
69 O Artega, I Astorga & AM Pinto, 'Inequalities in public health care provision in Chile', *Cuadernos de Saude Publica*, 18 (4), 2002, pp 1053–1066.
70 J Howell & J Pearce, *Civil Society and Development: A Critical Exploration*, Boulder, CO: Lynne Rienner, 2002.
71 V Schild, 'Engendering the new social citizenship in Chile: NGOs and social provisioning under neo-liberalism', in M Molyneux & S Razavi (eds), *Liberalism and its Discontents: The Politics of Gender, Rights and Development in a Global Age*, Oxford: Oxford University Press, 2002, pp 170–203.
72 J Gideon, 'Integrating gender issues into health policy', *Development and Change*, 37 (2), 2006, pp 329–252 and J Gideon, 'Consultation or co-option? A case study from the Chilean health sector', *Progress in Development Studies*, 5 (3), 2005, pp 169–181.
73 H Hofbauer, 'Gender sensitive budget analysis: a tool to promote women's rights', *Canadian Journal of Women and the Law*, 14, 2002, pp 98–117.

From the Girl Child to Girls' Rights

ELISABETH J CROLL

Despite the amount of attention given to Women in Development (WID), Gender and Development (GAD) and Children and Development (CAD), the question of how to address best the needs and interests of girls is a much neglected and under-studied one in the development context. Although there was evidence of widespread discrimination against girls, it was not until the 1990s that there was any concerted attempt to draw attention to the scale of the discrimination. Much of this new interest took place using the rubric 'the girl child', which was widely deployed in publications and on platforms to elicit support for the cause of girls. This brief paper, based largely on demographic, ethnographic and documentary research across East, South and Southeast Asia, suggests that, for the most part, the girl-child platform has not translated into effective, sustained or transformative national programmes or local projects in support of girls. Instead it argues that the cause of girls might be better served by an emphasis on girls' rights embedded in frameworks that gender both entitlements and expectations of children and take campaigns directly into the familial environment.

The girl child

In 1990 UNICEF's Board recommended that its strategy and programmes for the ensuing decade explicitly address the status and needs of the girl child.[1] During subsequent years UNICEF published a number of pamphlets emphasising that gender discrimination against girls was so routine as to be both pandemic and virtually invisible in many societies.

> To be born female is not a crime but you would never know it by looking at the deplorable conditions of girls in many parts of the world ... Beginning from birth, girls in many parts of the world experience that 'apartheid of gender' with her lesser claims decided at the moment her biological sex is known.[2]

Another identified girlhood as 'a perilous path' beset by a wide range of discriminatory and violent practices and described girlhood as a time of 'harsh lessons' when 'girls begin to deny themselves' and 'to expect little and to think less of themselves than of their brothers'—a lesson which they too will pass on to their own daughters unless 'this vicious circle' is broken.[3]

At the same time UNICEF also pledged itself to work with others to get girls on to an international agenda.

> If you are working for human rights and equal rights, human development, women's health, literacy, education, population control, economic development, foreign labour law, AIDS prevention, in fact almost any of today's pressing issues, then girls are your concern—and need your support.[4]

Indeed it was UNICEF's concern for the girl child that was an important contribution to raising her profile during the preparation for and events of the Fourth UN Conference for Women held in Beijing in 1995 where, for the first time, the girl child occupied her own place on an international agenda. Section L of the Beijing Platform for Action outlined nine strategic objectives for the girl child. These included eliminating all forms of discrimination against girls in education, health care and cultural practices; protecting girls from exploitation and violence; and encouraging all forms of girls' participation in social, economic and political life. Requiring statutory support, 189 governments committed themselves to taking concrete steps 'to end all discrimination against girls and to prepare girls to participate actively and equally with boys at all levels of social, political, economic and cultural leadership'.[5] Subsequently, country, regional and international meetings preparatory to both the Beijing+5 and Beijing+10 (years) in 2000 and 2005 encouraged further expressions of interest in and support for Section L. In addition, many regions had their own girl-child campaigns, several of which predated the Beijing Conference in 1995.

In the late 1980s the South Asian Association for Regional Co-operation (SAARC) designated the 1990s as the 'Decade for the Girl Child' and called for governments and other organisations to conduct research into the problems of discrimination and to provide positive media images for girls. In India, for example, a nation-wide project on 'The Girl Child and the Family Environment' was instigated to generate comparative data across the country to help in the planning of new programmes.[6] Simultaneously women's organisations publicised the 'silent' violence against daughters, including the different types of discrimination experienced before birth, in infancy and at marriage, as exemplified by worsening sex ratios at birth and the incidence of dowry-related deaths.[7] In China, too, the government and the women's organisations took a number of initiatives throughout the 1990s to raise awareness and investigate discrimination against girls. They held a national conference on 'The Girl Child in Poverty Stricken Regions', established a National Expert Group on the Girl Child and embarked on a popular education strategy to forward the cause of the girl child.[8] Other countries in Asia also took varying degrees of interest in the girl child, particularly in relation to education, and it could be said that all these initiatives helped to place her cause on global, regional and national platforms. However, an analysis of international donor and national programmes across East and Southeast Asia suggest the cause remained limited in scope and rarely generated transformative projects or other interventions at local levels that might meet the practical let alone strategic needs of girls.[9]

Even within UNICEF a mid-1990s history of that organisation noted that, while the girl child issue was prominent at UNICEF headquarters in New York, it was rarely taken up to the same extent in country programmes.[10] A few years ago I myself evaluated the discourse that conceptualised and positioned the girl child in UNICEF country programmes, including national situational analyses of children, programming operations for children and other supporting documentation from each of the countries in UNICEF's East and Southeast Asian region.[11] In these otherwise comprehensive and authoritative reports reflecting UNICEF's long experience in multifaceted programming across the region, references to the girl child were few and her cause was seldom incorporated into country programme, policy or project. In all the reports any references to girls were likely to be scattered throughout the texts and were rarely cross-referenced or co-ordinated into a separate profile or discussion of the girl child's specific needs and interests. There were almost no references to Section L of the Beijing Platform for Action and, despite UNICEF's commitment to gender-disaggregated data, child-related data was not disaggregated routinely outside of education. Where the data did show gender disparities, these were not always picked up and analysed in the text. Likewise textual references to gender disparities coexisted alongside non-gender disaggregated data, leading overall to a gender-neutral approach in child-focused programmes. Moreover, the very language of children, child labour, child prostitution, abused children and trafficked women and children camouflaged the gender of especially vulnerable categories which very often, although not exclusively, comprised girls. Indeed, the common use of the phrase 'women and children' masked the generational and gender disparities or inequalities experienced by girls in relation to both 'women' and 'children'.

In keeping with UNICEF's commitment to women's issues there was much interest in and space allotted to a variety of programmes in support of women. But, even where headings and phrases read 'women and girls', the contents that followed almost exclusively referred to women and made little reference to linkages between women's and girls' status. Despite adjunct references to 'today's girls' as 'tomorrow's women', there was little recognition of the linkages between girlhood and womanhood, including the proven relationship between maternal, infant and child mortality rates or low birth weights and the nutrition and health of adolescent girls; between gender socialisation in childhood and multiple and low-status roles in womanhood;

between the greater employment of women and increased domestic labour of girls; or between women's empowerment and the self-esteem of daughters.[12] UNICEF also promoted gender equality and introduced gender units, advisers and focal points throughout the region, but very rarely were children divided by gender. Rather its interest in gender inequality centred on the roles, status and empowerment of adult women, with almost no reference to inequalities in childhood entitlements, early socialisation into gender roles or the linkages between gender inequality in childhood and in adulthood. Even where a number of special studies of girls had been commissioned by UNICEF country offices, their findings seldom featured in the country-situation analyses of children or provided the rationale for programming. The exception to all these observations was to be found in girls' education.

Globally girls education has attracted high-level support from the UN Secretariat, the World Bank and other development agencies, donor nations and Asian governments. Indeed girls' education as the key to reducing fertility, educating subsequent generations and improving human capital has been represented as the jewel in the development crown. As the president of the World Bank has noted, 'girls' education is the single best investment that can be made in the developing world today'.[13] UNICEF too has designated girls' education as the prerequisite to sustainable development on the grounds that an educated girl is more likely to become a competent mother, a knowledgeable family planner, a more productive and better-paid worker, an informed citizen, a skilful decision maker and a self-confident individual.[14] Hence girls' education became the main objective of almost all UNICEF girl-child campaigns.[15] It is my own experience that any reference to the girl child almost immediately slips into a discussion of girls' education, so that the cause of girls is almost invariably defined in these narrow terms. Overall it has been an uphill struggle to broaden agendas at all levels to include other factors such as premature death, health and various forms of exploitation or violence. It has always seemed to me that today's almost exclusive emphasis on girls' education is reminiscent of an earlier phase in development programming which emphasised women's entry into social production to the exclusion of less visible reproductive roles. Finally, and perhaps the most important indictment of a limited approach, there are the trends showing increasing discrimination against girls, despite some development gains across parts of Asia.

Recent demographic and ethnographic studies show that daughter discrimination remains a feature of most societies in Asia and not only of their poorer and less developed rural regions characterised by high fertility and competition for scarce resources. These studies suggest that girls across the continent, whether in rural, urban, rich or poor sectors remain particularly vulnerable at two separate stages of their lifecycle. First, before birth, in infancy and in early childhood, young girls in South and East Asia experience types of discrimination which are reflected in unfavourable sex ratios at birth, high rates of female infant and child mortality and lesser access to educational and health facilities. In recent years these trends have been exacerbated by declining fertility, smaller family size and continuing son preference alongside new reproductive technologies.[16] In Southeast Asia it is adolescent girls who are most at risk and disadvantaged in education, nutrition, health, the labour market and in family and community participation. They also constitute a particularly vulnerable category in terms of sexual harassment and exploitation, especially in the labour-intensive industries of special economic zones and where prostitution and HIV/AIDS are widespread.[17] In most South and East Asian societies girls remain vulnerable in both lifecycle phases and not only in circumstances of natural disaster, economic crisis or socialist transition.

Very contemporary studies suggest that, although the advocacy in support of women, gender, children and the girl child has drawn attention to various and serious forms of gender discrimination in childhood, there have been fewer interventions that have made a difference to the survival, lives and life-choices of girls. One of the reasons why international platforms have not translated into transformative projects may be the lack of a ready framework within which the girl child can be located. So far, for reasons which become clearer in this paper, the concept of the girl child has not sat comfortably within the Women, Gender or Children and Development rubrics, so she has remained an outlier in these arenas. Outside education there have been few attempts to address the practical let alone strategic needs of girls as members of the female gender or as female children. Thus there may be a case for arguing that the focus on girls take more of a rights-based approach in advocacy, in programming and in local projects designed to address the practical needs and strategic interests of girls.

Girls' rights

Just in terms of nomenclature the label, 'girls' rights', appears less juvenile and less passive suggesting active agents engaged in rights dialogues and other participatory approaches. The label 'girls' rights' also fits well with the more general development interest in rights-based frameworks and constitutes a logical extension of two landmark conventions defining the rights of women and of children, both of which are cited as guiding principles in international, regional and country development programming on children throughout Asia. Interestingly, even in a region where the concept of human rights is much debated and not always supported in relation to Asian values, there is widespread government and civil society support expressed for women's and children's rights, with many references to the Convention for the Elimination of Discrimination Against Women (CEDAW) and the Convention on the Rights of the Child (CRC). However, largely because of their timing, neither of these two conventions make substantive references to girls or single out girls' rights for special attention. CEDAW, adopted in 1979 by the UN General Assembly, marked a most important milestone in support of the recognition and protection of women's rights but makes very few references to girls. Fifteen years later, in the mid-1990s, UNICEF and UNIFEM did attempt to rectify this omission by extending the mandate of CEDAW to include support for girls on the grounds that women's rights and girls' rights are inseparable and that the rights of girls today are the rights of tomorrow's women.[18] However, in spite of the combined sponsorship and a number of briefing pamphlets reflecting the joint support of UNIFEM and UNICEF for women's and girls' rights, it is women's rights that have remained the focus of UNIFEM's platforms and programmes while UNICEF has focused on children's rights.

The Convention on the Rights for the Child, adopted by the UN General Assembly in 1989 and ratified by most member states to become the most widely endorsed of human rights treaties, generally supports equality among children regardless of age, sex, social background and ethnicity.[19] Although it upholds equal opportunities for both boys and girls, there are very few references to girls or to gender disparities in childhood. Nevertheless, the advantages of extending this framework to support the needs and interests of girls are several. First of all, the rights language of the CRC has been taken up widely so that the child rights' framework is now a major and familiar component of government programmes across the Asian region. In support of the CRC and World Summit/Millennium Goals for Children, each country's National Plans of Action for Children (NPAs) help resolve tensions between universal standards and culture-specific variations, address inter-linked sectoral needs of children and compose a ready tool that could be easily adjusted to incorporate policies aimed at reducing discrimination against girls. Second, mechanisms for monitoring the implementation and documenting violations of child rights are in place internationally. Already in some of the international evaluation reports on country implementation of the CRC the International Committee on the Rights of the Child has listed continuing discrimination against girls as an important but neglected issue.[20] Third, in terms of conceptualising and operationalising girls' rights, the rights framework of the CRC embracing survival, development, protection and participation provides a pre-existing and comprehensive frame for broad-ening existing approaches. For instance, the focus on girls' rights to 'survival' and health care is appropriate where there is excessive infant and child mortality of girls. Equally girls' rights to 'development', embracing all forms and levels of education and training, would be helpful in overcoming continuing gender disparities in academic and vocational education leading to disadvantageous gendered divisions of labour in adulthood. Girls rights to 'protection' against all forms of abuse, neglect, exploitation and violence is necessary given the incidence of domestic and public sexual exploitation of girls in child labour, child prostitution, trafficking and physical abuse. Fourth, girls' rights to 'participation' in defining their own needs and interests and in family and community decision making are apposite in cultural traditions which exclude or disempower girls because of their age and gender, give them a lesser voice in families, school and communities and diminish their bargaining capacities and entitlements to familial resources.

Familial entitlements

If the need to address girls as a separate social category derives from evidence of their lesser chances of survival, access to health care or education and greater sexual and other exploitation, there are several additional reasons for singling out girls' rights. Documentary and field research across the region suggests not only that girls' rights have been overlooked within the larger rubrics women's and children's rights but also that their interests may be quite different from and even conflict with those of women and boys. One reason why an increase in attention to the rights of women seems not to have led to a correlative rise in attention to the status of girls is that, although girls and women have their female gender in common, they are also divided by generation. Girls as daughters are the only category to reside in natal as opposed to marital households and as transient members of the families of their birth, they have a quite different value to their families than do daughters-in-law, wives and mothers in patrilocal households. This is not only so in the patrilineal kinship systems common across the region but also in populations with bilateral kinship reckonings and in societies where a growing number of separate households are established by the younger generation following marriage. When generational hierarchies are added to gender hierarchies, daughters are not only devalued in relation to grown women, but familial allocations and investment in daughters may be quite different from those conferred upon their brothers.

Ethnographic studies in the region suggest that familial resource allocation to children may not be equal but is rather biased to the benefit of sons—and not only where there are scarce resources.[21] In children's programmes, there is still the assumption that the family is a benign institution operating in the best interests of the child with fair and equal allocation of resources to all children. However, recent research suggests that it is not so much the availability of services for education and health that are of import, but parental attitudes, behaviour and choices affecting familial resource allocation to food, health care and education. It could be argued that the different entitlements of sons and daughters, alongside the lesser claims of girls as temporary, short-term and thus liminal members of their families, is one reason why it is important to highlight the familial dimension which is often omitted in policy and programme formulation or implementation. If entitlements are so often linked to expectations, it is not surprising to find that these same ethnographic studies also show that the differing expectations of girls and boys have led to two major patterns in familial expectations of daughters across Asia.

Familial expectations

Although there is a variety of family structures which influence expectations of and values attached to girls and boys, one of the significant features in development strategies across Asia has been the central role assigned to the family in providing support, assistance and welfare for its members. In the absence of state-sponsored pensions, welfare and safety-nets, adults and children are reliant on resource flows between the generations.[22] The dependence upon the contributions and support provided by children governs long-term expectations of cash, goods or care and ultimately the value of children but interestingly the literature on this and on intergenerational contracts has not divided children by gender.[23] Yet ethnographic studies suggest that parents have very different expectations of girls and boys, in that sons are uniformly expected to live with or near parents, provide long-term support and succeed in education, careers or other income-generating activities. In societies of South and East Asia expectations of practical and ritual support from sons have meant that daughters who marry out are not expected to contribute to the support of their parents. Thus sons are preferred, perceived as an asset and the recipients of long-term investment, while daughters frequently are deemed a burden or liability and a 'double loss' in that they move out on marriage and are not expected to contribute to the support of parents. Where daughters do contribute to the support of their families before marriage, and this is more widespread than the beliefs and images would suggest or is acknowledged by parents, these contributions are often dismissed as short-term reimbursement for the expenses of their upbringing and certainly deemed a less significant contribution than that of their brothers.[24] In these circumstances it is the differing expectations of sons and daughters that result in son preference and privilege, leading in extreme circumstances to imbalanced sex ratios at birth, higher female infant and child mortality rates and less protection of girls.

There are signs that the greater income-earning opportunities for adolescent girls in South and East Asia, the greater incidence of smaller or single-daughter households and longer life expectancy with extended demand for physical care are leading to some changes in familial expectation of daughters, as in China's one- or two-child families or India's and Korea's smaller families.[25] However, the experience of girls in Southeast Asia shows that these circumstances will not necessarily be to the advantage of girls. In a second pattern of discrimination, especially evident in Southeast Asia, daughters have a higher value in infancy because it is expected that from a young age they will contribute to the support of their parents either in times of scarcity or for material gain. The extent to which families may rely on a daughter's contribution varies from culture to culture and with economic circumstance, but poverty and indebtedness tend to place an extra burden on the shoulders of young girls. A young daughter's domestic labour may substitute for that of her employed mother, while parents who have an urgent need of income for subsistence or for debt repayment, may exchange or sell their daughters directly or inadvertently into occupations that can be hazardous and exploitative. In many societies remittances from daughters have increased because of the growing opportunities for factory work, domestic service and commercial sex work which can provide instant returns to meet immediate familial needs. Indeed, adolescent girls may find themselves supporting parents, siblings and extended family members especially, but not only, in times of hardship. Their role is such that it is sometimes said that there are greater expectations of and dependence on daughters than there is on development!

It is an underlying premise of this paper that any shift in expectations of daughters within the development context is not only dependent upon a shift in platform from the girl child to girls' rights but also contingent on embedding the notion of rights within discourses on gender and the family and on resolving tensions between generalised or universal child standards and culture-specific imperatives that structure the lives of children.[26] As Burman has also observed, the needs and interests of girls in the development context have been abstracted from cultures of gender and divorced from discourses of the family.[27] Indeed, it can be argued that the exercise of girls' rights is contingent upon a parallel shift in interest to child-centred gender equality within and outside the family. My own years of first-hand development experience in Asia suggest that initiatives in support of children will only effect their goals if they gender children, separate out the gender-specific needs and interests of girls and boys and theorise the relations between gender and childhood.

Gender and girls

It is an underlying premise of this paper that gender divisions, hierarchies and stereotypes in childhood have to be challenged and changed if there is to be any reorientation in familial entitlements or expectations and any increase in girls' rights to survival, development, protection and participation. Although there are variations in the ways in which gender relations are defined and interpreted in everyday beliefs and behaviour, an extensive perusal of ethnographic field studies and personal narratives across Asia suggests that there is a pervasive theme which punctuates everyday conversation, interview and lifecycle event or ritual—namely, that children are gendered.

Among rural and urban, literate and illiterate, secluded and employed or rich and poor populations, parents and family members talk about boys and girls rather than use the collective category 'children'. Differential characteristics and values attached to girls and boys are assumed, articulated and unquestioned so that in everyday practice girls and boys are categorised, welcomed and represented quite differently.[28] In Asia there are also marked divisions of labour and separation of spaces with differentiated male and female spheres of activities and influence that are valued hierarchically. Most field investigations also suggest that the calculations of parents in planning and building their families are largely rooted in the expectations that sons and daughters will follow customary divisions of labour established at a very early age. Even though their earnings may be supporting entire households, the value of daughters' contributions to the family's budget and well-being are frequently overlooked or underestimated by parents and other family members.[29]

Most Asian cultures also emphasise gender difference in social, physical and emotional characteristics and stress complementarity of roles in separate spheres rather than the similar gender characteristics, overlapping activities and competition common elsewhere. It is because it is still difficult in many cultures for daughters to cross boundaries or substitute for sons in many familial functions that girls are most at risk either in infancy and/or later in adolescence.[30] Moreover, gender stereotypes, which commonly suggest that girls and boys ought to display quite distinctive characteristics, undertake specific activities and have different capabilities, are likely to limit the expectations of girls of their selves, diminish their self-esteem and instil a heightened sense of obligation to their families.[31] Many field researchers have concluded that it is this explicit sense of responsibility among the daughters themselves that has very often propelled them into exploitative conditions of work. Perceiving themselves to be temporary and lesser members of their natal households, they feel especially indebted to their families and particularly obligated to repay the expenses of their upbringing, regardless of the cost to themselves and whether or not there are major expectations that they will do so.[32]

If it can be argued that the operationalisation of any platform to achieve equality for girls is contingent upon a shift in rubric from the girl child, women's rights or children's rights to singling out girls' rights, and a parallel shift in focus from gender equality in adulthood to gendered strategic and practical needs in childhood, then it must be said that, so far, there are few models that have incorporated this dual shift. However, in one Southeast Asian country there is evidence of a number of building blocks which could potentially comprise such a comprehensive approach. In the Philippines there have been simultaneous projects to single out girls' rights, to question socialisation into gender roles and to raise the self-esteem of girls. Together these might comprise the stepping stones necessary to achieve such a dual shift.

Stepping stones

In the Philippines, the child-rights framework has been deployed specifically to draw attention to girls' rights. A widely disseminated and illustrated reader-friendly 30-page booklet entitled *Girls Have Rights Too* was published to counter common Filipino beliefs that men and women were already equal which disguised the more subtle areas of discrimination that still affected the life-choices for and opportunities for girls.[33] As the foreword noted, this booklet provided 'a good starting point for removing cultural blindness and establishing the truth that the girl child has rights too!'. It used statistics and stories to amplify the ways in which Filipino culture binds girls to gender stereotypes and fosters acceptance of exploitative practices so that Filipino girls are more likely to be underweight or stunted and physically vulnerable because of early marriage, the prevalence of HIV/AIDS or other sexually transmitted diseases and organised prostitution, trafficking, violence or abuse. Schools are accused of reinforcing and perpetuating gender-biased concepts, employers of exploiting girl children and the mass media of under-reporting the girl child and perpetuating gender stereotypes. The booklet places girls' rights in the context of the CRC, CEDAW and, unusually, Section L of the Beijing Platform for Action before concluding with a section entitled 'What You Can Do'. This identifies 12 ways in which all sections of society, ranging from policy workers and service providers to girls themselves, can document, monitor and intervene in cases to reduce discrimination against girls.

Around the same time a study of child rearing was commissioned by UNICEF and the Ateneo Wellness Centre in Manila to further understand how gender roles are transmitted and acquired during the process of socialisation and how families, school and the media influence the behaviours, attitudes and expectations of girls and boys. Entitled *How We Raise our Daughters and Sons*, this booklet drew attention to the ways in which 'child-rearing attitudes and practices are extremely potent tools for transmitting gender roles, expectations and even aspirations' and how 'families, especially parents, play a crucial role in shaping children's early attitudes and thoughts about themselves, their communities and the world at large'.[34] This booklet on gender socialisation concluded that Filipino girls are disadvantaged by behavioural restrictions and household responsibilities that, onerous and devalued, limit their future options within and outside the family. It made a number of recommendations to parents, school, the media, non-governmental organisations and governments.

Finally, a project entitled 'Improving Self-Esteem and Strengthening the Role and Capacity of Women and Girls' was designed to help girls build their own personal confidence and self-respect so that they could become agents in transforming the conditions of their own lives. The project aimed to identify the factors in Filipino culture which shaped and reinforced the self-images and low self-esteem of girls 'rendering them vulnerable to subordination and exploitation and limiting their life choices and opportunities'.[35] This project was unusual in that it not only emphasised girls' rights and gender socialisation and stereotyping but it also aimed explicitly to enhance the self-esteem of young girls. It was anticipated that this project would result in a gender and children's rights education module that would focus on the CRC, gender role socialisation, sexuality and human rights' education for girls, boys and service providers. How these programmes will combine to promote girls' rights in Filipino society remains to be seen, but together they comprise many of the stepping stones necessary to meet the strategic needs of girls: they single out girls and embrace both rights-based and gender frameworks. Without such a strategic and holistic approach, previous experience across the Asian region suggests that the cause of girls is likely to remain confined to international platforms, under-studied in analysis and girls the most neglected of social categories in country policies and programmes, at least within the development context.

Notes

This paper is based on field visits to China, Pakistan, Indonesia and Thailand, extensive reading of demographic and ethnographic studies and UNICEF and other donor documentation across East, South and Southeast Asia.

1 UNICEF, *Women and Girls: The Key to Development*, London: UNICEF, nd, p 4.

2 UNICEF, *To be Born Female...*, New York: UNICEF, 1994.

3 UNICEF, *Girls and Women: A UNICEF Development Priority*, New York: UNICEF, 1993, p 8.

4 UNICEF, *To be Born Female.*

5 UN, *Platform for Action and the Beijing Declaration*, Fourth World Conference on Women, New York: United Nations Department of Public Education, 1996.

6 J Bagachi, J Guha & P Sengupta, *Loved and Unloved: The Girl Child in the Family*, Calcutta: Stree, 1997, p 27.

7 V Ponacha (ed), *The Childhood that Never was: An Anthology of Short Stories on the Girl Child*, Bombay: Research Centre for Women's Studies, SNDT Women's University, 1993.

8 E Croll, *Endangered Daughters: Discrimination and Development in Asia*, London: Routledge, 2000, pp 174–181.

9 M Molyneux, 'Mobilisation without emancipation? Women's interests, state and revolution in Nicaragua', *Feminist Studies*, 11 (2), 1985, pp 232–233.

10 M Black, *Children First: The Story of UNICEF Past and Present*, Oxford: Oxford University Press, 1996, p 212.

11 This study included situational analyses, profiles and supporting documentation for China, South Korea, Mongolia, Indonesia, Philippines, Malaysia, Vietnam, Cambodia, Laos, Burma, Papua New Guinea, Fiji and the Pacific. For full report of this study see, E Croll, *Gender Inequalities among Children in the East Asian Pacific Region*, Bangkok: UNICEF, 2001.

12 UNICEF-GOI (Government of Indonesia), *Challenges to a New Generation: The Situation of Children and Women in Indonesia 2000*, Jakarta: UNICEF Indonesia, 1999, pp 67, 82; UNICEF China, *Children and Women of China: A UNICEF Situation Analysis*, Beijing: UNICEF, 1995, pp 25, 68; UNESCO, *Integrating Girl Child Issues into Population Education*, Bangkok: UNESCO, 1997, pp 14–15.

13 UNICEF, *Education for Girls: Lifeline to Development*, New York: UNICEF, 1995, p 3.

14 *Ibid*, pp 2–3.

15 UNICEF, *Children First*, Issue 38, New York: UNICEF, 1998, p 12.

16 Office of the Registrar General and UNFPA India, *Missing…Mapping the Adverse Child Sex Ratios in India*, New Delhi: Office of the Registrar General and UNFPA India, 2003; UNFPA China, *Sex Ratios— Facts and Figures*, Beijing: UNFPA China, 2004; E Croll, 'Fertility decline, family size and female discrimination: a study of reproductive management in East and South Asia', *Asia–Pacific Journal*, Economic and Science Commission for Asia and the Pacific, Bangkok, June, 2002, pp 11–38; M das Gupta and PNM Bhat, 'Fertility decline and increased manifestation of sex bias in India', *Population Studies*, 51, 1997, pp 307–315; UNDP, *Human Development and South Asia 2000: The Gender Question*, Oxford: Oxford University Press, 2000; S Sudha & SI Rajan, 'Female demographic disadvantage in India, 1981–1991', *Development and Change*, 30 (3), 1999, pp 585–618; B Gu & K Roy, 'Sex ratios at birth in China with reference to other areas in East Asia: what we know', *Asia and Pacific Population Journal*, September, 1995, pp 17–42; and AT Abeykoon, 'Sex preference in South Asia: Sri Lanka—an outlier', *Asia and Pacific Population Journal*, September, 1995, pp 5–16.

17 UNAIDS, *Reducing Girls' Vulnerability to HIV/AIDS: The Thai Approach*, Geneva: UNAIDS, 1999; WHO, *Adolescence: The Critical Phase*, New Delhi: WHO, 1997; S Baker & M Romejin, 'Girls at work: the situation in Asia', *ILO Discussion Paper*, 4, paper for discussion at the 'Asia Regional Meeting on the Worst Forms of Child Labour', Phuket, Thailand, 8–10 September 1999; H Berger & H van de Glind, 'Children in prostitution, pornography and illicit activities', paper for discussion at the 'Asia Regional Meeting on the Worst Forms of Child Labour'; K Archavanitkul, *Trafficking in Children for Labour Exploitation including Child Prostitution in the Mekong Sub-region*, Bangkok: ILO, 1998; and T Bond & D Hayter, *A Review of Child Labour, Street Children, Child Prostitution and Trafficking, Disability and the Family*, Hanoi: UNICEF, 1998.

18 UNICEF and UNIFEM, 'Girls' rights', Information Sheet, New York: UNICEF and UNIFEM, January 1995.

19 UNICEF, *First Call for Children: World Declaration and Plan of Action from the World Summit for Children and Convention on the Rights of the Child*, New York: UNICEF, 1990.

20 V Muntarbhorn, *A Sourcebook for Reporting under the Convention on the Rights of the Child*, Bangkok: UNICEF, EAPRO and Child Rights Asianet, 1997. See also Concluding Observations of International Committee on the Convention on the Rights of the Child, on China, 3 June 1995; on Burma, 21 September 1993; and on Micronesia, 3 June 1995.

21 For a summary of the findings of these and other ethnographic studies, see Croll, *Endangered Daughtes*; SH Potter & J Potter, *China's Peasants: The Anthropology of a Revolution*, Cambridge: Cambridge University Press, 1990, pp 228–229; C Ikels, 'Setting accounts: the intergenerational contract in the age of reform', in D Davis & S Harrell (eds), *Chinese Families in the Post-Mao Era*, Berkeley, CA: University of California Press, 1993, pp 307–333; CN Milwertz, *Accepting Population Control: Urban Chinese Women and the One-Child Family Policy*, London: Curzon Press, 1997, pp 145, 196; L Shuzuo & Z Chuzhu, 'Gender differences in child survival in rural China: a country study', paper presented at the Annual Meeting of the Population Association of America, New York, 25–27 March 1999; K Karpardia, *Siva and her Sisters: Gender, Caste and Class in Rural South India*, Boulder, CO: Westview Press, 1995; and P Jeffrey & R Jeffrey, *Don't Marry Me to a Plowman! Women's Everyday Lives in Rural North China*, Boulder, CO: Westview Press, 1996, pp 39, 69.

22 See E Croll, 'The intergenerational contract in the changing Asian family', *Oxford Journal of Development Studies*, forthcoming, December 2006.

23 M Nag, 'Economic value and costs of children in relation to human fertility', in N Eberstadt (ed), *Fertility Decline in Less Developed Countries*, New York: Praeger Publishers, 1981; D Friedman, M Hechter & S Kanawaza, 'A theory of the value of children', *Demography*, 31 (3), 1994, pp 375–380; 'Comment and reply', *Demography*, 33 (1), 1996, pp 133–139; JC Caldwell, 'Towards a restatement of demographic transition theory', *Population and Development Review*, 2 (3 and 4), 1976, pp 321–366; and Croll, *Endangered Daughters*.

24 D Wolf, 'Daughters, decisions and domination: an empirical and conceptual critique of household strategies', in N Visanathan, L Duggan, L Nissonoff & N Wiegerersma (eds), *The Women, Gender and Development Reader*, London: Zed Press, 1997, p 126; Bagachi *et al*, *Loved and Unloved*, p 27; Potter & Potter, *China's Peasants*, p 193; and Croll, 'The intergenerational contract in the changing Asian family'.

25 M King Whyte, 'The persistence of family obligations in Baoding', in King Whyte (ed), *China's Revolutions and Intergenerational Relations*, Ann Arbor: University of Michigan Press, 2003, pp 130–132, 168–188; Y Shengming & I Chi, 'Living arrangements and adult children's support for the elderly in the new urban areas of mainland China', in I Chi, NL Chappell & J Lubben (eds), *Elderly Chinese in Pacific Rim Countries: Social Support and Integration*, Hong Kong: Hong Kong University Press, 2001, p 216; Y Yunxiang, *Private Life under Socialism*, Stanford, CA: Stanford University Press, 2003, pp 180–181; JB Leung, 'Family support and community-based service in China', in Chi *et al*, *Elderly Chinese in Pacific Rim Countries: Social Support and Integration*, p 177; Sudha & Rajan, 'Female demographic disadvantage in India', p 275; and L Packiam, 'Caring for the aged: emerging alternatives' in LT Bhai (ed), *Ageing: An Indian Perspective*, New Delhi: Decent Books, 2002, p 217.

26 P Alston (ed), *The Best Interests of the Child: Reconciling Culture and Human Rights*, Oxford: Oxford University Press, 1994; J Boyden & V Rialp, 'Children's rights to protection from economic exploitation', in JR Himes (ed), *Implementing the Convention on the Rights of the Child: Resource Mobilisation in Low Income Countries*, Dordrecht: Martinus Nijhoff, 1995.

27 E Burman, 'Developing differences: gender, childhood and economic development', *Children and Society*, 9 (3), pp 121–147; Burman, 'The abnormal distribution of development: policies for Southern women and children', *Gender, Place and Culture*, 2 (1), 1995, pp 21–36.

28 For a summary of these ethnographic findings, see Croll, *Endangered Daughters*.

29 D Grover, *Tomorrow's Woman, Today's Child*, Bangkok: UNICEF, 2000, p 29.

30 Croll, *Endangered Daughters*.

31 H Rydstrom, 'Rural Vietnamese girls' socialisation', report for Swedish Save the Children Fund, September 1999, p 10; UNICEF and Ateneo Wellness Centre, 'How we raise our daughters and sons: child rearing and gender socialisation in the Philippines', Manila: UNICEF and the Ateneo Wellness Centre, 1999.

32 Potter & Potter, *China's Peasants*, p 193; CN Milwertz, *Accepting Population Control*, pp 136–138; S Chaturvedi, *Youth Career Development Programme: Making a Difference to Children and Youth in Thailand at Risk from Exploitation*, Bangkok: UNICEF, 1998, p 6; PF Kelly & D Bach Le, *Trafficking in Humans from and within Vietnam*, Hanoi: UNICEF and other agencies, September 1999, p 41; and Rydstrom, 'Rural Vietnamese girls' socialisation', p 9.

33 UNICEF, *Children Have Rights Too!*, Manila: UNICEF, 1999.

34 UNICEF and Ateneo Wellness Centre, 'How we raise our daughters and sons'.

35 Government of the Philippines and UNICEF, *Master Plan of Operations between the Government of the Philippines and UNICEF*, Fifth Country Programme for Children, 1998.

Revisiting Equality as a Right: the Minimum Age of Marriage clause in the Nigerian Child Rights Act, 2003

NKOYO TOYO

The UN Convention on the Rights of the Child (CRC) was ratified by Nigeria in 1991. In 2003 it was domesticated in the Child Rights Act (CRA).[1] Since the Constitution of Nigeria does not put the matter of child protection under the exclusive or concurrent jurisdiction of the national government, states which are sub-units of the federal government are obliged to apply the act as it is, or pass it as a state law. Some states of the Nigerian Federation—particularly in northern Nigeria—came to oppose the provisions of the CRA, claiming that it contravenes religious and cultural norms and practices. The clause in the CRA that stipulates a minimum age of marriage came to be the focal point for an emergent controversy, eliciting divergent reactions from various groups. The ensuing debate revolved around whose interpretation, knowledge and values matter in situations where practices embedded in cultural traditions define social realities. It also raised questions about how those who advocate women's rights come to present related issues of gender equality and women's empowerment.

The normative assumption that flows from the adoption of any international human rights treaty is that it will guarantee rights for people alike. As a result, its domestication into national law is believed to be more than a statement of intention; it is also a guarantee that citizens will be able to access such rights. But this assumption often overlooks locally existing cultural–religious norms and the infused relations of power which hollow out the real value of legal provisions. These cultural norms exist in and are asserted by groups with an interest to secure some advantage and/or to capture spaces which would otherwise be open to deliberative responses. Opposition to the CRA has largely occurred at the point of incorporation into sub-national legislation as, at this level, culture or religion can be easily evoked and claimed by or on behalf of populations whose interests are perceived to be threatened.

This type of opposition is not new to the struggles for rights by women nor is it lost on Nigerian feminists. Commenting on a similar development which canvassed for respect for international human rights standards within the context of the *shar'ia* penal code in northern Nigeria, Ayesha Iman, a leading feminist and Muslim scholar, argued that:

> Nigeria is in fact a state party to several international human rights covenants. However, although such agreements may give rise to obligations under international law, unless they have been specifically incorporated into domestic law, they give no basis for claims in national courts. The interplay between domestic Nigerian multiple and parallel legal systems of secular, Muslim and customary laws is also problematic as they give differential rights on different issues, and jurisdiction can be contentious.[2]

In addition to the legal dilemma presented by Iman, there is the politics of who and what determines the applicable legal regime in a given state and in whose interest such a decision is made. In a situation where the constitution recognises cultural and religious rights alongside what are referred to as 'fundamental human rights', there are bound to be conflicts. Although the Nigeria Constitution prohibits discrimination on the grounds of sex, it fails to extend the same clear standards of non-discrimination to issues of marriage, inheritance, divorce and other aspects of family life, which are consigned to the domain of personal law.

Tensions inherent in the process of negotiating between plural legal possibilities have had a long and complex history in Nigeria. An important question raised by the CRA controversy is why the present attempt to make laws on rights based on international influences is being 'reversed' and whether the dispute represents a step backwards. Furthermore, what are the implications of these contests over rights for women, especially in relation to prevailing cultural and religious norms and traditions?

This chapter takes up these questions, analysing how different women's groups and programmes have reacted to these challenges and the broader implications of the controversy that surround the 'age of marriage' debate for women's rights and gender equality. It begins with an account of the background to and content of the CRA and explores the different positions taken up by advocates and opponents of the provisions of the act. It goes on to reflect on how far state 'complicity' with those opposed to the act reveals shortcomings in its commitment and capacity to fulfil obligations to promoting equal rights for boys and girls.

Background to the Child Rights Act of 2003

The CRA was ratified by Nigeria on 16 April 1991 and the African Charter on the Rights and Welfare of the Child was subsequently adopted. In order to make the convention applicable within Nigeria, various stakeholders engaged in advocacy and awareness programmes to press home the importance of translating its aspirations into national and sub-national legal frameworks. The CRA was eventually passed as national law in 2003, but this was after a long and tedious struggle. The history of the Act began with the first bill on Children's Rights of 1993, which suffered a setback from groups who claimed that it contained provisions contrary to Christian and/or Islamic values. Muslim opponents at the time particularly objected to the provision setting 18 years as the minimum age for marriage. They claimed that this was incompatible with Islamic precepts, where girls were given into marriage at a much younger age.[3]

With the return of the country to civil rule in 1999, it was possible to re-present the issue, resulting in its passage as an Act in September 2003 by a majority in the National Assembly. The success was challenged by a powerful and vocal minority, whose public declarations were clearly linked to what one critic termed the 'neo-fundamentalist project',[4] a project intent on advancing a certain application of the new *shar'ia*-based penal code following its introduction into a number of northern States of Nigeria in 2000. Their continued dispute over the minimum age for marriage section of the Act raised questions about the fundamental rationale behind it and the possibility of equality of the sexes being addressed. For instance, following a meeting of the Supreme Council for Shar'ia in Nigeria (SCSN), one of its leaders captured the mood of others when he reported that:

> SCSN observed that this law (CRA 2003), if allowed to be passed by our state assemblies, will demolish the very basis and essence of the Shar'ia and our Islamic culture, and accordingly called on all Muslims and Islamic organisations to take appropriate steps in their States to prevent this from happening.[5]

Reviewing this challenge, the arguments on the efficacy of the CRA can best be situated within the domain of Nigeria's tripartite legal system, the political capacities of groups that are socially and culturally excluded from claiming rights, the positionality of those who speak for them, and interactions with those who oppose the CRA. By subjecting the analysis of the CRA processes to these variables, it becomes evident that a real constraint on implementation is the weakness of agency on the part of those who support it. As groups they have weak links to one another—both vertical and horizontal—and therefore little inter-group accountability. These weak linkages undermine the pursuit of rights-based approaches and compel advocates to seek alternatives, including adopting forms of political accommodation that contradict the very basis of their action.

The rights scenario

Rights frameworks have exposed poor indicators of development and the low socioeconomic status of girls and women in parts of Nigeria, and yet opposition groups continue to deny the connection between these and the withholding of rights such as those enshrined in the CRA. Yet the logic of rights can and has helped feminists make effective conjectures on how they can promote the ideals of international human rights treaties and their underlying principle of equality.[6]

Some of the situations considered in this paper show that those campaigning for rights enter the rights sphere with competing approaches which can capture solidarity across various constituencies. But competing notions and interventions can also undermine efforts to achieve certain principles. For instance, those who have carried out rights advocacy by de-linking it from the principle of equality have tended to jeopardise arguments against discrimination. Although these strategies have enabled access to certain constituencies, they have only partially succeeded in presenting the 'rights' arguments and so are unlikely to achieve social change. Expectations that rights-based approaches will be nurtured over time are continuously challenged by a host of contextual factors, including the fact that those promoting them are themselves immersed in patriarchal gender relations, producing a variety of localised interpretations of their meaning.

The Child Rights Act, 2003

The Child Rights Act of 2003 is divided into 24 parts with 275 sections. These sections seek to protect the child from all forms of abuses and discrimination. Rights covered in the Act include: the right to survival and development, the right to name (identity), freedom of association and peaceful assembly, freedom of thought, conscience and religion, the right to privacy, the right to freedom of movement and the right to freedom from discrimination. Others are: the right to dignity, the right to health and health services, the right to parental care, protection and maintenance, the right to free, compulsory and universal primary education, the right of a child in need to special protection measures, the right of the unborn child to protection against harm and the contractual right of the child. In addition to the list of rights, the Act sets out the responsibilities of government and parents to provide structures and facilities, homes and a conducive environment for the full development of children. It empowers the court to make protection and supervision orders in respect of children in need of care and protection, as well as to establish a child justice system for the protection of children in court. The Act makes special provisions for the care of children with disabilities and gives courts the power to arrest, summon, search and order forfeiture and then impose penalties.[7]

Under Sections 21 and 23 of the CRA it is illegal for a parent to marry off his or her daughter if she is below 18 years old. The sections provide for a fine of N500 000 (or US$7000) or a jail term of five years. In addition, it is an offence punishable by imprisonment for a husband to consummate a marriage with a child under 18 years. He is considered to have raped the girl, who is illegally his wife under the provisions of the Act. The CRA provides that adoption of children who are non-biological relations is permitted but that to marry an adopted son or daughter is null and void, with punishment of up to 14 years imprisonment (Sections 141 and 147). The Act further makes for equal inheritance between male and female children (Sections 10 and 12). The contention around Sections 10, 12, 21, 23, 141 and 147 of the Act are particularly crucial, because they not only challenge notions of rights under Muslim law, they also challenge existing case law under *shar'ia*.

For instance, with the introduction of *shar'ia* law, the age of criminal responsibility became an issue and was variedly interpreted. Some groups decreed it to be 18 years, others decided on puberty and, in cases involving fornication or adultery, which can attract flogging or the death penalty, respectively, the age of responsibility was set at 15. This implies that, in cases where children reach puberty earlier than 18 years, no distinction is made between them and adults in dispensing *shar'ia* punishments. In January 2001 a young girl, Bariya Ibrahim Magazu, whose age was variously put at between 13 and 17 years, was subjected to 100 strokes of the cane in public in Zamfara State, after she gave birth to a child without being married.[8] This sentence raised several legal issues, including under *shar'ia* law. Advocates of rights under *shar'ia* law argued that changes in the way Muslim law was being applied had to be made known to people if they were to be punished meaningfully and if respect for legal procedures was to be established.

The 'Minimum Age of Marriage' and the related issues of gender equality

The CRA tried to resolve some of the legal and practical difficulties associated with the differential use of age of marriage and related punishments. It defined a child as a person who has not attained the age of 18 years and consequently is not in a position to fully enter into a contract of marriage. However, other pieces of legislation have created definitional confusion, making the relevant age uncertain. For instance, Section 2 of the Children and Young Persons Act (CYPA), states that 'a child' means a person under the age of 14 years, while 'a young person' means a person who has attained the age of 14 years and is under the age of 17 years. The Immigration Act stipulates that any person below 16 years is a minor, whereas the Matrimonial Causes Act puts the age of maturity at 21. What is evident from the Bariya Ibrahim Magazu case is that, while the legal question of the age of a child remains unsettled, the contention is mainly about when a child is no longer a child for the purpose of marriage or punishment.

The politics of the private sphere

A minimum age of marriage has an impact on state as well as Muslim personal law, and is seen as controversial partly because the conception of minimum age emanates not from national law but from the international arena of the CRA. This is viewed by some Muslim critics as an international imposition which is also an invasion of what is basically a private sphere. Such is the importance people place on the private sphere that all constitutions of Nigeria have embodied respect for the divergent forms of identities, expressions and values. For instance, in the 1999 constitution there are provisions in Sections 275–279 for the Shar'ia Court of Appeal and in Sections 280–284 for the Customary Court of Appeal.[9]

In much of the public sphere the discourse about the nature of the private sphere has been muted. Dominant thinking seems to be that 'private' spaces should be protected as spaces for the alternative ethnic, religious and social norms which inform the daily lives of people in Nigeria. The dispute over the minimum age of marriage reveals a classic example of how the imposition of certain interpretations of marriage is actually a function of dominant influences within the private sphere—a sphere whose regulation is nevertheless contested by a variety of forces. In this case, however, the myth of an absence of politics in the private sphere has bolstered conservative interpretations of *shar'ia* law by the Muslim right wing. As Iman comments:

> the myth of a single uniform (conservative) Shar'ia, has enabled the Muslim religious rightwing to prevent progressive Muslim scholars and rights' activists from establishing the legitimacy of their positions in fiqh (jurisprudence), Shar'ia, or non-religious laws.[10]

Advocates of the CRA point to how child marriages limit opportunities for girls in education and account for many of the 36 million Nigerian women and girls said to be without education.[11] They highlight the physical, mental and emotional health impact of early marriage on girls and the fact that girls engaged in child marriages are deprived of the right to control their bodies and reproductive health.

Reproductive health issues form a major part of the CRA and the African Protocol, and both they and the Convention on the Elimination of All Forms of Discrimination Against Women (CEDAW) protect against child marriage. It seems that, while there is broad international agreement in favour of a minimum age for marriage of 18 years, the practice of forced and arranged early marriages continues unabated and seems to be the norm in some parts of the country.

Obstacles to implementation

The tripartite legal system

In setting out the functions of the various tiers of government—national, state and local—the 1999 constitution empowers the federal legislative to make laws for the country but also requires that State Houses of Assembly should pass similar laws at state level. In addition to this legislative requirement, the constitution recognises three distinct traditions of law: the English common law, the Islamic *shar'ia* law (religious law) and the customary law (based on communal traditions). In Section 4 of the 1999 constitution, there is provision for the judiciary to be fair in the determination of any question of civil rights and obligations. Notwithstanding the existence of this formal arm of government, the same constitution allows other legal systems to run concurrently with it. Taking advantage of the gaps created by this complex web of legal systems, some states have passed laws and pronounced judgements which challenge the constitution and put principles of human rights to the test.[12]

Observing the challenges this tripartite legal arrangement has presented to the dispensation of justice, some members of the Expert Committee set up by the UN Commission on the Status of Women to monitor compliance with the CEDAW (ratified by Nigeria in 1985) have expressed concerns about the contradictions and inconsistencies created by the application of Nigeria's three legal systems. They cautioned against the perpetuation of customary and religious practices which negatively affect the situation of Nigerian women and emphasised the need for the government to take urgent action to harmonise its legal framework to ensure the uniformity of human rights protections.[13] The conflict of laws is particularly visible at the state level, where laws are passed and interpreted with little regard for the constitution and national acts, and where by 2005 only four states had passed a child rights law.

Mobilisation by the opposition

The CRA has suffered the additional obstacle that advocacy groups have been less successful than opponents in mobilising support and steering the discourse around rights, with the result that alternative discourses are lacking. Opposing groups not only stated their objection, but mobilised clerics, visited legislatures in the *shar'ia* states of the north and confronted members of the National Assembly on their adoption of the CRA. In addition, they engaged in a widespread media campaign including naming those that were working against the interests of Islam.

States such as Kaduna, with a mixed Muslim and Christian population, instead of responding to opposition challenges, have chosen to reword their version of the CRA in order to make it more acceptable. In the predominantly Muslim state of Bauchi, rather than engage in the controversy over the CRA, the state legislature opted for and passed the Girl Child Education Law, which prohibits the withdrawal of girls from school (ostensibly for marriage) before they have finished their secondary education (usually at about the age of 18). The law also guarantees free schooling for girls, as well as payment of national examination fees. The manner in which the legislature de-linked education from rights in this case raises questions about the extent to which gender equality and women's empowerment is being addressed.[14] It also draws attention to the failure of many of the strategies that have been used to domesticate international human rights.

Women's organisational development and the challenge of strategies for the domestication of human rights in Nigeria

After many years of heightened national involvement with international conferences and events there has been an exponential growth in the number of women's groups working for greater recognition of rights and empowerment for women. Notwithstanding this development, there remains a wide gap between activism and practice that can bring about change. The delay in achieving rights as enshrined in and protected by international instruments such as the CRA remains a huge concern. NGO accounts of rights practices show that they often do not address how women relate to laws and the effect these laws have on their perception of rights. Furthermore, not enough is even known about the notions of rights being used by NGOs.

The international and the internal

Different groups also take different positions on the extent to which the establishment of rights must be an internal, organic process, and on the forms that such a process should take. Bilkisu Yusuf, President of the Federation of Muslim Women Associations of Nigeria (FOMWAN) argues that, in Islamic family law as historically constructed and constituted, there are well defined notions of rights which are different from rights that are stated in the constitution. These rights are 'reformable' but such reforms can only come from within the Islamic legal system.[15] Her view is supported by Iman, who disagrees with some of the ways in which the role of international solidarity around women's rights have been portrayed. She states that:

> While international solidarity is important to local rights struggles, and campaigns...the international media and protests have largely ignored the existence of dissent among Muslims, and have downplayed the existence of protests and campaigns enacted within Nigeria.

Pereira also argues that there has been an oppressive denial of the diversity of thought in the development of Muslim laws.[16] She recounts the ways in which the penal code for northern Nigeria was passed after much consultation with diverse ethnic and religious groups in the region, an important departure from the way in which the expansion of the jurisdiction of the Shar'ia Court of Appeal beyond family and personal status law has been achieved. The penal code process was also open to international influences, and many aspects were adopted from similar legislation in India and Pakistan. This process suggests that there is indeed scope for what Iman terms the constant reconstruction of international treaty rights to enable local people to claim them and/or have them respected by their local culture.[17]

132

Many interest groups and actors involved in rights advocacy come from being leaders of NGOs or bureaucrats committed to the pursuit of rights. Within this group of leaders some operate at the international level, while most remain at the national/local level or both. Wherever they find themselves, there remains a spatial distance between the international actors and the local, with each unable to fully respond to the other. This separation gives scope for divergence in action and views which creates space for the kind of opposition associated with the CRA to materialise. At the same time people working on the same issues find themselves positioned on different sides of an argument.

For negotiations at the international level to be useful and able to influence the reform of state laws, better ways of reaching agreement have to be worked out. For instance, many intermediary organisations working on Muslim laws responded differently to the Amina Lawal case and it took a lot of time before any of them worked together. Even then, groups such as Baobab for Women Rights and Women's Rights and Protection Alternative (WRAPA) had a different approach from that of FOMWAN or the Muslim Sisters Organisation. Amnesty International (AI) had a different approach again: when Amina Lawal was convicted of adultery in March 2002, AI made a statement describing the punishment as cruel, inhuman and degrading—a statement that FOMWAN, for example, could not have made.

Such have been the differences in strategy and in the organisations' conversation around rights and power. Some agreements were also reached, however, between faith-based organisations such as FOMWAN, on the one side, and women's rights groups such as Baobab and WRAPA, on the other, to work together in prosecuting some cases in court. As a minimum basis for action, both groups agreed that international instruments were important and should be adhered to. Baobab was less supportive of using state-centred approaches, working more to animate reactions from the public sphere where NGOs and other interested constituencies could act. Nevertheless, Baobab and Amnesty International signed a statement in 2002 stating that:

> By ratifying the Convention Against Torture in June 2001, the Federal Republic of Nigeria has decided to bind itself not to apply such punishments. Since 2000, amputation and flogging have been carried out in several states of northern Nigeria...

The way groups have reacted to the CRA can usefully be traced to their histories and origins. The UN Decade for Women (1975–85) and the period thereafter produced a lot of issues which are important in describing the positionality of groups today. For instance, under the military, elite women and wives of military leaders 'working' for the advancement of women adopted a style which allowed them to access the resources of the state. Some of their notions conflicted with more populist views of rights but, through their proximity to the state, they were able to undervalue other forms of agitation for substantive rights. One of the programmes of a first lady, the Family Advancement and Empowerment Programme (FEAP), promoted women's empowerment only where it was linked to the advancement of families (in this case the family support was determined by the husband). Feminists' organisations such as Women in Nigeria (WIN) rejected this approach, and turned to developing and canvassing their own notions of rights.

As a result, by the end of military rule in 1999, competing meanings and notions of rights had emerged, many of which, including WIN's, did incorporate the issue of equality. For some other groups equality was less fundamental and not necessarily a requirement for the achievement of development opportunities for girls and boys. Reform from within the *shar'ia* was also emphasised in rights language: Bilikisu Yusuf, the Amira of FOMWAN stated that:

> The various Islamic groups should organise seminars, workshop etc to educate the people so that they know their rights and are capable of analysing issues and making balanced judgement on Shar'ia. The SCSN should work with the Federation of Muslim Women's Associations in Nigeria FOMWAN and its over 500 affiliates nationwide and other civil society organisations to build awareness of Muslim women on their rights under the Shar'ia.

Disagreements amongst women's groups around the nature and content of rights should not exclusively be framed as obstacles, however, for they have allowed the varying discourses and strategies for the realisation of rights to emerge. The challenge now is how to move forward on the implementation of rights; how to struggle for rights in ways that encompass and stimulate social action; and how to use the logic of rights-based approaches to respond to different interpretations. In other words, the challenge for the domestication and effectiveness of the CRC lies in finding strategies that work.

Strategies for realising rights and working on equality

Legal options

Resort to legal action can be useful but slow and time consuming. In January 2005 the official interaction with the 38th Session of the Committee on the Rights of the Child reported that only four out of 36 states had passed the Child Rights law, and another 20 were in the process of enacting it. They noted that the remaining 12 were yet to indicate when they would address the law. These figures show some level of acceptance of the Act but also foretell the need to pressurise others to act. Action is particularly needed in the light of the alternative report to the committee, which states that

> OMCT and CLEEN are deeply concerned about the situation of children in Nigeria, in particular, that children are at a high risk to be subject to various forms of abuse and cruel, inhuman, or degrading treatment and punishment.[18]

134

The implementation of the CRA,[19] where it has been enacted, has also been largely ineffectual. Apart from work by NGOs in the area of child education, not much else has happened. Nevertheless, courts and judges have an important role to play in implementation, by providing and compelling certain unambiguous interpretations of actions and/or laws in order to settle the messy business of multiple legal systems.

Within the *shar'ia* legal system, both better information and reform remain important strategies. Clear accounts of the meaning of *shar'ia* law are sometimes elusive: Pereira analyses the offence of *Zina* in the Amina Lawal case and notes that there is a distance between the legal view of the offence and the common sense understanding of *Zina*. Consequently, she makes a case for people to be properly informed about the transgressive nature of laws. Reform of *shar'ia* also has many proponents: the Honourable Saudatu Sani (Chair of the House of Representatives Committee on Women Affairs and Youth Development) argues for legislative solutions that are accommodative of other legal systems. She said:

> I am a Muslim and I will never be a party to anything that will allow the Islamic legal System to be abused. I agree that the Islamic legal system is protective of the child: it supports the family system. But I will not allow myself to use culture to dehumanize the child.[20]

As a result, she thinks that the passage of the Act in northern states should be 'subject to the provisions of Shar'ia law which not being fully settled in terms of case law is reformable'. Proponents of *shar'ia* law reform will have to make their case loudly and clearly, though, in the face of strong opposition like that expressed by Dr Ibrahim Datti Ahmed (President of the Supreme Council of Shar'ia in Nigeria). He sees the CRA as 'a conspiracy against Islam . . . and a direct attack on Islam and . . . no Muslim will obey this law. It doesn't matter who passes it'.[21]

With this in mind it seems likely that proponents of reform will need to take into account ways of linking or referencing it to international human rights laws. It remains difficult to see how this can be achieved if the reform is completely alienated from human right treaties.

Public institutions and deliberation

There is also a need to look beyond the law and its implementation to the role of public sphere institutions in transforming and diffusing public opinion, and creating spaces in which public deliberation can contribute to administrative decision making. Building local institutions that provide counter discourses on issues of rights, and can generate debates within local communities, may be key to addressing local power structures. According to Iman:

> using local structures and mechanisms (as a means of resisting retrogressive laws or interpretations of laws and the forces behind them) is the priority. It strengthens local counter-discourses and often carries greater legitimacy than

135

'outside' pressure. Further, it can really address the local political power struggles that are behind the political use of religions and ethnicities in Nigeria.[22]

Politicising the private sphere

Meanwhile, mutual rights and obligations between husband and wife in particular, and family members in general, cannot be treated as mere private concerns of individual marriage partners but are ones which the Islamic and other communities have vested interests in. Many sections of the Islamic community recognise their interest in reviewing and building upon these relations.[23] This recognition means that, while the context of human rights can be challenged by those who claim to speak for Islam, there are alternative ways of pushing for change.

Research

Making the Act effective and accepted calls for a lot more research into understanding the various actors and locations, their religious and cultural contexts and identifying approaches for domesticating rights which will work in these different contexts. Where there continues to be resistance, new approaches are required which can only come from new knowledge along with the application of progressive interpretations of religion and culture.

Resolving conflict

The Nigerian Constitution places an obligation on the state to protect cultural and religious rights, but this does not mean that all practices associated with culture and religion should be protected as rights. Even in the present instance where the constitution has created courts for customary and religious norms, what amounts to a right under these varying contexts can be contested. For example, although there is a religion or culture which permits child marriages, there is nevertheless a legitimate need to question how this affects the child and to investigate whether gender gaps are being reinforced. If they are, the two interpretations of the law are in contention and determining whether to allow or disallow a particular cultural or religious norm will be the subject of inquiry and legal test. Questions of the proper limitations that must be placed on the exercise of cultural and religious rights when they conflict with other human rights will inevitably arise. In the presence of some demonstrable harm, individuals and groups are entitled to demand that cultural or religious practices are set aside and interventions to protect the affected initiated.

Remaining questions

The CRA case study shows that, although supportive legislation can achieve the promotion of rights, it can also lead to a disconnection between the exercise of rights, their realisation and the promotion of greater gender justice based on the notion of equality. While international instruments such as the CRC provide a rigorous process for ascertaining rights and a framework for applying them, within the plural legal system that exists in Nigeria their progress cannot be straightforward. As a result, the domestication of the CRC has raised many issues and presented huge challenges for those working to make rights realisable. The intervention of NGOs, activists, advocates and others has created space for active discussion and for society at large to be heard. This will probably influence how decisions are made and enable the public sphere to become the arena for resolving the contested definition of rights.

Within Nigeria the choices for feminists and rights-based advocates are several but the outcomes remain largely uncertain. Many questions remain unanswered and unexplored: what are good rights-based practices arising from the domestication of an international human rights framework? What are the criteria for assessing the success of such approaches in the future? Put another way, what will be the value of promoting international human rights for boys and girls if this will not result in equality? Since the CRC aims to achieve equality, should it omit to canvass equality or will this have consequences for the ultimate realisation of the CRC itself? In assessing rights-based approaches under the CRA is there a balance between cultural and religious relativism and human rights effectiveness?

Ultimately the lesson that emerges from this case is that, for international human rights treaties to make a difference to vulnerable groups such as children, they have to go beyond being evoked and advocated by groups to become tools for political action, which also means the creation of mechanisms that challenge powerful agents in society and compel accountability by states.

Notes

1 UNICEF/Federal Government of Nigeria, *Children's and Women's Rights in Nigeria: A Wake-up Call— A Situation Assessment and Analysis*, 2001. This analysis is in keeping with the historical context of gender inequality across all sections of the Nigerian population.
2 A Iman, *Northern Nigeria Women's Reproductive and Sexual Rights and the Offence of Zina in Muslim Laws in Nigeria*, 2006, at www.pambazuka.org.
3 UNICEF, quoted in Integrated Regional Information Networks (IRIN), *Nigeria: Focus on the Challenge of Enforcing Children's Rights*, November 2002, at http://www.irinnews.org/.
4 SL Sanusi, 'Discourses, subjectivities and family law in Nigeria', paper presented at the International Conference on Muslim Family Law in sub-Saharan Africa, Centre for Contemporary Islam, University of Cape Town, 11–14 March 2002, argues that the radical departure in the implementation of *shar'ia* in parts of northern Nigeria is the latest manifestation of the neo-fundamentalist project. The project has an overt political religious agenda of a 'return to Islam'.
5 Reported in *This Day* newspaper as 'Nigeria: Shar'ia Council against Child Rights Act', 21 August 2005.
6 Ideals of the indivisibility and universality of rights.
7 Report of a two-day workshop on Child's Rights Act Advocacy and the Nigeria Movement for Children organised by the Akwa Ibom State Social Mobilization and Technical Committee, at http://www.akwaibomstategov.com/edit2-2.asp?ID=1106.
8 IRIN, 26 August 2002. Also in F:\ecoi_net - Focus countries » Nigeria » Current Issues (Shar'ia).txt.
9 OMCT–CLEEN Foundation, 'Report on the implementation of the Convention on the Rights of the Child by Nigeria', prepared for the Committee on the Rights of the Child, 38th Session, Geneva, January 2005.
10 Iman, *Northern Nigeria Women's Reproductive and Sexual Rights*.
11 OMCT–CLEEN Foundation, 'Report on the implementation of the Convention'.

12 The rights guaranteed include the right to life (Sec 33); the right to personal liberty (Sec 35); the right to a fair hearing (Sec 36) and the right to freedom of movement (Sec 41). Section 42 prohibits unjustifiable discrimination on the basis of 'ethnic group, place of origin, sex, religion or political opinion'.

13 Press release of the Committee on the Elimination of All Forms of Discrimination against Women following its 637th and 638th meetings.

14 There is a lot of justification for this law but its attempt to keep girls in school for as long as possible subtly supports the views expressed. There is wide gender disparity in Nigeria's literacy rate, with the UNDP *Human Development Report* reporting literacy rates of 62.5% for men and 37.5% for women. J Suara, 'Gendered minorities in Nigeria: a review of the educational status of women', in M Abba & M Kanu (eds), *Education of the Disadvantaged Groups in Nigeria: Challenges for Universal Basic Education*, Conference Proceedings, Yola, 2000, p 25.

15 B Yusuf, 'Women and empowerment in Islam', *Weekly Trust*, 13 December 2002.

16 Pereira is the National Co-ordinator of the Network for Women's Studies in Nigeria. C Pereira, 'Zina and transgressive heterosexuality in northern Nigeria', *Feminist Africa, Sexual Culture*, 5, 2005, at http://www.pambazuka.org.

17 Iman, *Northern Nigeria Women's Reproductive and Sexual Rights*.

18 OMCT–CLEEN Foundation, 'Report on the implementation of the convention'.

19 Some states, particularly in the southern parts of the country, have gone ahead with integrating the CRA into their state laws but, with the obstacles listed, their application is nominal and therefore unable to make a significant impact on the other parts of the country.

20 *Weekly Trust*, 10–16 September 2005.

21 *Ibid.*

22 Letter circulated by Baobab for Women's Rights, an NGO, calling for caution by international rights groups and sympathisers campaigning against a sentence of death by stoning on a woman found to have committed adultery by a *shar'ia* court in northern Nigeria.

23 Centre for Islamic Legal Studies, Ahmadu Bello University and DFID, 'Nigeria's security, justice and growth programme: promoting women's rights through Shar'ia in northern Nigeria', mimeo, 2005.

Rights and Realities: limits to women's rights and citizenship after 10 years of democracy in South Africa

MARY HAMES

> In order for the rights and freedoms embodied in constitutions to be realised, they must become a part of the everyday reality of citizen's lives, and the institutions protecting them must be deeply entrenched. (Nelson Mandela, in the foreword to the National Action Plan)[1]

This chapter takes a critical look at the institutions put in place by the South African state to support the promise of the 1996 South African Constitution, and at how they have promoted or protected women's rights. In doing so, it problematises the meaning of liberal citizenship for black women who live in poverty in South Africa. It asks how these paper rights can be translated into more substantive gains for women, and to what extent the women to whom rights are accorded in the constitution actually understand and exercise these rights.

The currency of citizenship in South Africa was for decades located in the right to vote and remained the privilege of white males. White women were given the right to vote in 1930, while policies that sought to control influx to cities and towns forced black women to carry passbooks as a form of identity document. From 1913 onwards black women orchestrated protests in opposition to carrying passbooks, as this severely impeded their freedom of movement and their rights as citizens of the country. 1994 was therefore a watershed year in more ways than one when all women were afforded the right to vote and to become 'equal' citizens. Since 1994 South Africa has been signatory to numerous international and regional agreements and conventions. The government has to report on a regular basis to these bodies on progress made towards eradicating inequalities, social injustices and violence, and on efforts made to level the playing field.

The 1996 South African Constitution gave women unprecedented rights. For the first time in the country's history all women were legally regarded as equal citizens at all levels. The liberal democracy and constitutional mechanisms that have been introduced over the past decade aim to be inclusive in redressing previously discriminating and harmful practices against marginalised groups. One of the groups specifically targeted for redress through new non-discriminatory mechanisms was the women of South Africa. However, many of the new laws fail to acknowledge how women in different race groups are differently privileged, dealing with them as if their lived experiences were homogeneous.[2] Black African women, in particular, have historically been the most marginalised, and inequalities continue. According to the research done by the Gender Advocacy Programme (GAP):

> Black women generally tend to have fewer opportunities for education, employment, economic and political participation, etc. In addition, class and cultural differences intersect with race and gender distinctions, making it more problematic to simply distinguish between black and white women, as if these are at least uniform categories.[3]

This chapter questions the notion of the equality of citizenship for all women. Gouws argues that the liberal model of rights presumes 'equality on the grounds of sameness between women and men and between women'.[4] She goes on to show that differences are often ignored because 'liberalism constructs a unified/universal political subject'.[5] The contradictions between the liberal rights discourse and the lived experiences of many South African women's lives form the central focus of the chapter. It begins with an account of the policies and laws that were introduced in an attempt to eradicate and redress past inequalities. It then sets the context for the analysis that is to follow in the lived realities of the majority of black women in the Cape Town region. It goes on to explore how black women living in a peri-urban area of Cape Town understand, express and experience these rights and realities, drawing on insights from a series of workshops that highlight the significance of issues of race, class and language.

Measures for gender equality in the New South Africa

The 1996 South African Constitution affirmed the responsibility of the state to ensure women's socioeconomic and political equality. This is entrenched in the supreme law of the country. Section 9 (3) of the constitution states:

> The state may not unfairly discriminate directly or indirectly against anyone on one or more grounds, including race, gender, sex, pregnancy, marital status, ethnic or social origin, colour, sexual orientation, age, disability, religion, conscience, belief, culture, language and birth.[6]

The constitution also makes provision for the creation of 'gender machinery' in order to affect the Bill of Rights. The 'gender machinery' is commonly referred to as the Chapter Nine institutions and includes, among others, the Public Protector, the Human Rights Commission, the Commission for Gender Equality (CGE) and the Electoral Commission. These constitutional mechanisms proved to be insufficient to ensure that gender inequalities were effectively eradicated. Consequently, the government proceeded to promulgate subsidiary legislation. 'Gender equality' was even further entrenched as a rights-based concern. Over the course of the 1990s 'gender mainstreaming' became the operating method through which the state increasingly became the custodian of 'women's concerns'.

A variety of legal instruments and mechanisms came to be created as measures for ensuring women's equality. This rights-based approach was premised on the assumption that *all* women could seek legal recourse when their rights were violated. Such legal mechanisms included the Constitutional Court, the Equality Court, the Commission for Conciliation, Mediation and Arbitration (CCMA), special Family Courts and labour courts. A national Office on the Status of Women (OSW) was established and located in the Office of the Deputy President. The OSW was mandated to draw up a National Gender Policy. Another function of the OSW is the monitoring of state policies with regard to women and gender within the different government ministries and departments.

The Office on the Status of Women is emulated in the different provincial structures, and the different 'gender focal points' in the departments have to ensure that issues of gender equality are observed. The monitoring body in parliament is the Joint Committee on Improvement of Quality of Life and Status of Women. This Joint Committee's primary function is to ensure that the Convention on the Elimination of All Forms of Discrimination Against Women (CEDAW) and the Beijing Platform of Action are implemented. It also monitors procedures, policies and checks on legislation as they are conceptualised and manifested within parliament, and conducts open hearings where civil society is invited to submit either oral or written submissions.

The South African government has also promulgated a myriad of progressive laws to ensure that proactive measures are taken to protect women's constitutional rights. Labour laws are especially 'women sensitive' and give those women who are 'gainfully employed' special protection. For instance, the Labour Act of 1995 includes a Code of Good Conduct that compels workplaces to have formal sexual harassment policies in place; the

Basic Conditions of Employment Act ensures that there is a minimum requirement for maternity leave which includes ante-natal, post-natal and family responsibility leave; the Employment Equity Act includes women as a special category, as candidates for affirmative action employment; and the Skills Development Act ensures that women, as previously disadvantaged workers, receive education and training in an effort to gain the necessary skills. The Basic Conditions of Employment Act makes provision for minimum leave (maternity and vacation), minimum wages, housing and health care for previously excluded groups of women, such as domestic and farm workers, who were never regarded as part of formal employment.

Other 'women sensitive' policies and legal provisions include the Basic Child Support Grant, which gives financial support to children up to the age of 14. Another important policy gives all pregnant women and children up to the age of six years free health care. The Maintenance Act of 1998, in theory, compels both partners to financially support their children. It further makes allowance for the employer to deduct money from a parent's salary or wages in order to contribute financially to the support of the child/children. The Domestic Violence Act (DVA) of 1998 is an example of a law that is particularly proactive in its defence of women's rights to bodily integrity and freedom from violence. The definition of domestic relationships is broad and includes relationships irrespective of marriage, as well as same-sex partners, parents or persons having parental responsibility, family members related by blood, affinity or adoption, people in a romantic or sexual relationship, including dating or a customary relationship, and people who have recently shared a home. The DVA also places responsibility and obligation on the police to assist survivors of domestic violence. It further states that members of the South African Police Service who do not comply with the obligations set out will be disciplined. The Act also regards stalking, harassment and intimidation as offences. It includes emotional, physical, verbal and economic abuse.

Legislation on sexual and reproductive rights has been especially progressive, and ground-breaking in relation to other African countries. The Choice on the Termination of Pregnancy Act 1996 recognises the right to the bodily integrity of women and allows for early, legal and safe abortions. The preamble to the Act makes it clear that is it the state's responsibility not only to provide reproductive health care but also to provide safe conditions under which the right of choice can be exercised without fear or harm. It also permits the girl child to terminate unwanted pregnancy without the permission of the parent. Another important constitutional provision is the inclusion of the right to sexual orientation. South Africa is the only country in Africa where homosexual partnerships and the right to sexual orientation are constitutionally recognised and protected. Other socioeconomic and political rights for same-sex partners have been slowly gained through protracted litigation processes. Some of these rights include the right to a partner's medical and pension benefits, the right to adopt children as same-sex partners and immigration rights for same-sex partners. Currently 1 December 2006 is set aside for the legal recognition of same-sex marriage.

Rights and realities

Over the past decade women's and feminist issues have increasingly become the responsibility of the state. Although initially advocated by feminists, the application of 'gender mainstreaming' has become increasingly problematic. The liberal gender paradigm of 'gender mainstreaming' has rendered the vibrant and radical South African women's movement passive and increasingly receptive to 'state feminism'. As Gouws notes, the institutionalisation of feminist demands within the state meant that discursive spaces were created within which 'gender' became the operative term to deal with 'women's issues'.[7] Women's and gender issues have come to be dealt with in a very technocratic manner.

Although juridical political inequalities have been removed on paper, the fact remains that the economic and social injustices have to a large extent remained deeply entrenched within the broader societal framework.[8] The intention of the progressive laws was to open up legal space for women, but custom and tradition still offer barriers to efficaciousness. There are certain anomalies within the constitution itself that contradict the substance of 'gender equality'. One of the most obvious is the recognition of traditional leaders in Chapter 12. According to Nhlapo, this recognition compromises gender equality, as traditional leadership remains the domain of 'unelected, usually male, senior members of cultural or linguistic groups'.[9] This, he argues, contributes to the unequal status of women as 'traditional powers and authority' remain entrenched in the patriarchal sphere.[10] The authority and power of traditional leaders are reflected in access to land, especially in rural areas. The patriarchal culture of domination and inherited legislation on allocation of land resources prohibits women's claims to property, residential rights and land use. These laws particularly affect black women in rural areas, where traditional authorities to a large extent still control communal land. Customs and customary practices still exclude women from the right to own, inherit or profit from land.[11]

The Basic Conditions of Employment Act and the unions that have surfaced in the past decade are indications of the considerable scope that economically vulnerable women have to pursue their rights in the 'new South Africa'. The Act has made it possible, for example, for farm workers to organise and form unions. But this scope presupposes powers, authority and confidence that many women simply do not have. Domestic work remains one of the most racialised, gendered and exploitative forms of 'employment' in the country. The majority of employers exploit their workers' dependence and basic need for employment at any cost. Workers continue to be often employed without contracts, for example, and many employers are able to avoid complying with the Act entirely. Koen illustrates this, observing that trafficking in people includes trafficking in women as domestic workers in the Western Cape, their desperation for a reasonable livelihood making them comply with employment practices that border on slavery.[12] Labour laws are only effective in as far as women are formally employed; because the majority of black women are located in employment that effectively remains outside this category, they do not have access to most of this liberal legislation.

Further challenges for realising women's rights arise in respect of 'women-friendly' provisions. The Basic Child Support Grant is a case in point. The allocated amount per child is currently only R170 per month. Women's organisations are consistently arguing that both the amount and the ages of the 'children' should be increased. Fester notes in this regard that, although the move to institutionalise the Basic Child Support Grant was led by a feminist minister and advised by a team of 'women-friendly' researchers, social scientists and bureaucrats, the outcome of the grant is not sufficient to redress poor women's circumstances.[13] Similar concerns arise in respect of the provision made by the 1998 Maintenance Act. A study commissioned by the Commission for Gender Equality found that, six years after its implementation, many women were still experiencing major obstacles in accessing the maintenance payouts, ranging from unco-operative respondents to an unfriendly if not gender-biased system.[14] An analysis of the court proceedings also found that 98% of the respondents were men. The study further found that those claiming maintenance from the partner/ex-partner often reported high levels of domestic violence.

Levels of gender violence remain appallingly high, despite the enabling legislation put in place by the Domestic Violence Act. Concerns have arisen among feminist activists that funding is increasingly being directed to men's movements, to the detriment of women's organisations. Gertrude Fester draws attention to some of these concerns, mentioning as an example that the organisation Men as Partners received funding to the amount of R500 000, in comparison with the R200 000 received by the Network of Violence Against Women, an umbrella organisation that has over 300 affiliated organisations in the Western Cape.[15]

South Africa's enabling constitutional provisions and progressive legislation may have opened up avenues for women to seek their rights, but prevailing societal norms continue to present significant barriers to the deeper structural change that is needed if women are to realise these rights. In the current political climate the prospect of securing the promise of these rights is further imperilled by reactionary societal forces that are finding resonance within the political system. A case in point is the contentious programme launched by government, and which has now become part of the nation-building vision: the Moral Regeneration Movement (MRM). The MRM promotes abstinence and proposes that girls should remain virgins until marriage, using patriarchal family values as its point of departure. It originated in a meeting between President Nelson Mandela and key South African religious leaders in June 1997.[16] A 'Moral Summit' took place in the following year, attended by religious, political, business and traditional leaders. During 2002 various programmes were conducted that endorsed faith-based overtures, including religious parliaments, Days of Prayer and Moral Regeneration Rallies, and a project to promote sexual abstinence by a Christian faith organisation. The first annual conference took place in 2004. All government departments are expected to adhere to the implementation of this programme, which is chaired by and monitored from the deputy president's office. The discourse of the programme is overwhelmingly heteronormative, and it makes deeply conservative assumptions about women's sexuality and role in society.

The contradictions of the Moral Regeneration Programme emerged most acutely in the developments that took place over the course of 2005 which implicated the then Deputy President, Jacob Zuma, in rape charges, and led to his suspension and recent trial, and to the continuing investigation into charges of corruption. During his period as chair of the MRM the former deputy president made public statements to endorse his and the government's commitment to the eradication of corruption and particularly violence against women. These included the statement that:

> We all speak in one voice in denouncing such things as violence, corruption and rape of our mothers, children and infants, beating our partners and wives, and exploitation of the poor.[17]

Although he was eventually acquitted of the rape accusation, the rape trial itself has generally been regarded as problematic for the advancement of women's concerns. Feminists and gender activists are of the opinion that the trial was conducted in an atmosphere of misogyny.[18] Gqola and others, for instance, question the fact that the judge allowed the sexual history of the accused to play such a prominent role; that the dress code of the accuser was used as a 'weapon' by the accused and the defence; and that culture was used in an ugly and oppressive manner against African women.[19]

The Zuma trial proceedings reversed the advances that women have made by 11 years. Stereotypes of women, their sexuality, their sexual orientation and their bodily integrity, and stereotypical perceptions about women's position in society surfaced during the trial. The paradoxical nature of progressive laws, on the one hand, and the conservative nature of the court system and the remaining archaic laws, on the other hand, exemplify some of the barriers to the advancement of women's rights that remain in South Africa. The verdict also emphasised the urgency of the repeal of the outdated Sexual Offences Act (Act 23, 1957), which discriminates against women in various ways. What becomes clear is that measures for protecting women's bodily rights and integrity coexist with discourses that continue to position women as passive sexual subjects, or to demonise their sexuality.

These contradictions are compounded by the multiple obstacles faced by South African women in gaining the opportunity to exercise their entitlements. Reasonable access to the legal mechanisms that exist presupposes some knowledge of the rights as laid out in the constitution. Access implies *all* women have the time, energy and finances to pursue their rights. In reality, however, even where women are able to go as far as seeking legal recourse, most legal procedures take a very long time before justice and legal remedies are awarded. The legal language, court procedures, court dates, and long distances to and from the physical legal structures are some of the deterring factors that ultimately make seemingly progressive mechanisms inaccessible for many women. For many poorer South African women, however, there are more entrenched barriers still to realising their rights: awareness that these rights exist and that they are in a position to claim them. As I go on to explore, through the example of a series of workshops held with black women living in poverty in the Western Cape, the yawning gap between the rights South African women hold on paper and their opportunities for realising them present a complex set of challenges for making these rights real.

Challenges for realising gender equality: the case of the Western Cape

Since the first democratic election in 1994 the Western Cape has been one of two provinces out of nine where it is very difficult for the ruling African National Congress (ANC) to get an outright majority vote. The province has always had a turbulent political history and this may in part be ascribed to the legacy of apartheid. Up to the mid-1980s 'coloured people' received privileged opportunities to live and work in the province. Since then the Coloured Labour Preference Act has become obsolete and the right to work in this province has become much more relaxed. With the dawn of the new democracy, the former Bantustans were abolished.[20] The Cape metropole became the place of preference for people who were looking for employment. However, the provision of adequate housing for all did not match the pace of urbanisation.

Before the abolition of the Coloured Labour Preference Act only three townships were built for 'Africans'. The larger percentage of low-cost, high-density housing, which became more popular when the Group Areas Act was enforced, was developed to accommodate the 'coloured' population. During the peak of apartheid other 'race groups' had to apply for formal permits to enter 'African' townships. The apartheid architects operated from the principle of divide and rule and townships were developed either close to industrial sites or along railway lines or major roads away from the central business and white residential areas. There were separate but unequal amenities developed for each of the race groups.

After the first democratic elections new informal settlements—also referred to as 'shanty towns' or 'squatter camps'—mushroomed overnight. Shacks were built consisting of wood, plastic and iron. Settlements were named by the residents after the political leaders in the new democracy—Mandela, Tambo, Joe Slovo. Sometimes they had names that reflected the destitute and helpless situation of those who lived there: Witsand (White Sands: a place where the wind endlessly blows to form white sand dunes), Bloekombos (Eucalyptus Bush) and Vrygrond (Free Land: land occupied without having to pay rates and taxes). In some of these informal settlements electricity and sanitation, in the form of outside toilets and communal water taps, were provided. From 1994 onwards low-cost housing was built under the auspices of the then Reconstruction and Development Programme (RDP). However, the rate at which these 'match box' houses were constructed was not fast enough to meet existing housing demand or the influx resulting from rapid urbanisation. These houses tended to be built outside the 'formal' towns or next to existing townships. The locals refer to these housing developments as 'Smartie Towns' because they look like coloured sweets from a distance. There are currently 156 informal settlements in and around the city. It is estimated that between 20 000 and 30 000 new families enter the urban area per annum. Many of the new immigrants are poor, originate from one of the poorest provinces, namely the Eastern Cape, and are isiXhosa speaking; like other residents in low-income areas, their education levels are low, they are mostly unemployed, and they come to compete with existing residents for housing as well as for jobs.

In 2005 the Social Services Division of the Cape Metropolitan Council approached the Gender Equity Unit (GEU) at the University of the Western Cape to conduct a series of workshops with regard to 'women's rights' and to explore the gains that women had made under the new dispensation.[21] These workshops were an opportunity to deconstruct the meaning and value of citizenship to marginalised women who were not in a position legally to contest their constitutional rights or whose main interest was mainly to make a living in hostile socioeconomic environments. Held in areas where the socioeconomic conditions described here prevail, the workshops took place over a period of one month and participants numbered between 25 and 45 women per session, all of whom were black and the majority of whom were unemployed. The following discussion explores what the GEU was to learn about these women's lives and about what they understood of the rights they had gained since 1994.

Exploring women's lived experiences and needs

The workshops were designed using a standard format, using the constitution with the Bill of Rights as the primary resource tool. The facilitators were not provided with profiles of the participants and therefore had no clue what the education level or the socioeconomic positions of these women were. The only common factors in the groups were that all the women were black and the majority were unemployed: the groups were otherwise very mixed. It became evident early on that using liberal rights language as a starting point for the workshop would make little sense; many participants had very low levels of education, and diversity of culture, language and religion within the groups posed challenges for communication and learning. Some of the participants have never left their respective townships and some did not even have identity documents. Others were new arrivals from the Eastern Cape and could only speak Xhosa, others could only speak Afrikaans. A number had never voted because they did not have any identification documents; only one had ever left the country. Their ages ranged from 17 to 70. In some of the groups there were very young women who had left school in grade three and could hardly read. Other groups included one or two retired nurses or teachers, indicating class differences.

It was therefore very difficult to negotiate priorities, especially when it came to interpreting a language of rights that is alien to the lived experiences of some of the participants. The truth in the statement by Yuval-Davis found echo in the approach to the meaning of citizenship in this context when we had to look at the concept in a 'multi-tier construct which applied to the women's membership in a variety of collectives—local, ethnic and national'.[22] Subsequently it was decided to conduct participative workshops, where specific rights would be deconstructed and reconstructed in an effort to make provision for the level of understanding, language differences and to work with women's lived experiences.

Lister argues that in contemporary theorisations of citizenship the argument arises that there is a notion of autonomy or the ability to determine the conditions of one's life and to pursue one's life projects.[23] However, it was clear that the participants in these workshops did not have that luxury and could ill-afford such notions. One immediate indication of this was the evidence of women's having responsibilities which made their workshop attendance extremely difficult in the first place. At one of the workshops two women brought their babies (one of whom was one month old) with them as there was nobody at home to take care of them. At another workshop one of the women fetched her child after normal school hours as she could not afford after-care. The child remained at the back of the hall for the remainder of the workshop. Even getting to the workshop was difficult for some: at many of the venues the workshops started late because participants were picked up at central points far from their homes which they had to walk to, setting out early in the morning (as early as four o'clock). For some, the workshop primarily meant being able to eat for the day. The early tea served at the workshops was in many instances their first meal of the day.

During the workshops it became apparent that another crucial impediment to women's using the available mechanisms for claiming their rights concerned their lack of basic literacy, a legacy of many years of inferior education stemming from gender, racial and class discrimination. Although there was only one woman who could not read or write, only two women had some form of higher education. For example, at one workshop a number of women returned home and came back with their identity books because they were under the impression that the advertised workshops would be offering employment. This showed their desperation for employment as well as their limited understanding of the dominant English language. They interpreted the concept 'workshop' as a place/shop where work is provided.

True to one of the basic human rights—*the right to be taught in your own language*—the workshops were conducted in the three official languages of the province. The issue of language proved to be very important, as many of the women could only speak and understand their mother tongue. At five out of the seven workshops the women started to dance and sing spontaneously, because some of them had never been in any kind of workshop, while others had never had facilitators who could translate their rights into a language that they fully understood. Some indicated that for the first time they understood what their rights were. At some of the workshops participants said that it was the first time that they understood what the constitution meant. Participants were allowed to speak and respond in the language that they were most comfortable in. For some of them it was the first time in their lives that they could express themselves, and many deeply appreciated the fact that the facilitators could speak their language.

In order for the facilitators to negotiate space for learning, emphasis was placed on the political rights and choices that every citizen could make with respect to forming or joining political parties. Although many of the women had a fair knowledge of what their rights were, they had no clue how all this connected with their rights as citizens. At all the workshops there were some women who occupied leadership positions within the local political party branches. These women tended to play the role of informal monitors of the process of the workshops, as well as unofficial spokespersons of the ruling party. The presence of these 'informal' political representatives tended to inhibit many of the women, who were not interested in formal politics. The Western Cape is well known for tensions that exist among the different political parties. It was therefore important to establish boundaries.

Although the facilitators' brief was to teach women about their rights, it became clear that the prevailing discourse in academic and political circles excluded a clear understanding of the lived realities of the participants. The facilitators decided to concentrate on those rights that specifically pertained to the everyday lives and needs of workshop participants. In an effort to establish their needs, the women were asked at the beginning of each workshop to share with the group their lived experiences: they shared their socioeconomic status, where they came from and what their expectations of the workshops were. Since many of the participants could only speak and understand one language, to enable them to participate fully it was necessary to translate the main concepts, which absorbed a large part of the time.

The focus of the workshop was on the Bill of Rights and especially on the equality clause, which has become the focus for many feminists, individuals and civil rights groups as a means of ensuring that the democratic values and principles of the constitution are upheld. Included in the Bill of Rights is the right to assembly, demonstration, picket and petition. However, none of the women saw the need to demonstrate or petition for their rights as they believed that the state would provide. Incidentally, during the period in which the workshops took place there was a series of demonstrations against non-service delivery throughout the country. It can be argued that these women were so marginalised and destitute that even marching for their rights was no option. Interesting factors that contributed to the absence of vocalising their right to demonstrate were the notions of nation-building, obedience and loyalty to the political party to which they belonged. Although the presence of political party representatives may have exacerbated participants' reluctance to air their grievances around taking part in strike action, it was clear that they were too scared to do so. It is also worth bearing in mind that these workshops were organised by the Social Services Division, which dampened the prospect of criticism given the dependency these women had on services provided by the state.

The issues that emerged from workshop discussions touched on all areas of women's everyday lives. The institutions of the state featured in all of these discussions; the stories that emerged spoke vividly not only to the shortcomings of state capacity to respond to the very real challenges affecting these women's lives, but also to the limits of 'rights' to affect these realities. All the women were concerned about the socioeconomic conditions in which they lived. Drug trafficking and drug use were among the most prominent concerns, which were attributed as major factors in the increase in sex work and violence in their areas. The prevalence of HIV and AIDS also remained a constant theme. In one of the workshops it was reported that food gardens and soup kitchens had been started so that the community members who were on medication, but unemployed, could enjoy at least one substantial meal per day. These services were provided on a voluntary basis by the women as community upliftment projects.

A large proportion of the women were new immigrants to the city, and many had left school early. Most lacked formal employment. Informal employment included selling fruit, sweets, cigarettes or meat on the street, caring for the family or neighbourhood children, and volunteering as care givers or street cleaners. Many of the women did not regard themselves as entrepreneurs, even those who they sold meat, sweets, cigarettes or fruit on the street. For them this was a means to provide for the family. The mainstream industries in the Western Cape are still largely owned by white men, and artisans and contractors are men. The traditional occupations and employment opportunities for black women in this region were in the leather and textile industries, as shop assistants and domestic workers. There are still very few women who have ventured into male-dominated occupations.

Participants who lived in informal settlements raised concerns about sanitation and access to health care. At one of the workshops, the residents of an informal area reported that their homes had burnt down months before and that the non-provision of proper sanitation since then was a major health risk. Some of the women who lived in council housing reported that they could not afford the maintenance and rent of the houses, because they were unemployed and had to pay both legal expenses incurred in being taking to court for non-payment and arrears. The lack of provision of adequate safety and security facilities, such as magistrates' courts and police stations, was mentioned. In the few circumstances in which formal complaints had been made, participants reported that they found the processes, attitudes and language hostile.

Domestic and other forms of violence were rife in many of the communities. The women wanted more mobile police stations and magistrates' courts, especially in areas where the community was rapidly growing. Court dates were deemed unrealistic. The judicial process was also seen as too slow. Participants expressed fears for the safety of their school-going children and young adults. A lack of parks and playgrounds was reported. According to a study done by the non-governmental organisation, Molo Songololo, on the vulnerability and sexual exploitation of children, it was found that there has been an increase in child pornography, child prostitution and the rape of young children. Some of the factors contributing to this state of affairs are poverty, unemployment, lack of effective social welfare support, high levels of domestic violence and an increased demand for children from local and foreign sex exploiters.[24]

Access to social security benefits was one of the biggest problems that the women experienced. Many of them were single parents and had no clue how to access the Child Maintenance Act or Child Grants. Some of the women who had recently moved to the city did not know where the social services departments were located, nor did they have extensive networks to help them gain access to social security. Access to day hospitals, clinics and other health-care facilities was a huge problem in all but one of the areas. Inequalities manifested themselves in different ways. It was obvious that these women often have to bear the brunt of care-taking responsibilities. Since most participants did not have formal employment, they did not have access to work-related benefits and had to rely on the public health care systems. Some reported that they had to get up as early as two o'clock in the morning to stand in the queue at the day hospitals that opened at seven o'clock. This did not guarantee that they would receive treatment, because there would always be patients waiting. With the advent of HIV and AIDS many of them have had to be responsible for unpaid home-based care of family members. The majority of the women had not heard of the Gender Commission or other gender mechanisms such as the Office of the Status of Women and could not see how these institutions could enhance the quality of their lives.

Conclusion

Reflecting on the proceedings of these workshops it was clear that that for the majority of black women even the notion of liberal citizenship is still a pipe dream. In spite of the progressive laws and the much celebrated gender machinery, these women were more interested in 'bread and butter' issues. As the workshops demonstrated, 'paper rights' have not yet been translated into 'substantive' rights for South African women, especially for those who have been subject to the historical disadvantage that is the legacy of apartheid. While much has been written about the marginalisation experienced by the rural poor, these workshops demonstrated just how acutely this margin-alisation is experienced by those who live in urban areas. For those who migrate to the city with the expectation of a better life, the realities of existence in urban informal settlements are those of extreme deprivation. Without an extended support system, living in contexts where crime and violence are a constant menace, where floods and fires threaten lives, and suffering from a chronic lack of employment, life for these women is exceptionally hard and hostile. Language barriers serve as further obstacles to seeking state support of any kind, including from the police and the judicial system.

The workshops opened up new challenges for feminist teaching, research and understanding of the knowledges and lived realities of women on the margins of society. They reminded us how little could be taken for granted about our constitutional rights and the machinery of legal mechanisms and formal institutions put in place to guarantee them. Manicom rightly argues that the inclusion of 'generic women's rights' is problematic because the different power modalities involved in racialised oppression, and the discrimination prevalent under customary law, increase existing inequalities among women.[25] Although the equality clause in the constitution took issues of marginalisation into account, it failed to elaborate on differences in societal perceptions. It is left to litigation to claim those rights. Efforts to make the legal system more accessible have included the establishment of the Family Court and the Equality Court, which are free, but marginalised groups experience a variety of other obstacles in gaining access to them, including their physical location and the fact that they are not fully operational because of under-resourcing.

Manicom frames a question that is of paramount importance in the South African context: how can this language of rights be translated into substantive civil, political and social rights where these different power modalities and such entrenched discrimination and gender inequalities exist?[26] This was an issue that was consistently raised during the workshops. How accessible are these rights when women do not know that they exist? When the laws and procedures are written in a legalistic language? When the structures are hostile and remote? When women do not have the financial means to access them? South Africa's rights-based constitution and its progressive legal framework grants everybody the opportunity—in principle—to access legal justice. This case is a poignant reminder of just how much addressing poverty and inequality matters if the rights that women are accorded as citizens are ever to be realised.

In the past few years feminists have become increasingly disillusioned with the role of the state. The under-resourced gender machinery institutions are in no position to adequately address women's needs and concerns. The appointment period for gender commissioners has been reduced to two from the original five years; more often than not these commissioners and gender focal point personnel are political appointees. It is indicative that there are currently no gender commissioners in post. A prominent feminist in parliament, Pregs Govender, recently left the government because of its stance towards HIV and AIDS and the bloated allocation to the Defence budget. Instead, women are increasingly organising outside the parameters of the state to raise awareness and have been consistently active in revitalising and mobilising civil society around women's concerns. This has been demonstrated by organisations such as Women on Farms in their 'Stop the Evictions Campaign' and the recent 'One in Nine' campaign spearheaded by People Opposing Women Abuse (POWA) and other organisations during the Zuma rape trial.

In conclusion, I want to reiterate the need to reassess the 'gender mainstreaming' approach and the role of the 'gender machinery'. I also want to underscore the importance of a robust women's movement that is separate from state interference and allegiance to party politics. The workshops discussed highlighted the contribution that can be made by feminist interventions and by understanding poverty, health, sexual violence and socioeconomic conditions. Policies and laws can only be meaningful and just if the most marginalised in society benefit. The gap between the rights that exist and the everyday realities of women that emerged from the workshops point to an urgent need for systematically restructuring the architecture of the existing 'women sensitive' laws so that these interventions ensure that substantive equity can take place, bringing meaningful change to ordinary women's lives. Only then can South Africa's 'paper rights' be made real.

Notes

1 *National Action Plan for the Protection and Promotion of Human Rights*, Houghton: Co-ordinating Committee on the National Action Plan, 1998.
2 The apartheid race classification had different race groups: African, coloured, Indian and white. The current classification divides the races into two broad categories: black (African, coloured, Indian) and white.
3 Gender Advocacy Programme (GAP), *Water and Sanitation in Smartietown: Looking at Municipal Service Delivery Transformation through a Gender Lens*, Cape Town: GAP, 1999.
4 A Gouws (ed), *(Un)thinking Citizenship: Feminist Debates in Contemporary South Africa*, Cape Town: University of Cape Town Press, 2005, p 4.
5 *Ibid.*
6 *Constitution of the Republic of South Africa*, 1996.
7 A Gouws, 'Gender mainstreaming and the politics of discourse construction', paper delivered at the Writing African Women: Poetics and Politics of African Gender Research conference, Bellville, University of the Western Cape, 19–22 January 2005, p 5.
8 K Bentley, 'Women's rights & the feminisation of poverty in South Africa', *Review of African Political Economy*, 100, 2004, pp 247–261; and M Szeftel, 'Two cheers? South African democracy's first decade', *Review of African Political Economy*, 100, 2004, pp 193–202.
9 T Nhlapo, 'Women's rights and the family in traditional and customary law', in S Bazilli (ed), *Putting Women on the Agenda*, Johannesburg: Ravan Press, 1991, pp 112–113.
10 *Ibid*, p 113.
11 S Meer (ed), *Women, Land and Authority: Perspectives from South Africa*, Cape Town: David Philips and Oxford: Oxfam, 1997.
12 K Koen, 'Production of feminist knowledge', paper delivered at the Feminist Intellectual Activism—Within and Beyond the Academy conference, Bellville, University of the Western Cape, 14–16 September 2005.
13 G Fester, 'State feminism', paper delivered at the Feminist Intellectual Activism—Within and Beyond the Academy conference, Bellville, University of the Western Cape, 14–16 September 2005.
14 Commission on Gender Equality, *Implementation of the Maintenance Act in the Magistrate's Courts*, 2004.
15 Fester, 'State feminism'.
16 J Rauch, 'Crime prevention and morality: the campaign for moral regeneration in South Africa', Monograph 114, April 2005, at http://www.iss.co.za/pubs/Monographs/No 114.pdf, accessed 22 May 2006.
17 Closing Address by Deputy President Jacob Zuma at the Moral Regeneration Summit, Waterkloof Airforce Base, Pretoria, 18 April 2002, at http://www.anc.org.za/ancdocs/history/zuma/2002/jz0418.htm.
18 Kerry Cullinan, former MP, resigned over AIDS denialism. See http://www.health-e.org.za/news/article.php, accessed 23 May 2006.
19 Pumla Dineo Gqola, 'Bleeding on the streets of South Africa', *Mail and Guardian*, 14 May 2006.
20 'Bantustans' were the areas designated as tribal 'homelands' for African South Africans during the apartheid era. See footnote 2 for racial classifications.
21 The GEU is the policy and activist arm of the University of the Western Cape, whose activities include developing and monitoring gender and race policies, training, lobbying and advocacy.
22 N Yuval-Davis, *Gender & Nation*, London: Sage, 1997, p 68.
23 R Lister, *Citizenship: Feminist Perspectives*, Basingstoke: Palgrave Macmillan, 2003.
24 K Koen, 'Children on the edge: strategies towards an integrated approach to combat child exploitation in South Africa', paper commissioned by WomensNet, 2005, at http://genderstats.org.za/documents/ChildSexExploit.doc, accessed 13 February 2006.
25 L Manicom, 'Constituting "women" as citizens: ambiguities in the making of gendered political subjects in post-apartheid South Africa', in Gouws, *(Un)thinking Citizenship*, p 35.
26 *Ibid.*

Is the Rights Focus the Right Focus? Nicaraguan responses to the rights agenda

SARAH BRADSHAW

Democracy and human rights moved up the international development agenda in the 1990s and became seen as a key characteristic of development priorities.[1] A wide range of actors has adopted a 'rights-based approach' to development, including the United Nations, the UK's Department for International Development (DFID) and non-governmental organisations (NGOs) working in the global South.[2] The potential of the rights approach for increasing recognition of women's demands as legitimate claims has made it particularly attractive to women's movements,[3] and has strengthened political efforts to advance women's agendas.[4] Some of the most effective organising over the past 25 years has been around rights-related claims, such as violence against women and sexual and reproductive rights.[5] The rights discourse has been said to provide the 'conceptual connection' that allows differing concerns to be consolidated under one thematic umbrella and this has produced a degree of stability within the global women's movement.[6] In turn, the use of rights discourse within women's movements has been seen to advance understandings of rights-based approaches.[7]

In contrast to this positive evaluation of rights-based approaches, others have taken a more critical stance.[8] The rise of rights has been seen as reflecting the institutionalisation and professionalisation of women's movements, a process linked to the dominance, during the 1990s, of the UN framework for determining women's rights.[9] This is also seen to correspond to ongoing concerns, at least within Latin America, about the 'NGO-isation' of the women's movements of the region.[10] Far from being viewed as a force for change the rights-based approach has been seen by some as depoliticising.[11]

What is meant by a rights-based approach has become a major analytical concern. The lack of an agreed definition has left the approach open to criticism and the suggestion that it is no more than a metaphor, 'a concept that catalyses a set of values into a phrase that many people can adopt and adapt'.[12] The UK's Overseas Development Institute has suggested a rights based approach 'sets the achievement of human rights as an objective of development. It uses thinking about human rights as the scaffolding of development policy'.[13] The Association of Women in Development talks of rights as a 'unifying set of standards and a common language, providing both a common vision and a set of tools'.[14] There are many different definitions that organisations offer when they claim to adopt a rights approach, although a number of elements have been highlighted as common across these.[15] Tsikata has suggested that enthusiasm for the rights-based approach among gender activists rests on their particular interpretation of what this approach means.[16]

Clark et al argue that one of the most important contributions of gender to understanding rights is in foregrounding the issue of power and unequal power relations.[17] This suggests that a rights focus alone may not necessarily make this link or promote a questioning of unequal power relations, but that power needs to be explicitly addressed. However, for others the construction of rights 'implies the rebalancing of power relations',[18] and the rights-based approach is seen to put power relations explicitly at the centre of analysis.[19] Miller et al also contend that work on rights (and participation) is ultimately about challenging and transforming power relations but they argue that 'confusion abounds' as to what rights-based approaches mean in practice and how they relate to questions of power.[20] This is especially difficult in relation to addressing 'invisible' mechanisms of power. The invisible mechanisms or power relations that operate in the private sphere are of particular concern when discussing gendered power relations. There are also many valid concerns that rights are being technically packaged in ways that ignore power.[21] The extent to which a focus on rights actually and automatically challenges existing unequal relations of power, therefore, has as yet to be demonstrated.

This chapter explores the different meanings, perceived usefulness and limitations of a rights approach to promote women's demands and as a means to unify women's actions in pursuit of these demands. How women's organisations have used rights to mobilise and promote change is explored using Nicaragua as a case study. Semi-structured interviews were conducted with representatives of women's groups and key actors in the national women's movements in 2005.[22] The research also utilised discussions

156

with members of a feminist NGO (Puntos de Encuentro) that has used a rights-based approach in its work,[23] as well as more informal, and ongoing discussions generated by presentation of the initial findings in Nicaragua.

Contemporary Nicaraguan women's movements

The women's movements of Nicaragua have been relatively well documented, particularly the role of women in the revolution and during the period of government of the Frente Sandinista de Liberación Nacional (FSLN).[24] Many of the existing gender-based and women-led NGOs emerged as a consequence of growing disillusionment with the revolutionary government and with its associated women's movement (AMNLAE). Electoral defeat in 1990 brought an abrupt political transition to the country and a crisis for AMNLAE. The early 1990s saw feminist activists working together to build a diverse and independent movement encompassing wider gender concerns such as violence and sexuality under its slogan 'Unity in Diversity'. As elsewhere, over time tensions were revealed within the movement, as attempts to forge common agendas highlighted fundamental differences between the key actors.

Analysis of the state of the region's women's movements undertaken by five feminist organisations in 2002 noted how they were passing through a 'difficult period'.[25] Despite the large number of active groups and local and national networks, the movement had become 'weakened and divided', suffering from disagreements over 'political strategy', particularly in the wake of Hurricane Mitch in 1998.[26] One positive outcome of the hurricane was a resurgence of civil society organising, with the formation of civil co-ordinating bodies in the affected countries and related action among some actors of the women's movements.[27] In Nicaragua 'cleavages' in the women's movement as a result of activities post-Mitch were also apparent.[28] Babb's analysis highlights the decision by a leading feminist NGO, Puntos de Encuentro, to 'remain apart' from a newly reunified National Feminist Committee (CNF) and its call for the formulation of an independent feminist platform for post-Mitch reconstruction. Bradshaw and Linneker's analysis also highlights 'fragmentation' of the women's movement in this period, with differences concerning participation in the newly formed Civil Co-ordinator for Emergency and Reconstruction (CCER).[29] Puntos de Encuentro took a lead role in the formation of the CCER as a mixed (male and female) advocacy organisation, while the CNF chose to remain outside it. This illustrates the existence of differences in opinion at that time within the women's movement about how best to present demands and promote change. While the nature of these differences may have changed, they continue today despite a new apparent unity.

The women's movement in Nicaragua has an appearance of co-ordination and suggests a new era of collective action. The recent launch of the 'Women's Health Agenda' in 2005, published in the name of the Autonomous Women's Movement, the Movimiento Autónomo de Mujeres (MAM), could be taken to exemplify this new unity.[30] The MAM has emerged as a dominant force over the past two years and the 'Health Agenda' is the most formalised of its activities to date. The agenda was the product of a two-year consultative process that included over 50 women's organisations. This suggests a move back to earlier efforts to formulate common platforms and away from activities focused on smaller groupings. The agenda presents a series of demands to the state around the themes of women's health, sexual and reproductive health, HIV/AIDS and gender-based violence. It contextualises these demands by reference to human rights and the international rights discourse.

The agenda was launched at a high-profile event in one of Managua's best-known hotels in June 2005. The event opened with speeches by a number of key feminist activists, who provided an overview of the state of women's rights in the country. A number of individual women participants each presented a copy of the agenda to an invited minister or representative of a ministry or public service, personalising the general claims laid out in the agenda. This event saw the MAM making a public claim on the state to fulfil its responsibilities for ensuring women's rights to health and well-being.

The MAM also makes use of the rights discourse when stating its case in and to the public. For example, in July 2004 when therapeutic abortion was again under threat, the MAM utilised the national press to state that, in countermanding therapeutic abortion, the Nicaraguan government would become a 'violator of rights'. In this piece readers were asked to reflect on 'where are women's and children's rights in this country?', concluding with 'demands', first calling for fulfilment of national and international agreements focused on the protection of the human rights of women, children and adolescents.[31]

The language and tactics of the MAM demonstrates how the rights discourse is being used to promote claims on the state. However, while the nature of recent collective actions could lead them to be labelled 'rights-based', this is not a label that has been adopted by the movement itself. The importance of the rights discourse in promoting this collective action is also questionable. The women interviewed from the MAM explained the reasons for the new-found collective spirit through reference to the changing national context and changes in individuals, rather than through reference to a particular agenda in common.

The 'autonomous' part of the MAM title means that those women who are part of the movement should have no political or religious affiliation and should participate in the movement as individuals, not as representatives of the groups or organisations that they work with. At the core of the MAM are around 20 well established women leaders and activists providing 'leadership' for the movement. Past conflicts appear to have been overcome to allow the MAM to function. Those involved suggest this is a result of what has been described as a new 'maturity' among the women involved, often with reference to particular groups who had 'matured', become willing to adapt, become more tolerant and able to unite with others within a single movement. The suggestion seems to be that changes in individual attitudes and actions have been more important than changes in the movement's practice.

In the interviews the new unification was also linked to the changing context in which women's groups were operating. The increasing power of the institutionalised Catholic Church in particular was noted, and its close relationship to both the existing government and the opposition FSLN party. The pact between these key actors is seen by many to challenge both notions of democracy and of Nicaragua as a secular state, with Church power manifesting itself in threats to organisations and individual women seen to challenge its doctrine.[32] The Church's ability to influence the dominant political discourse is also demonstrated by the recent withdrawal from the school system of a government-sponsored sex education manual after objections were raised by the Cardinal. Its influence on public policy is also apparent, and the Church has itself utilised the rights discourse to attack the 'right' to therapeutic abortion. These recent attacks on women's sexual and reproductive rights are challenged within the MAM Health Agenda, which includes a demand to 'regulate and punish' those public functionaries found to be violating the secular nature of the state.

While the publication of this set of collective demands in such a hostile political and economic environment is a real achievement, the MAM does not encompass all women activists. It must be understood in relation to what has now become labelled the 'wider movement', defined in relation to the MAM as a vague articulation of other women's groups and the actions of these groups. While the language of the MAM is a language of rights, what appears to keep the MAM separate from the 'wider movement' is also the issue of rights. The MAM as yet remains a young and evolving grouping and its final nature is still to be determined. Those who are part of the MAM define their position with respect to 10 guiding principles. While these remain unpublished, interviewees suggested that they included democratic rights, with specific reference to notions of the secular state, and gender-based rights such as the right to live without violence. Also included were some 'rights' that are highly contested—such as the right to abortion. As a result, the number of women who choose to be part of the MAM or who are 'eligible' to be so may be relatively limited. The new unification, while focused on agreement with a set of rights, may also impede wider unity, given the contested nature of these 'rights'.

Understandings of rights-based approaches in Nicaragua

In all the interviews with representatives from women's groups and organisations the importance of rights and rights discourse for their work became clear. Those interviewed as individuals and activists also talked the language of rights. However, when describing themselves and their organisations, most did not foreground rights or see themselves as 'rights' organisations. Moreover, when asked if they had heard of the 'rights-based approach' to development, the majority said no. This should not be read as suggesting a lack of knowledge or understanding on the part of the interviewees, but as a limitation of the concept and of the ease with which it can be recognised. It highlights the rather obvious fact that notions such as

159

rights-based development (RBD) and the rights-based approach (RBA) are constructions and, as such, mean little unless first explained and defined. Just like 'mainstreaming', for which no satisfactory Spanish equivalent has yet been agreed upon, RBD, and much less RBA, does not translate well into Spanish.

One advantage of a rights-based approach is said to be that rights can find resonance in diverse situations and, as Molyneux and Lazar have noted, 'the language and practice of human rights has become a global reality'.[33] However, this apparent resonance may mean we assume that we and others know what a rights-based approach looks like, since we 'know' what rights look like. During the interviews none of the women challenged the notion of 'rights'; they talked instead of a set of rights as if they were a given, a known. However, as the separation of the MAM from the 'wider movement' highlights, this set of rights may in fact not be universally agreed upon, not a 'given', for all actors within women's movements.

There was also an apparent difference over how to claim 'women's rights' between those operating in the capital city and within the MAM and those women working with women's groups outside Managua, or as part of the 'wider movement'. The MAM, as noted above, tends to make claims on the state to uphold women's rights in general and actively utilises the media in order to promote these claims. Women's groups outside the capital tended to employ a variety of tactics. Their actions tended to be less part of an articulated programme and more based on perceived local needs and focused on local actors rather than on the national government. The representatives from the women's groups interviewed noted how the legal path to rights fulfilment was an important one to follow. However, simultaneously the notion of the judicial system as patriarchal was noted, and as such the process of making claims was also accepted as being rather futile. This was not seen to mean that claims should not be made, rather it was translated as implying the need to adopt a more holistic approach or to provide a 'fall back' position for women when the legal system (inevitably) failed them.

The approach is not so much to 'domesticate' international rights,[34] or to 'link rights to daily life',[35] but rather to make up for the shortcomings of non-compliance with rights in daily life by evoking a set of (other) rights. For example, one organisation suggested that women in situations of violence should fight for their right to live free from violence, collectively and through training as local 'defenders of rights', and that in instances of violence women should use the judicial system to claim protection. However, at the same time the need to be able to live independently, and more importantly to believe they could live independently, was also noted, promoting a complementary focus on psychosocial services and economic skills training. Interviewees highlighted notions of agency and autonomy as important and these were presented as complementing rather than arising from a rights focus, additional to, but not the same as rights.

When asked what 'development based on rights' might look like, many of the women interviewed did not explain explicitly but instead described what they did that might fit the 'rights-based' label. The description of the work of one of the organisations was 'text book' RBA (in my understanding at least): it sought to empower women to claim their right to health and education services from the state rather than provide them to the women directly, or indeed, rather than demand them on the part of the women it worked with. What is interesting is that the notion of rights is nowhere made explicit in the organisation's own literature. In fact the organisation is generally described (by others) as a micro-credit organisation.

Although the interviewees did not recognise the notion of a 'rights-based approach' to development, all did utilise rights in their work and saw the gains that had been made collectively by focusing on rights. It was noted how the focus on rights had added legitimacy to women's claims and allowed advancement. Some suggested that the current attacks on women's rights were evidence of this, and demonstrated the power of rights discourse to bring about change. One feminist thinker in particular felt current threats to women's position and situation should be seen as a backlash, a reaction to the gains made. As such she felt we should be focusing on understanding how we were able to get where we are, and learning from this to advance in the future. That is, rather than questioning the rights focus, we should be learning from it. Others, however, were less clear about the utility of rights to advance gendered claims.

This notion of the utility of focusing on rights alone was questioned explicitly by a number of those interviewed, albeit in different ways. The representative of a feminist organisation, when asked if the organisation used rights and rights discourse in its work, suggested that what they did could be translated into rights language, but why would they want to do that? The feminist discourse they used, for them, needed no translation. More importantly it was felt that the rights discourse had, like much gendered language, been 'stolen' by other actors such as the World Bank, while feminist discourse had still not been co-opted. The discussion sparked reflection on the idea of translating the work of women's and feminist organisations into rights discourse, since a 'consultant' brought in to help the organisation with funding proposals had recently suggested they rename their training and consciousness raising activities as their 'rights package'. Another interviewee from an organisation that promotes the health and education of women and girls in rural areas described how they had recently started to think about using the language of rights explicitly in their work. This had arisen from participation in a European Union-funded project on rights. She noted how in general they 'learnt' from the people themselves how best to present ideas but that participating in the programme had led them to reflect on the fact that the work they had been doing did have a rights focus, and on the importance of naming it as such, at least in terms of ensuring finance.

The women interviewed saw the utility of the rights discourse as an 'acceptable' and 'comprehensible' approach to furthering the advancement of women. It was seen to be a discourse that is 'acceptable' to other non-gendered actors and NGOs and most notably to donors. In the current climate it was noted how it is increasingly difficult to find finance for women-only projects or those focused on raising gender consciousness. There is money available for projects focused on rights, on participation, on citizenship—the elements that make up a rights-based approach. This may lead organisations to use the language of rights to 'sell' their gendered projects. While this may be beneficial to all involved (women's organisations get funding for their work and donors are able to fund gendered projects), such a repackaging of gender as rights has wider implications. It raises questions over what a 'rights-based approach' to development is, whether the repackaging of gender as rights should be seen as a 'rights-based approach', and the extent to which this should be welcomed.

Doing the 'rights thing'

One organisation that has used the 'rights label' is the feminist NGO Puntos de Encuentro, one of the case study organisations in Molyneux and Lazar's work.[36] Puntos de Encuentro (Meeting Points) assumes a gender and generational focus in its work, utilising multiple- and multi-media, including radio, TV and printed materials, to 'critique traditional and official discourses', to reveal how they reinforce the subordination of women and young people in order to promote alternative ways of thinking.[37] Their focus on 'Diversity with Equity' and the organisation's work with young people, including young men, marks it as distinct from many other feminist and women's organisations. Its explicit reference to rights-based development is also atypical in Nicaragua.

Molyneux and Lazar noted, however, that during their study of the organisation there was initially a negative reaction to the idea of focusing attention on rights.[38] This arose from a conceptualisation of rights within the organisation as 'human rights' and the implications of adopting a human rights approach in the particular political context of that time. The study itself influenced thinking in the organisation through its suggestion that the notion of rights could be broadened to include rights in daily life. This was partly responsible for moving Puntos towards a more explicit rights-based approach, and was linked with the idea that rights language could bring 'legitimacy' to the organisation's work and proposals for change.[39]

Despite this recent refocusing, as one of the founders has made clear, the conceptual entry point of the organisation's work was never rights. This may help to explain why members of the organisation find it easy to highlight how they use rights to further their aims but find identifying this as a 'rights-based approach' less straightforward. That the organisation's work and aims are consistent with 'flexible notions of rights-based approaches is not in dispute.'[40] However, the extent to which this rights-based approach is recognised and named as such within the day-to-day activities of the organisation appears still to be somewhat limited. The notion originally used within Puntos to provide a focus to its work was 'autonomy', the aim being to promote individuals' rights along with collective rights and the capacity to participate in decisions that affect their lives. This notion continues to provide the overarching focus for its work and its overall aim. The recent strategic plan suggests the organisation aims to 'promote social dialogue' and to 'create capacity for critical thinking' for the formulation of collective proposals for change.[41]

Within this context rights are seen as providing a good entry point. It was thought that rights language allowed discussion with groups and individuals that otherwise might not have entered into dialogue with a feminist organisation. This is seen as invaluable in the organisation's work in building alliances between organisations. One example used was that of sexuality and sexual orientation, a key aspect of Puntos' work. The focus on rights established links between this topic and other issues more acceptable to non-feminist and non-gender specific organisations. Drawing on rights opened the door to dialogue with these organisations. Similarly, invoking rights was seen to be positive in prompting people to favour the issue or else be seen to be against fulfilment of another person's 'right'. This draws on the notion that working with a rights framework suggests a legitimacy that doesn't need to be explicitly stated or discussed, a deliberative process that would invariably raise doubts and differences but which, with the rights discourse, can be left unsaid.

The rights-based approach can be seen as providing the tools for change,[42] and as a 'strategic entry point'.[43] However, discussions also suggested doubts over the ability of this approach to be more than a tool, over the ability to produce advancement past the 'entry point' and thus over the ability for a rights approach alone to produce the desired change. While rights were seen as invaluable for the organisation's work in building alliances between organisations, its work does not stop there. Puntos looks to build alliances with and between organisations in order to help change the social context and in this way promote change. It seeks to influence what organisations discuss and how they discuss it, to generate discussion around the unequal power relations that are at the basis of rights non-compliance, rather than focusing only on generating agreement around the need for compliance with a set of rights. Doubts were raised over the extent to which a focus on rights actually and automatically challenges existing unequal relations of power.

The role of rights in challenging unequal power relations

Those that reflected on the relationship between rights and power in the study suggested a change in power relations would not necessarily or automatically arise from focusing on rights. It was suggested that both issues need to be addressed explicitly and that the two approaches are not synonymous but complementary. The example of abortion was used by one interviewee to illustrate this point. She noted how claiming the right to safe abortion, while important, does not address those factors that lead to unwanted pregnancy or which limit a woman's ability to exercise a legal right to abortion, such as unequal power relations in the home or social stigma. The assumption that claiming rights implies rebalancing power, or that a focus on rights does challenge relations of power, may detract from the important task of challenging unequal power relations, and the discourse of power may be silenced as it is subsumed within the rights discourse.

Claiming an 'agreed' right, such as the right to education or reproductive health services, may shift the focus away from those factors that hinder women's ability to exercise any rights, the multiple relations of power that determine each individual woman's situation. Such an approach may promote a static rather than dynamic understanding of any situation, in that a set of claims are made rather than a set of diverse and evolving relations analysed and challenged. Issues of diversity and difference may also be ignored, as the aim becomes the promotion of a common goal.

One feminist thinker suggested that rights be seen as 'the lowest rung on the empowerment ladder'. Seeing rights as the end goal rather than part of a process focused on challenging unequal power relations would mean we progress no higher. In a similar vein the current director of Puntos talked of the need to take the rights approach to its 'logical conclusion' in that for women to exercise their rights rather than simply having their rights recognised requires an explicit challenge to the multiple power relations that negate women's ability to live their rights on an individual and collective level. The focus on power and the questioning of power relations is what ensures that a rights focus is not left to an interpretation of only the visible and acceptable.

It is perhaps for this reason that organisations such as Puntos de Encuentro continue to highlight the notion of autonomy and the fundamental importance of challenging unequal power relations. The organisation's most recent Strategic Plan makes this clear when it highlights the institutional aim as being to design 'strategies and methodologies that allow the analysis of, and change to, the unequal power relations experienced in daily life'.[44] Rather than suggesting Puntos work from a rights-based approach to claim existing rights, it was suggested by one long-standing member of the organisation that it is in the process of creating new rights, naming as rights those claims that arise from the process of challenging unequal relations of power. For some this is what a gendered rights-based approach does entail; the distinction here is that the focus is firmly on the issue of power and the process of challenging existing power relations as being of central importance rather than the privileging of rights as the dominant focus.

Concluding comments

Women's movements and groups in Nicaragua utilise the rights discourse and find it useful for furthering collective aims. The recent publication by the Autonomous Women's Movement of a women's health agenda demonstrates how the language of rights is being used to promote and legitimise women's interests. The agenda has been able to mobilise a large amount of support. At the core of the MAM is a group of women activists who, after many years of differences, have found a new ability to work together thanks to individual life-course changes and the changing political context. The continued unity of the MAM appears to be related to rights in that the notion of what are legitimate women's rights binds this grouping. This new unity, however, highlights old divisions around what are 'rights', and those who are not part of the autonomous movement have become defined in relation to it, as the 'wider' movement.

The promotion of women's rights, however understood, has become a central component of the work of the majority of women's groups and movements in Nicaragua. However, few label themselves as 'rights' organisations and much less identify with the 'rights-based approach', despite some level of donor pressure to do so. There does appear to be some resistance to repackaging gender as rights and this may have something to do with how well the idea translates across time and space, but also with the perceived limitations of rights to further women's interests. What is being questioned is the extent to which a focus on rights can transition into a change in social relations, a change that demands a rebalancing of unequal power relations. Rather than seeing a rebalancing of power as inherent within a rights focus, rights are seen as a tool that can help to challeng unequal power relations and promote women's autonomy. The focus is on those factors that lead to rights non-compliance rather than seeking compliance with a set of rights. This shifts the focus back explicitly onto power and to challenging unequal power relations.

This need to remain focused on power and issues of unequal power relations may be increasingly necessary, as other language, such as the language of rights, continues to be co-opted by a whole range of actors and used to promote their own agendas. The World Bank's recent adoption of gender and rights language is a concern, given the continued neoliberal policy context in which it is being applied. More worrying is the apparent neutralisation of the global rights framework as constructed through UN agreements and conventions, reducing wide-ranging rights into a minimum set of basic needs to be delivered to the poor. The Millennium Development Goals (MSGs) lack any clear engagement with earlier rights frameworks and specifically with hard-won women's rights. If the 1990s saw a shift in development priorities, with democracy and human rights moving up the international development agenda,[45] the early 2000s have seen them slide back down.[46] That collective feminist action to claim every woman's right to live without violence could succeed in renaming gender-based violence as a human rights violation demonstrates the power of the rights discourse. However, recent events suggest the need to reflect on how well the rights focus can not only bring about but also sustain change.

Notes

1 M Molyneux & S Lazar, *Doing the Rights Thing: Rights-Based Development and Latin American NGOs*, London: Intermediate Technology Development Group, 2003; and R Eyben, 'The rise of rights: rights-based approaches to international Development', *IDS Policy Briefing*, 17, Brighton: Institute of Development Studies, 2003.
2 Institute of Development Studies, *IDS Bulletin, Special Edition: 'Developing Rights'*, 36 (1), 2005.
3 Bjork, 'Feminists are seeking spaces to move from fragmentation towards common grounds for action', *Les Penelopes*, 17 January 2004.
4 S Wölte, 'Claiming rights and contesting spaces: women's movements and international women's human rights discourse in Africa', in M Braig & S Wölte (eds), *Common Ground or Mutual Exclusion: Women's Movements and International Relations*, London: Zed Books, 2002, pp 171–188.

5 P Antrobus, *The Global Women's Movement: Origins, Issues and Strategies*, London: Zed Books, 2004, p 118.

6 U Ruppert, 'Global women's politics: towards the 'globalising' of women's human rights', in Braig & Wölte, *Common Ground or Mutual Exclusion*, p 156.

7 C Clark, M Reilly & J Wheeler, 'Living rights: reflections from women's movements and gender and rights in practice', *IDS Bulletin*, 36 (1), 2000, pp 76–90.

8 T Dzodzi, 'The rights based approach to development: potential for change or more of the same?', *IDS Bulletin*, 35 (4), 2004, pp 130–133.

9 S Bracke, 'Different worlds possible: feminist yearnings for shared futures', in J Kerr, E Sprenger & A Symington (eds), *The Future of Women's Rights: Global Visions and Strategies*, London: Zed Books, 2004, pp 97–115.

10 SE Alvarez, 'Advocating feminism: the Latin American feminist NGO "boom"', *International Feminist Journal of Politics*, 1 (2), 1999 pp 181–209.

11 Bracke, 'Different worlds possible'.

12 B Pratt, 'Rights or values?', *ONTRAC* (newsletter of the International NGO Training and Research Centre (INTRAC)), 23, January 2003, p 2.

13 ODI, 'What can we do with a rights-based approach to development?', *Overseas Development Institute Briefing Paper*, 3, London: Overseas Development Institute, September 1999, p 1.

14 AWID, 'A rights based approach to development', *Women's Rights and Economic Change*, 1, Association for Women's Rights in Development, August 2002, p 1.

15 L Piron, 'Rights-based approaches and bilateral aid agencies: more than metaphor?', *IDS Bulletin*, 36 (1), 2005, pp 19–30.

16 Dzodzi, 'The rights based approach to development'.

17 Clark *et al*, 'Living rights'.

18 S Correa, 'From reproductive health to sexual rights: achievements and future challenges', *Reproductive Health Matters*, 10, 1997, pp 107–116.

19 Piron, 'Rights-based approaches and bilateral aid agencies'.

20 V Miller, L Vene Klasen & C Clark, 'Rights-based development: linking rights and participation—challenges in thinking and action', *IDS Bulletin*, 36 (1), 2005, pp 31–40.

21 J Pettit & J Wheeler, 'Developing rights? Relating discourse to context and practice', *IDS Bulletin*, 36 (1), 2005, pp 1–8.

22 Many thanks to all those interviewed for sharing their time and their thoughts. Particular thanks to Amy Bank, Vilma Castillo, Ana Criquillion and Teresa Hernández in Nicaragua, and to Andrea Cornwall, Maxine Molyneux and Brian Linneker in the UK for comments on earlier drafts of this paper. Thanks also to International Cooperation for Development/Progressio for their continued support and funding.

23 The author has worked with Puntos de Encuentro for many years and is not an 'objective' outsider in the processes discussed here. The paper reflects the author's views only and not the institutional position of Puntos de Encuentro. For more information on Puntos de Encuentro, see T Hernández & V Campanile, 'Feminism at work: a case study of transforming power relations in everyday life', in H van Dam, A Khadar & M Valk (eds), *Institutionalizing Gender Equality: Commitment, Policy and Practice. A Global Source Book*, The Netherlands: Royal Tropical Institute (KIT), 2000; and www.puntos.org.ni.

24 See, for example, F Babb, *After Revolution: Mapping Gender and Cultural Politics in Neo Liberal Nicaragua*, Austin, TX: University of Texas Press, 2001; J Deighton *et al*, *Sweet Ramparts: Women in Revolutionary Nicaragua*, London: War on Want/Nicaragua Solidarity Campaign, 1983; M Molyneux, *Women's Movements in International Perspective: Latin America and Beyond*, Basingstoke: Palgrave, 2003; M Randall, *Sandino's Daughters Revisited: Feminism in Nicaragua*, New Brunswick, NJ: Rutgers University Press, 1994; and M Randall & L Yanz, *Sandino's Daughters: Testimonies of Nicaraguan Women in Struggle*, London: Zed, 1981.

25 M Clulow, *The Central American Women's Movement and Public Policy: Analysis by Five Feminist Organizations*, Building Women's Citizenship and Governance, European Commission and the UK Lottery Fund, 2002.

26 Babb, *After Revolution*, p 40.

27 S Bradshaw & B Linneker, *Challenging Women's Poverty: Perspectives on Gender and Poverty Reduction Strategies from Nicaragua and Honduras*, CIIR-ICD Briefing, London: Catholic Institute for International Relations, 2003.

28 Babb, *After Revolution*, p 44.

29 Bradshaw & Linneker, *Challenging Women's Poverty*.

30 Movimiento Autónomo de Mujeres de Nicaragua, *Agenda de Salud Integral de las Mujeres*, Managua: Si Mujer/Forum Syd/Planned Parenthood, 2005.

31 *El Nuevo Diario* (Managua), 9 July 2004 (author's translation).

32 S Bradshaw, B Linneker & R Zuniga, 'Social roles and spatial relations of NGOs and civil society', in C McIlwaine & K Willis (eds), *Challenges and Change in Middle America: Perspectives on Development in Mexico, Central America and the Caribbean*, Harlow: Pearson Education, 2002, pp 243–269.

33 Molyneux & Lazar, *Doing the Rights Thing*, p 89.

34 Wölte, 'Claiming rights and contesting spaces'.

35 Molyneux & Lazar, *Doing the Rights Thing*.

36 *Ibid.*

37 Puntos de Encuentro, *Gendered Social Communication Strategies: The Case of Puntos De Encuentro in Nicaragua*, Report for MS Denmark, Nicaragua, 2001.

38 Molyneux & Lazar, *Doing the Rights Thing*.

39 *Ibid.*

40 *ibid*, p 134.

41 Puntos de Encuentro, *Strategic Plan*, Managua: Puntos de Encuentro, September 2005.

42 AWID, 'A rights based approach to development'.

43 C Moser & A Norton, with T Conway, C Ferguson & P Vizard, *To Claim Our Rights: Livelihood Security, Human Rights and Sustainable Development*, London: Overseas Development Institute, 2001.

44 Puntos de Encuentro, *Strategic Plan*.

45 Molyneux & Lazar, *Doing the Rights Thing*, p 1.

46 See Women's International Coalition for Economic Justice, *Seeking Accountability on Women's Human Rights: Women Debate the Millennium Development Goals*, New York: WICEJ, 2004.

Index

Page numbers in *italics* represent tables.